ATLAS OF
TWENTIETH CENTURY
WORLD HISTORY

ATLAS OF
TWENTIETH CENTURY
WORLD HISTORY

Michael Dockrill

HarperCollins*Publishers*

G
1035
D63
1991

FIRST U.S. EDITION

An Ilex Book

Created and produced by Ilex Publishers Limited 29–31 George Street, Oxford OX1 2AJ, England.

Project editor Nicholas Harris
Text editors Elizabeth Miles, Simon Adams
Map editors Nicholas Harris, Zoë Goodwin, Alan Mais
Design Wolfgang Mezger, Phil Jacobs
Picture research Linda Proud
Index Peter Barber

Maps produced by Lovell Johns Ltd., Alan Mais
Typesetting by Opus, Oxford and Getset, Oxford
Printed by Eurograph s.p.a. - Milano - Italy
ISBN 0 06 055169 0

Photograph Credits

KEY: AP – Associated Press, London; EQ – Equinox Archive, Oxford; FRL – French Railways Limited; FSP – Frank Spooner Pictures, London; H-DC – Hulton-Deutsch, London; M – Magnum, London; P – Popperfoto, London; PNL – Pictorial Nostalgia Library, West Wickham, Kent; RA – Retrograph Archive Collection, London; VM – Vintage Magazine Company, London. b bottom; bc bottom centre; bl bottom left; br bottom right; cr centre right; t top; tl top left; tr top right.

Front Cover tl AP; bl FSP; br FSP; cr P; tr P.
Page 2–3 H-DC; p7 FSP; p8 H-DC; p9 tr H-DC; b VM; p10 t1 EQ; p10–11 H-DC; p11 t EQ; p22 EQ; p23 P; p36 P; p37 H-DC; p38 bl RA; br H-DC; p39 EQ; p42 H-DC; p44 H-DC; p45 VM; p52 H-DC; p54 H-DC; p55 tl PNL; tr H-DC; p57 H-DC; p70 H-DC; p71 tr H-DC; cr EQ; p77 EQ; p92 H-DC; p93 tl H-DC; tr P; p96 bl P; bc H-DC; p102 H-DC; p103 t AP; b FSP; p107 H-DC; p117 FSP; p118 FSP; p119 FSP; p127 P; p138 FRL; p139 tl M, Ferdinando Scianna; tr FSP; p140 M, Stuart Franklin; p141 tr P; b FSP.

Ilex and the author wish to acknowledge the assistance of Anna Bramwell in the preparation of this book.

Other acknowledgments: Nicola Barber, Andras Bereznay, Malcolm Day, Designers and Partners (Oxford), Saki Dockrill, Asad Ismi, Latha Menon, Richard Rowan.

Contents

84187

Preface

Since the beginning of the twentieth century the world has been transformed from the Eurocentric one in which Britain, France, Germany and Russia held economic and political dominance, to that of 1991 in which the United States of America, despite its increasing economic problems, polices the globe. It is a period which has seen the rise, spread and fragmentation of communism; the decline of European colonial empires and the growth of non-European nationalism; the economic dominance of the Western powers and the debt burden and economic hardships of developing countries; the growth of religious fundamentalism and fanaticism; and the threat of international terrorism. Over the same period, there have been spectacular developments in transport, communications, medicine, military technology and space exploration, along with changes in attitude to social welfare and the exploitation of the planet.

In providing a graphic illustration of these political, social and technological changes by means of maps, the **Atlas of Twentieth Century World History** provides an accessible introduction to this complex period. The 94 maps, employing a wide range of cartographic techniques, cover both global and local themes. On the one hand they chart global shifts in territorial control and political power and on the other they scrutinize a particular region, revealing for example how wars were won or lost or how the patchwork of ethnic distribution has been − or may prove to be − a major cause of historical change.

The events of 1989 and 1990 in Eastern Europe show just how quickly these changes can occur. The reunification of Germany, unthinkable at the start of 1989, has become a reality, while other countries in Eastern Europe are beginning to experience the problems of adapting to democracy. Meanwhile, the Soviet Union, against whom the United States and Western Europe allied and rearmed after 1949, has ceased to be a major threat as it grapples with a wide range of internal problems. The Atlas contains up-to-date maps to illustrate the changes in Eastern Europe and the USSR.

Such changes, with their opportunities and difficulties, are by no means peculiar to the present but have been magnified by the complexity of events in recent years and by the rapidity with which modern technology allows them to take place. Moreover as the threat of nuclear war recedes we are now faced with the potential consequences of environmental pollution, itself a product of the technology that has contributed to human betterment. Although environmental problems, and diseases such as AIDS, threaten life today as much as any military weapon, the close of the Cold War has still created a mood of optimism in the West. But progress is not predictable and in the twenty-first century human ingenuity will continue to be tested as efforts are made to share out resources and to contain war, poverty, disease and world-wide pollution.

THE CRACKS IN THE EDIFICE

Commercial, industrial, imperial and military competition created a potentially unstable Europe.

The early 20th century marked the zenith of European dominance throughout the world. Western Europe controlled, directly or indirectly, most of the world's surface and the bulk of its trade and investment. It shared with the United States a virtual monopoly in technological innovation. As colonial powers, the European nations justified their control of foreign lands by claiming that they were engaged upon a 'civilizing mission', bringing to backward peoples the benefits of Western civilization – Christianity, justice, efficient government, modern transport, education, sanitation and medicine.

Yet cracks were beginning to appear in the edifice of Western power. Given the smaller population of the West, which had to rule huge numbers of people in Africa and Asia, European dominance depended to a large degree on a mixture of self-confidence and bluff, although superior military and naval technology could always be brought to bear if these failed to convince. The West was also beginning to experience the first manifestations of nationalism in India, Indo-China, China, Turkey, Persia and Ireland. Countries such as Britain and France, which prided themselves on their constitutional freedoms, were faced with a dilemma when they continued to deny these blessings to the peoples of India or Indo-China, especially when the growing middle class in these possessions, most of whom had received a Western education, was able to turn such principles against its rulers. Nor was socialism, whose growth in the West after 1900 so alarmed the propertied classes, entirely sympathetic to empires that appeared to exploit their overseas subjects as ruthlessly as they did their working classes at home.

The country that most felt these pressures was Britain. The death of Queen Victoria in 1901, and the elaborate ceremonial surrounding her funeral, which was attended by all the crowned heads of Europe, were seen by many contemporaries as marking the end of more than 60 years of unfettered British industrial and imperial progress. Other nations were now challenging Britain's industrial pre-eminence. In particular, the rapid industrialization and increased urbanization of Germany had created a formidable economic rival, which had overtaken Britain in many of the indicators of national power, especially in iron and steel production, the basis of military strength. Not only did Germany possess the strongest army on the continent, but also after 1898 it began to construct a large ocean-going battle fleet. At the same time, the United States, while not so immediately threatening to Britain, was becoming an even more formidable

◄ **Wilhelm II (1859–1941) became German Emperor in 1888. He was ambitious and vain, personifying the spirit of Imperial Germany. After Germany's defeat in 1918 he went into exile.**

▶ **The British in India enjoyed a privileged life style. British men monopolized the major administrative and military posts, while their wives led a pampered existence.**

Where the Money Was

At the turn of the century, standards of living were highest in the industrialized nations and in those areas of European settlement where raw materials and land were abundant. Statistics for this period are, however, unreliable. For example, in poor economies there is always a large non-cash element owing to factors such as self-sufficiency, barter and a reluctance to disclose information to revenue officials. Furthermore, figures for standards of living and national income are averages and do not clearly indicate the sharp differences between rich and poor. On the whole, however, while this difference was relatively large in the industrialized West, it was smaller in the United States and Canada.

During the first decade of the 20th century, world trade in primary and manufactured goods almost doubled, but by 1910 Europe's share of industrial production began to decline, as that of the US, Japan and Russia rose. Russia's industrial expansion relied on foreign capital, particularly from France, which alone held one third of Russia's total debt. This debt was serviced by high taxes on the peasantry, which led to increasing resentment against foreign capitalists.

Capital for industrial expansion was still provided mainly by West European investors. Joint-stock companies were formed to build railways in Egypt and tramways in Warsaw. Most of the utilities in South America were constructed through money raised from British shareholders.

To start with, there was little fear of expropriation. When Venezuela threatened to default on her debt repayments in 1902, British and German warships blockaded her ports. In reality however, investment in areas not under the political control of the investing nations was vulnerable to political change, and much European capital invested in Russia, Latin America, China and elsewhere was expropriated or lost as a result of internal upheaval in the years during and following the First World War.

World Development

In 1900 the world was shrinking: continents were now linked internally and externally by metalled roads, railways, steamships and the telegraph. The Trans-Siberian railway was all but completed in 1904 and the Andes were crossed by a railway in 1910. Over 600,000 miles of railways had been built by that year, mostly by British, French and North American engineers. The steam locomotive allowed an expansion of markets for industrial goods. Oil-fired instead of steam-propelled ships were making their first appearance. Important technological developments were also taking place during this period, notably in the United States: the first powered flight occurred in 1903, while the first mass production motor car – the Model T Ford – rolled off the production line in Detroit in 1907. These developments were all helping to increase the pace of industrialization throughout the world.

Britain, formerly the 'workshop of the world', was slipping behind her major competitors, notably Germany and the United States, which were not only overtaking it in coal, iron and steel production but were also developing newer industries and techniques, such as electrical engineering and chemicals. Japan too was advancing industrially in this period. Most countries in Western Europe, however, remained dependent on Third World countries (then mostly colonial or semi-colonial societies) for their raw materials, such as cotton, oil or rubber, which they turned into manufactured goods. Most also had to import large quantities of food, as France was the only country self-sufficient in agriculture.

industrial power than Germany. France, Austria–Hungary and Russia had also made considerable economic strides during the 1890s and by the 1900s, when France had recovered from the effects of the scandalous Dreyfus Affair, the country became increasingly confident that it could defeat Germany in a war. Commercial, industrial, imperial and military competition were all therefore helping to create a potentially unstable continent.

This was not how the situation was viewed in Europe. The Western bourgeoisie believed that the rapid advances since the mid-19th century in technology, communications, medicine, sanitation and in wealth-creation of all forms would continue unabated in the future, spreading the benefits of progress and prosperity throughout the world. That these benefits were restricted to the well-to-do was ignored. Indeed the new rich, whose wealth was based on profits from industrial, commercial and banking enterprises, enjoyed a most opulent lifestyle, while throughout Europe the old landed aristocracy lived a life of extraordinary elegance and formality.

In the political sphere, although the imperial governments of Germany and Austria–Hungary remained autocratic, constitutions had been granted and were based on universal manhood suffrage. Even in Russia, the most politically backward nation, a limited constitution based on a severely restricted

▲ The Krupp factory in Essen, showing Germany's industrial strength early in the twentieth century. Steel is being prepared for tanks.

franchise was granted by the Tsar in 1905. However the parliaments in these imperial governments were little more than debating chambers, and carried no real powers.

There were also some improvements in the social conditions of the working classes, at least in the West. Germany had introduced a system of unemployment insurance and old age pensions in the 1880s, and Britain and France began to follow suit in the 1900s. Liberal middle-class consciences had been pricked by the appalling conditions that existed in the urban areas, a legacy of the Industrial Revolution. In the United States, the Progressive Movement, and in Western Europe, numerous municipal reformers, began to work towards improving housing, sanitation and medical facilities and providing better recreational and educational facilities for working class families. Yet in the years leading up to 1914, working-class dissatisfaction with wages and conditions manifested itself in numerous strikes and demonstrations, particularly in Britain and France, while St Petersburg was gripped by a General Strike on the very eve of the Great War. Social forces were at work across the continent that would eventually bring the entire edifice tumbling down around its rulers' ears.

◀ Anti-imperialism in China led to a siege of European embassies in Beijing in 1900 by the nationalist group, the Boxers. The embassies were eventually relieved by a six-nation force but the harsh means used to subdue the rising only served to exacerbate nationalist feeling. The picture shows a public execution in front of European troops.

11

The Imperial Powers

GREENLAND
(Denmark)

SPITSBERGEN
(Norway)

ICELAND
(Denmark)

FAEROES
(Denmark)

CANADA

UNITED
KINGDOM

DENMARK

LABRADOR

NETHERLANDS
BELGIUM

GERMANY

NEWFOUNDLAND

FRANCE

AUSTRIA -
HUNGARY

ST. PIERRE & MIQUELON

ITALY

PORTUGAL

SPAIN

UNITED STATES

AZORES

SPANISH
MOROCCO

Gibraltar (Br)

MALTA

CYPRI

BERMUDA

MADEIRA

MOROCCO

BAHAMAS

CANARY IS

ALGERIA

LIBYA

EGY

TURKS & CAICOS IS

RIO DE ORO

BRITISH
HONDURAS

CAYMAN
IS

JAMAICA

C. VERDE IS.

FRENCH WEST AFRICA

FRENCH
EQUATORIAL
AFRICA

ANGL
EGYPT'
SUDA

PUERTO
RICO

GAMBIA

TRINIDAD AND
TOBAGO

PORT.
GUINEA

TOGO

NIGERIA

CAMEROON

Panama
Canal

Caribbean Is.

GUIANA

SIERRA
LEONE

GOLD
COAST

FERNANDO PO

RIO
MUNI

UGAN

ARUBA

SÃO TOME & PRINCIPE

BELGIAN
CONGO

CURAÇAO

ANNOBON

GERM
AFRI

BONAIRE

BR. VIRGIN IS.

ASCENSION

DANISH VIRGIN IS.

ANGOLA

N. RHO

ANGUILLA

S. MARTIN

ST. HELENA

S.
RHO

S. BARTHOLOMEW

MARQUESAS
IS

ST. EUSTATIUS & SABA

ST. KITTS-NEVIS

BARBUDA

BECHUANA-
LAND

ANTIGUA

TUAMOTU ARCHIPELAGO

MONSERRAT

GERMAN
SOUTH-WEST
AFRICA

SWAZILAN

GUADELOUPE

PITCAIRN I.

DOMINICA

BASUTO

MARTINIQUE

ST. LUCIA

UNION OF
SOUTH AFRICA

ST. VINCENT

BARBADOS

GRENADINES

GRE...

TRISTAN DA CUNHA

FALKLAND IS

12

SOUTH GEORGIA

Of the major colonial powers, Britain in 1914 possessed the largest overseas empire, occupying about 11 million square miles of territory on every continent and ruling over some 400 million people. The older settlements of Canada, Australia and New Zealand had achieved self-governing status by 1907, but remained united to the motherland by close cultural, defence and economic ties. In addition, Britain controlled an 'informal empire' of protectorates and defensive alliances over the Sudan, Egypt (including the Suez Canal), southern Persia and the Persian Gulf; investments in, and trade with, China and South America gave Britain considerable influence in those countries as well.

France possessed the second largest overseas empire, with extensive territories in Africa, Indo-China, the Caribbean and the Pacific. Although it was an important source of manpower and raw materials, France had acquired most of its empire after 1870 in order to strengthen its prestige as a European great power. After 1900 France sought to take over Morocco, the last remaining independent state in North Africa, an ambition finally achieved in 1911.

Germany had arrived late in the scramble for overseas colonies. By 1914 it had acquired territories in South-West and East Africa, Togoland and Cameroon in West Africa, several islands in the Pacific, and had seized Jiaozhou from China. Germany was not satisfied with these gains, believing that as a leading industrial and military power it was entitled to a much greater share of the world's resources. In the late 1890s, it began to construct a large battle fleet with the intention of forcing Britain to share some of its colonial holdings with Germany. The ensuing naval race poisoned Anglo–German relations down to the outbreak of war in 1914.

In contrast the United States acquired its colonies during the 1890s almost by accident. Victory in a war with Spain in 1898 over Cuba enabled it to annex Puerto Rico, Guam and the Philippines. Hawaii and the eastern Samoan Islands also fell to the United States in 1898, followed by other Pacific islands.

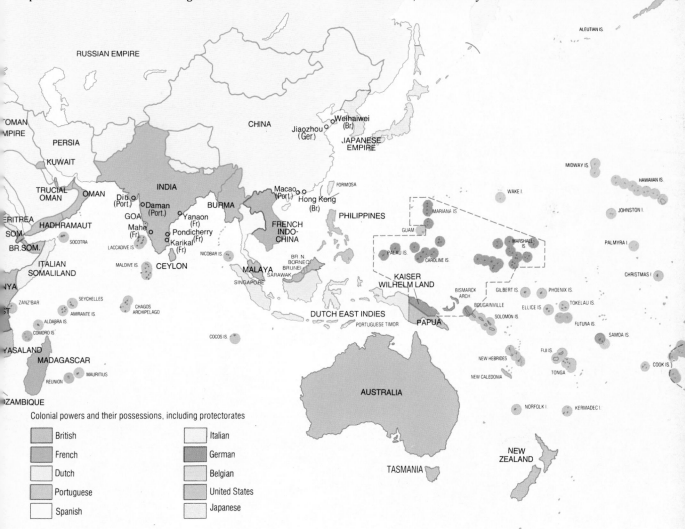

Colonial powers and their possessions, including protectorates

- British
- French
- Dutch
- Portuguese
- Spanish
- Italian
- German
- Belgian
- United States
- Japanese

The Doomed Empires

Maximum extent of
Ottoman Empire, 1683

Losses 1683–1878

Losses 1879–1914

Ottoman Empire, 1914

1878 Date of independence

International boundary,
1914

RUSSIAN EMPIRE

Kiev

GERMAN
EMPIRE

Vienna •Budapest

AUSTRO-HUNGARIAN
EMPIRE

Belgrade•

Odessa

KHANATE
OF CRIMEA
Tributary state

1774

CASPIAN
SEA

ROMANIA
1878 •Bucharest

Crimea
Sevastopol

BLACK SEA

SERBIA
1878

Tiflis

Baku

Rome•

MONTENEGRO

ALBANIA

MACEDONIA

Sofia•
BULGARIA
1908

Constantinople

Erzurum

ITALY

ADRIATIC SEA

1913

GREECE

Athens•
1830

Smyrna

Ankara

Berlin–Baghdad railway

Tributary
states

Tehran•

PERSIA

Algiers•

Sicily

Aleppo

ALGERIA   Tributary states

1710

Tunis•

TUNISIA
French protectorate,
1881

Malta (Br.)

MEDITERRANEAN SEA

Crete

Dodecanese
Italian, 1912

Cyprus
Br prot.,1878

SYRIA

MESOPOTAMIA

Baghdad

Tripoli•

Benghazi•

CYRENAICA
Italian, 1912

Alexandria•

Damascus•

PALESTINE
Jerusalem•

Basra•

KUWAIT
Br prot.,1899

TRIPOLI
Italian, 1912

FEZZAN
Italian, 1912

EGYPT
British occupation, 1882

Cairo•

Arabia

HEJAZ

Medina•

RED
SEA

0   km   750

0   mls   500

Mecca•

Boundary of Russia , 1914

Acquisitions, 1855–1914

Under Russian occupation
or protectorship

Russian sphere
of influence

Murmansk•

FINLAND
Helsingfors•

Arkhangelsk•

YAKUTSK

Anadyr•

to Alaska,1867

KAMCHATKA

Riga•

St. Petersburg

Turukhansk•

Yakutsk•

Okhotsk•

Petropavlovsk•

Warsaw•

POLAND

Moscow•

YENISEYSK

Kiev•

Kazan•

TOBOLSK

Nikolayevsk•
Sakhalin

Odessa•

UKRAINE

Tobolsk•

Tomsk•

IRKUTSK

TRANS-
BAYKAL

AMUR
REGION

USSURI

TOMSK

Irkutsk•

Turgai•

Semipalatinsk•

TANNU TUVA
Russian prot. 1912–21

Chita•

MANCHURIA
Russian occupation, 1900–05

OTTOMAN
EMPIRE

Tiflis•

Russian protectorate,
1873

Baku•

Khiva•

SYR DARYA

Tashkent•

1871–81

MONGOLIA

Mukden•

KOREA

Port Arthur
1898–1905

TRANSCASPIAN
REGION

Tehran•

Bukhara•

Samarkand•

Beijing•

PERSIA

Kabul•

Russian protectorate,1868

AFGHANISTAN

CHINA

0   km   1500

0   mls   1000

14

The Ottoman (or Turkish) Empire was in continuous decline from the end of the 18th century. The inefficiency of the Sultan's government in Constantinople resulted in the loss of a large part of its Balkan lands; Serbia, Greece and Romania had all emerged as independent nations by 1878. By 1900 the Ottoman Empire was struggling to retain a hold over its remaining European possessions in Macedonia, where rival Serbian–, Greek– and Bulgarian–backed guerrillas fought to overthrow Turkish rule. Its weakening power was made worse by the rivalry between Austria–Hungary and Russia for predominance in the Balkans, which had nearly resulted in conflict between them several times during the 19th century. War had, however, been prevented by the intervention of other European powers, anxious to avoid involvement in a major struggle if the Ottoman Empire collapsed. Their attempts to persuade the Turks to ameliorate the situation in Macedonia by introducing reforms were all frustrated by Turkish opposition. In the Middle East, Germany, Britain, France and Italy competed to wrest economic concessions from the Turks. By 1900 German influence was supreme: it had secured the right to build a railway from Berlin to Baghdad and was equipping the Turkish army.

Austria–Hungary was also facing increasing unrest in its multi-national empire fanned by Serbia and Romania, which hoped to secure a share of the spoils if the empire collapsed. The emperor, Francis Joseph, ruled over a state that included Germans, Hungarians, Poles, Czechs, Italians and Romanians. In 1867 the empire had been divided between the Austrians and Hungarians, by which time other nationalities also demanded autonomy.

Unlike Austria–Hungary and the Ottoman Empire, the Russian Empire did not appear to be in a state of decline. A country of enormous economic and military potential, Russia had made considerable industrial strides in the 1890s. Moreover, having consolidated its earlier gains in Central Asia, Russia was extending its influence into Persia and Afghanistan, and was also advancing into Manchuria and northern China. However, seemingly the strongest of the three eastern empires, Russia was the first to suffer defeat in war (against Japan) and the outbreak of revolution, both in 1905.

Boundary of Austro-Hungarian empire, 1914

Ethno-linguistic divisions

German	Polish	Serbian
Italian	Czech	Croatian
Rhaeto-Romance	Slovak	Slovene
Romanian	Ruthenian	Hungarian

0 km 200

0 mls 150

15

World Population 1900

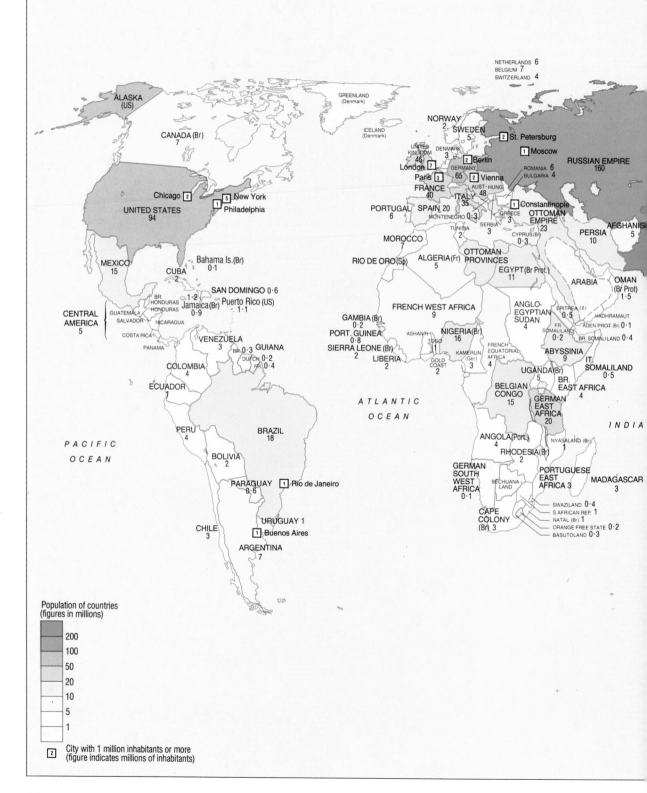

NETHERLANDS 6
BELGIUM 7
SWITZERLAND 4

ALASKA (US)

GREENLAND (Denmark)

NORWAY 2
SWEDEN 5

2 St. Petersburg
1 Moscow

RUSSIAN EMPIRE 160

CANADA (Br) 7

ICELAND (Denmark)

UNITED KINGDOM 46
DENMARK 3
2 Berlin
GERMANY 65
2 Vienna
AUST·HUNG 48
ROMANIA 6
BULGARIA 4

London 7
Paris 3
FRANCE 40
ITALY 35

Chicago 2
5 New York
1 Philadelphia

UNITED STATES 94

PORTUGAL 6
SPAIN 20
MONTENEGRO 0·3
GREECE 3

1 Constantinople
OTTOMAN EMPIRE
SERBIA 3
CYPRUS (Br) 0·1
OTTOMAN PROVINCES 23

AFGHANIS 5
PERSIA 10

MEXICO 15

Bahama Is.(Br) 0·1

CUBA 2

MOROCCO 7

TUNISIA 2

RIO DE ORO (Sp)

ALGERIA (Fr) 5

EGYPT (Br Prot.) 11

ARABIA

OMAN (Br Prot) 1·5

SAN DOMINGO 0·6
Puerto Rico (US) 1·1

BR HONDURAS
HONDURAS 1·2
Jamaica (Br) 0·9

CENTRAL AMERICA 5
GUATEMALA
SALVADOR
NICARAGUA
COSTA RICA
PANAMA

VENEZUELA 3

BR 0·3 GUIANA
DUTCH 0·2
FR 0·4

GAMBIA (Br) 0·2
PORT. GUINEA 0·8
SIERRA LEONE (Br) 2
LIBERIA 1

FRENCH WEST AFRICA 9

ASHANTI
TOGO 1
GOLD COAST 2

NIGERIA (Br) 16

KAMERUN (Ger)

FRENCH EQUATORIAL AFRICA

ANGLO-EGYPTIAN SUDAN 4

ERITREA (It) 0·5
FR SOMALILAND 0·2
BR SOMALILAND 0·4
ADEN PROT. (Br) 0·1
HADHRAMAUT

ABYSSINIA 9

IT. SOMALILAND 0·5

COLOMBIA 4

ECUADOR 1

UGANDA (Br) 5
BR. EAST AFRICA 4

BELGIAN CONGO 15

GERMAN EAST AFRICA 20

INDIA

PERU 4

BRAZIL 18

ANGOLA (Port.) 4

NYASALAND (Br) 1

ATLANTIC OCEAN

BOLIVIA 2

RHODESIA (Br) 2

PACIFIC OCEAN

PARAGUAY 0·6

1 Río de Janeiro

GERMAN SOUTH WEST AFRICA 0·1

BECHUANA LAND

PORTUGUESE EAST AFRICA 3

MADAGASCAR 3

CHILE 3

URUGUAY 1

1 Buenos Aires

CAPE COLONY (Br) 3

SWAZILAND 0·4
S.AFRICAN REP 1
NATAL (Br) 1
ORANGE FREE STATE 0·2
BASUTOLAND 0·3

ARGENTINA 7

Population of countries (figures in millions)

- 200
- 100
- 50
- 20
- 10
- 5
- 1

[2] City with 1 million inhabitants or more (figure indicates millions of inhabitants)

There are two striking features about the population of the world between 1900 and 1913. The first is that while Europe was densely populated, most of what we now describe as the Third World, together with the United States, was sparsely populated. Europe had a population of about 325 million, Africa only 13.5 million; Canada, Australia and most of Asia, except India and China, similarly had low population densities. The second feature is that while the populations of China, Japan, Russia, the United States and South America increased rapidly, that of Western Europe barely changed. Indeed France suffered from a falling birth rate, which weakened it economically *vis à vis* Germany, whose population had soared in the last two decades of the 19th century.

Across the world, the rise in population was largely due to improved medicine and hygiene. However, much of the increase in the American population was the result of immigration. During the 19th century millions of Europeans had emigrated to North and South America. As death rates fell in Europe, the growing populations of countries as diverse as Norway, Italy and Germany could not be absorbed into new industries or agriculture, and people left to find better wages, land and space in the New World. In addition, many emigrants sought the political and religious freedoms denied to them in their own countries, especially after the failure of the 1848 revolutions in Europe. The same was true of emigrants from Russia and Central and Eastern Europe in the early 20th century.

During the first decade of the 20th century, emigration to the United States continued at a high level both from southern European countries, such as Portugal and Italy, and Eastern Europe, all of which were still dependent on agriculture. On the other hand, greater prosperity in Western Europe after 1900 resulted in a decline in emigration to the New World. Thus in Germany, economic growth meant a higher demand for labour, and workers began to pour in from Poland and Italy. Moreover, German workers benefited from state pensions and insurance schemes introduced during the 1880s. As a result, German emigration decreased dramatically between 1910 and 1914.

In Russia, too, the situation changed in the years before the First World War. Five out of every fourteen emigrants who had left Russia in the previous 30 years had returned by 1914. This process was encouraged by the progress of Russia's industrialization before 1914, which led to the growth of an urban middle class which hoped that the limited constitution granted in 1905 would be followed by more comprehensive political reforms.

Chronology 1900–1914

EUROPE	AMERICAS

1900

	EUROPE		AMERICAS
Feb	● British Labour Representation Committee founded (Labour Party)		
Sept	● Founding of Socialist Revolutionary Party of Russia		

1901

	EUROPE		AMERICAS
Jan	● Death of Queen Victoria and accession of Edward VII in Britain	Mar	● William McKinley becomes US President for second term
		Sept	● President McKinley is assassinated and is succeeded by Vice-President Theodore Roosevelt

1902

	EUROPE		AMERICAS
Apr	● Peasant revolt in Russia suppressed	Dec	● Venezuela blockaded by Britain and Germany over non-payment of international debt
June	● Triple Alliance of Germany, Austria and Italy renewed		
Dec	● Secondary education provided by the state in England and Wales		

1903

	EUROPE		AMERICAS
Jan	● Ownership of land for peasants in Ireland as the landlords are gradually bought out	Jan	● Alaska frontier question settled between USA and Canada
Apr	● Massacre of Russian Jews at Kishinev, Bessarabia	Nov	● US–Panama treaty places Panama Canal Zone in US hands
Aug	● Pope Pius X succeeds Pope Leo XIII (died July)	Nov	● Panama declares itself independent of Colombia
Nov	● Russian Social Democratic Party splits into Mensheviks and Bolsheviks		

1904

	EUROPE		AMERICAS
Feb	● Outbreak of Russo–Japanese War	Nov	● Theodore Roosevelt elected President of USA
Apr	● Entente Cordiale between Britain and France following agreement on territorial disputes over Morocco, Siam (Thailand), Newfoundland and Egypt		
Oct	● Russian fleet mistakenly fires on British trawlers at Dogger Bank in North Sea		

1905

	EUROPE		AMERICAS
Jan	● Russian Revolution follows 'Bloody Sunday' massacre (22nd) in St Petersburg		
June	● Norway declares independence from Sweden		
July	● Separation of Church and State in France		
Oct	● First of Russian soviets (councils) formed in St Petersburg under Leon Trotsky		
Nov	● Foundation of Sinn Féin ('Ourselves Alone') party in Ireland		
Dec	● Uprising in Moscow crushed by government troops		

1906

	EUROPE		AMERICAS
Jan	● Liberal landslide in British general election leads to sweeping social reforms	Apr	● Earthquake in San Francisco kills more than 1,000 people
Mar	● Algeçiras Conference: Spain and France confirm Morocco's independence	July	● Peace treaty ends war between Guatemala, El Salvador and Honduras
May	● First meeting of Duma (elected parliament) in Russia	Oct	● Insurrection in Cuba on President Palma's re-election; Roosevelt intervenes to establish provisional government to carry out reforms
June	● Anti-Semitic pogroms in Russia		
July	● Russian Duma dissolved and martial law declared		
Nov	● Leon Trotsky exiled to Siberia		

1907

	EUROPE		AMERICAS
Aug	● Anglo-Russian agreement defines spheres of influence in central Asia and Persia	Nov	● Oklahoma becomes state of USA

AFRICA, ASIA, AUSTRALASIA	SCIENCE & CULTURE

AFRICA, ASIA, AUSTRALASIA

Jan • British Protectorate established over northern Nigeria
Feb • Boer War in South Africa: relief from Boer siege of Ladysmith by British forces
May • Orange Free State annexed by Britain
May • Mafeking relieved by British forces after 217 days siege
May • Russians occupy Manchuria and massacre 45,000 Chinese
June • Boxer Rebellion in China

Jan • Foundation of Commonwealth of Australia, with Edmund Barton as first Prime Minister
Feb • North West Frontier Province created in India between Afghanistan and Punjab
Sept • Peace Protocol between China and European powers ends Boxer Rebellion
Sept • Ashanti kingdom annexed to British Gold Coast colony

Apr • Russo–Japanese Convention: Russia agrees to evacuate Manchuria
May • Peace of Vereeniging ends Boer War
Sept • White settlement of Kenya highlands begins

Feb • Kano, Nigeria, submits to Britain
Mar • British occupation of northern Nigeria complete

Feb • Russo–Japanese war begins as Japanese attack Russian fleet
Aug • British troops, led by Francis Younghusband, arrive in Tibet
Oct • Revolt of Hereros and Hottentots against Germans in South-West Africa (until 1908)
Oct • Reorganization of French possessions as French West Africa, with capital at Dakar

May • Destruction of Russian fleet by Japanese at Tsushima
July • Muslim uprising in German East Africa
Sept • Treaty of Portsmouth (US): Japan establishes protectorate over Korea and secures leasehold of Port Arthur and Sakhalin Island after its defeat of Russia
Nov • Government of Papua transferred from Britain to Australia

Mar • Britain pays compensation for damage caused in the Boer War
Dec • Aga Khan founds All-India Muslim League
Dec • Transvaal colony is granted self-government in South Africa

Mar • Anarchy in Morocco: French troops move in
July • Orange River colony gains autonomy as Orange Free State
Sept • Revolt of Hereros crushed by German troops
Sept • New Zealand receives dominion status

SCIENCE & CULTURE

• Giacomo Puccini *Tosca*
• Edward Elgar *Dream of Gerontius*
• First Zeppelin flight in Germany
• Quantum theory is formulated by Max Planck
• Browning revolver invented by John M Browning
• Sigmund Freud *Interpretation of Dreams*
• Second Modern Olympic Games are held in Paris

• Ragtime jazz develops in USA
• Sergei Rachmaninov 2nd Piano Concerto
• First Nobel prizes awarded
• Trans-Siberian railway completed
• Adrenalin discovered by Jokichi Takamine
• Guglielmo Marconi achieves first transatlantic radio transmission

• Claude Debussy *Pelléas et Mélisande*
• Completion of Aswan Dam in Egypt
• Hormonal action demonstrated by William Bayliss and Ernest Starling

• Jack London *The Call of the Wild*
• Henry James *The Ambassadors*
• Leos Janáček *Jenufa*
• Ford Motor Company formed in Detroit, USA
• Wright brothers make first successful flight in aeroplane with petrol engine

• Joseph Conrad *Nostromo*
• Auguste Rodin *The Thinker*
• Rolls-Royce company formed
• Giacomo Puccini *Madame Butterfly*
• Abbey Theatre, Dublin opened
• Anton Chekhov *The Cherry Orchard*
• New York Broadway subway opens with first electric trams
• Silicone developed by F S Kipping

• Claude Debussy *La Mer*
• First cinema opens in Pittsburgh, USA
• Theory of Relativity formulated by Albert Einstein
• Antonio Gaudi builds Casa Mila in Barcelona
• Les Fauves (Wild Beasts) group led by Henri Matisse and André Derain

• Gamma rays discovered by Joseph Thomson
• Vitamins discovered by Frederick Gowland Hopkins
• Roald Amundsen crosses North West Passage and determines position of magnetic North Pole

• Mahler 8th Symphony ('Symphony of a Thousand')
• Pablo Picasso *Les Demoiselles d'Avignon*
• Ivan Pavlov studies conditioned reflexes
• Pablo Picasso and Georges Braques evolve Cubist Movement

EUROPE	AMERICAS

EUROPE

Feb	• Assassination of Carlos I and Crown Prince of Portugal
July	• 'Young Turk' revolutionaries promise elections in Ottoman Empire
Oct	• Bulgaria declares its independence from Turkey
Oct	• Austria annexes Turkish provinces of Bosnia and Hercegovina
Dec	• Disastrous earthquake in south Calabria (Italy) and Sicily

Apr	• Sultan Abdul Hamid II of Turkey deposed by 'Young Turks': Muhammad V succeeds until 1923
Aug	• Anti-government revolutionary rising in Barcelona, Spain, crushed

May	• Edward VII of Britain dies and is succeeded by George V
Sept	• Italy declares war on Turkey
Oct	• Revolution in Portugal: Manuel II abandons throne, Portugal is declared a republic

Aug	• Strikes and industrial unrest in Britain
Nov	• Italy annexes Turkish province of Tripoli
Nov	• Suffragette riots in Whitehall, London

Jan	• German elections leave Socialists the largest single party in the Reichstag
May	• Italy bombards Dardanelles and seizes Rhodes
May	• Greece signs anti-Ottoman alliance with Bulgaria (joined by Serbia in July)
Oct	• Treaty of Ouchy ends Italo–Turkish war: Italy secures Tripoli
Oct	• First Balkan War: Serbia, Montenegro, Greece and Bulgaria drive Turkey out of Macedonia

Jan	• German Army Bill expands size of German army
May	• Albania declares its independence from Turkey
June	• Second Balkan War: Bulgaria fights Serbia, Turkey, Greece and Romania, but loses substantial territory in peace settlement (in Aug)
Aug	• Treaty of Bucharest ends Second Balkan War

Mar	• Curragh 'mutiny' of British Army against Home Rule in Ulster
May	• Irish Home Rule Act introduces self-government for all of Ireland
June	• Assassination of Archduke Francis Ferdinand, heir to the Austro-Hungarian throne, at Sarajevo in Bosnia

AMERICAS

May	• North Carolina becomes a 'dry' (no-alcohol) state
Aug	• Cuba holds first general election under US supervision: Liberal victory, with José Gomez as President (until 1913)

Dec	• Dr José Madriz elected in Nicaragua to succeed ousted President Zelaya

May	• Mexican Civil War: Porfirio Díaz overthrown, Francisco Madero becomes President

Jan	• New Mexico and Arizona (Feb) become states of USA
Apr	• SS Titanic sinks, drowning 1,500 people
May	• US marines land in Nicaragua to prevent renewal of civil war

Jan	• Woodrow Wilson becomes President of USA
Feb	• General Victoriano Huerta takes power in Mexico and murders Madero. Wilson refuses recognition and US arms embargo ensues

Jan	• President Oreste of Haiti abdicates during revolt and US marines land to preserve order
Mar	• Unrest in Brazil: Rio de Janeiro in state of siege
Mar	• President Wilson sends US troops into northern Mexico to crush bandits
Apr	• Civil government established in Panama Canal Zone
Apr	• General civil disorder in Mexico: many local dictators: Aluaro Obregon is dictator of three-quarters of Mexico
July	• President Huerta succeeded by Venustiano Carranza
Aug	• Universal Negro Improvement Association and African Committees formed in Jamaica

May	• Pan-Islamic Hijaz railway opened in Arabia as far as Medina
Aug	• Léopold II hands over control of the Congo to Belgian government
Nov	• Labour government elected in Australia

• Ford Motor Company produces first Model 'T'
• Béla Bartók 1st String Quartet

Oct	• Prince Ho Hirobumi assassinated after establishing Japanese control in Korea
Dec	• Union of Cape Colony, Transvaal and Orange Free State

• Robert Peary reaches North Pole
• Sergei Diaghilev launches *Ballets Russes* in Paris

Jan	• French Congo reorganized as French Equatorial Africa
May	• Louis Botha and James Hertzog found South African Party and win first elections
July	• Cape Colony, Natal, Orange Free State and Transvaal form independent Dominion of South Africa

• Vasili Kandinsky *Improvisation XIV* one of the paintings to herald the start of purely abstract painting
• Excavation of Knossos and discovery of Minoan culture by British archaelogist Arthur Evans
• Edward Elgar Violin Concerto
• Igor Stravinsky *The Firebird*

Mar	• French troops occupy Fez, Moroccan capital, after tribal revolt
July	• Agadir crisis in Morocco with arrival of German gunboat, *Panther*, to protect its interests in Morocco
Sept	• Italo–Turkish War begins in Libya
Oct	• Famine and revolution in China: Manchu dynasty overthrown (Dec)
Nov	• French protectorate imposed on Morocco

• First fighter plane built by Anton Fokker
• Aircraft first used for offensive measures by Italians in Libya
• Roald Amundsen reaches South Pole
• Georges Braque *Man with a Guitar*
• Richard Strauss *Der Rosenkavalier*

Jan	• Chinese republic proclaimed under leader Sun Yixian (Sun Yat-sen)
Feb	• Sun Yixian replaced by General Yuan Shikai
Apr	• Tibetans expel Chinese troops from Lhasa
Aug	• Japan and Russia reach agreement over spheres of influence in Mongolia and Manchuria

• Robert Scott and companions die after reaching South Pole
• Glenn Curtiss constructs first sea-plane
• Stainless steel invented by Howard Brearley
• Maurice Ravel *Daphnis et Chloé*
• Arnold Schoenberg *Pierrot Lunaire*

July	• China agrees to grant Mongolian independence
Nov	• Mohandas Gandhi, leader of Indian Passive Resistance Movement in South Africa, is arrested after protesting against Transvaal government's discrimination against its Indian population

• First Charlie Chaplin motion picture
• D H Lawrence *Sons and Lovers*
• Marcel Proust first part of *À La Recherche du Temps Perdu* (completed 1927)
• Igor Stravinsky *Rite of Spring*
• Thomas Mann *Death In Venice*

Jan	• Northern and Southern Nigeria united as single British colony
Dec	• Egypt declared British protectorate

• See page 35

THE WAR TO END ALL WARS

A relatively stable order was smashed in an orgy of blood and violence.

On the outbreak of the First World War in 1914, Sir Edward Grey, the British Foreign Secretary, remarked to a friend that "the lamps are going out all over Europe. We shall not see them lit again in our life-time." In retrospect many contemporaries shared Grey's view that a relatively stable order, one marked by continuous progress and prosperity, had been smashed in an orgy of blood letting and violence. The resurgence of European intellectual culture and a vibrant experimental art that had occurred before the war – itself the origin of the post-war modern movement – was swamped under a tide of jingoism and militarism.

The pre-war pageantry of the ruling classes – the balls, fêtes, spas and country houses of the well-to-do, the poetry and literature of the younger intellectuals – had always been merely a veneer masking profound social unease. All countries experienced increasing labour unrest, strikes and riots in the years prior to 1914. Britain faced civil war in Ireland and suffragette violence in England. Revolutionary outbreaks in Russia culminated in the assassination of the Prime Minister, P.A. Stolypin, in 1911, while increasing nationalist fervour throughout Europe and virulent anti-Semitism in both Austria–Hungary and Russia disfigured what often seem in hindsight to have been peaceful and civilized societies. At the same time the rise of the socialist movement in Europe terrified the propertied classes.

Nor was the likelihood of a long and destructive war lacking its prophets. Ivan Bloch, a Polish banker, in a vast study written during the 1890s, warned his readers that gigantic strides in modern military technology, allied to the conscription of millions of young adult males, would cause the next war to be a long drawn-out, bloody stalemate, leading eventually to revolution and the collapse of Western civilization. Norman Angell, a British writer, believed that the intricate peace-time mechanism of international finance, investment and trade would collapse on the outbreak of war, leading to immense suffering and chaos. Such forebodings were dismissed by European generals, who planned to wage a short, victorious war, brevity made necessary, in their view, by the colossal expense of the undertaking. In the event Bloch was proved to have been largely accurate in his prophecy. During the war the trenches, barbed wire, machine guns and artillery dominated the battlefield, cutting a swathe of death and mutilation through an entire generation of young men.

The war did, however, bring some transient benefits to previously deprived elements in all the belligerent nations. Governments found themselves forced to intervene industrially and socially in an unprecedented fashion to mobilize all their resources to meet the insatiable demands of the war machines. The effort created conditions of almost full employment, and the working classes were now in a position to bargain for improved wages and better working conditions. Women had to be called upon in large numbers to replace the men who had gone to fight, and many left domestic service, the chief source of female employment before 1914, to work in the new munitions factories or in non-combatant roles in

The Russian Revolutions of 1917

In February 1917 the Tsarist regime collapsed in Russia, a victim of its own incompetence in managing a world war. The transport system was in chaos, there were acute shortages of food and clothing, and munitions were not reaching the war fronts. In addition, the armies were demoralized by a long succession of defeats and large number of casualties.

The revolution began when strikers demonstrating about food shortages in Petrograd (then the capital) were joined by the Petrograd military garrison which had been ordered to crush them. The Tsar's ministers were arrested and the Tsar was forced to abdicate on 2 March. The insurrectionists then set up soviets, or workers' and soldiers' councils, to monitor events and the Duma (parliament) which met on 27 February, fearing mob rule, hastily set up a Provisional government consisting of liberal politicians under Prince Lvov. It was hoped that this government would administer the country until a Constituent Assembly, elected by the Russian people, could be established. The soviets and the Provisional government co-existed uneasily until the Bolshevik revolution in October.

Imprisoned members of the various revolutionary parties, including the Bolsheviks, an extreme Marxist group, were released, while the German government, anxious to disrupt Russia's war effort further, allowed Vladimir Illyich Lenin, the Bolshevik leader, to travel in a sealed train from his exile in Switzerland across Germany to Petrograd. The Bolsheviks soon began to penetrate the soviets. The Provisional government meanwhile announced that it would continue to prosecute the war, and prepared for a new Russian offensive in the summer. This decision was not popular with the mass of the population, which was suffering from food shortages and war weariness. Meanwhile, the peasants were clamouring for the seizure of the estates of the nobility and their redistribution, which the government insisted must be done legally through an eventual Constituent Assembly. When A.F. Kerensky, the Minister of Justice, replaced Lvov in July, all he could offer was a more vigorous prosecution of the war. His position was further weakened when General Kornilov, the Army Supreme Commander, attempted unsuccessfully to overthrow the government in July. As the economy continued to deteriorate, and with the transport system at a complete standstill, Russia's armies, after further defeats during the summer, began to disintegrate as troops deserted in large numbers. The Provisional government staggered on until after an almost bloodless coup in October, Lenin and the Bolsheviks seized power in Petrograd. They had triumphed as a minority party because of Lenin's shrewd tactical skill in striking at the most favourable moment, because of the divisions among their opponents, and because of the disorder and confusion inside Russia.

◀ **With the majority of men called-up to fight, young women and the elderly formed the workforce in munitions factories.**

the armed services. (Many of these gains were lost during the post-war slump as demobilized ex-servicemen swelled the unemployed, although British women were given the vote. Dissatisfaction with the meagre results of war-time sacrifices became widespread after the war.)

The length of the war did encourage the growth of a strong popular movement in the West, spearheaded by the US President, Woodrow Wilson, which called for a new morality in politics and international affairs. War should be outlawed and conflicts prevented by a world founded on the principle of national self-determination, with an international organization to arbitrate disputes and maintain peace. This system was to replace the pre-1914 balance of power politics and alliance systems, and prevent the frenzied arms races associated with them, which many felt had been responsible for the war.

Wilson's vision was challenged, however, by an alternative programme put forward by Vladimir Illyich Lenin and the Bolsheviks, who had seized power in Russia in 1917. The European socialist movement had disintegrated on the outbreak of war, with the majority of socialists in every country supporting their governments' war efforts. However, Lenin's revolutionary Marxist party was bitterly hostile to moderate socialism, which had failed to act internationally to prevent the war and which had showed itself to be the ally of capitalism. Lenin's communist ideology envisaged a peaceful world based not upon capitalist exploitation and violence but on the victory of the proletariat worldwide. Communist propaganda seeking to undermine the loyalty of the proletariat in the West to the existing order terrified the bourgeoisie, and at the end of the war added a new and menacing source of instability to an irreparably fissured world order.

The Causes of World War I

Legend:
- International boundary 1914
- Central Power at outbreak of war
- State later allied to Central Powers
- Entente Power at outbreak of war
- Ally or associate of Entente Powers
- Neutral State later allied to Entente Powers
- Neutral throughout the war
- → Schlieffen plan
- Slav–inhabited areas of Austria-Hungary
- Ottoman lands gained by Balkan states 1913

0 km ———— 400
0 mls ———— 300

SWEDEN

NORWAY

FINLAND

L. Lad

Bergen
Christiania
Stockholm
St. Petersbu

NORTH SEA

DENMARK

BALTIC SEA

Riga

Mins

Gothenburg

Glasgow
Edinburgh
Belfast

UNITED KINGDOM

Dublin

Manchester

Birmingham

London

Copenhagen

Danzig
Königsberg

Hamburg

Berlin

Warsaw

GERMAN EMPIRE

Cologne
Leipzig
Breslau

Oder

Vistula

NETHERLANDS
Amsterdam

Brussels
BELGIUM
LUX.

Frankfurt
Nuremberg

Prague

Krakow
Lemberg

Dn

ATLANTIC OCEAN

Brest

Seine

Paris
Reims

Rhine

ALSACE – LORRAINE

Munich

AUSTRIA -

Vienna

Tisza

Loire

Tours

Berne
SWITZERLAND

Danube

Budapest

Yassy

FRANCE

Bordeaux

Lyon

Rhône

Milan

Turin

Venice

Trieste

HUNGARY

Sava
BOSNIA
Annexed by
Austria 1908–9
Sarajevo

Belgrade
SERBIA

Bucharest

ROMAN

Danube

Var

Toulouse

Marseille

ITALY

Florence

Rome

ADRIATIC SEA

MONTENEGRO
Cetinje
Uskub

BULGARIA

Sofia

PORTUGAL

Lisbon

SPAIN

Tagus

Madrid

Ebro

Barcelona

Corsica

Sardinia

Naples

Durazzo

ALBANIA

Salonica

Gall

Balearic Is.

Tangier

Gibraltar
(Br)

SPANISH
MOROCCO

Algiers

Palermo

Sicily

GREECE

Athens

Aegean Sea

Crete

Tunis

MOROCCO
(Fr)

ALGERIA
(Fr)

TUNISIA
(Fr)

Malta
(Br)

MEDITERRANEAN SEA

Tripoli

LIBYA
(Italian)

The immediate cause of the First World War was the murder of the heir to the Austrian throne, Francis Ferdinand, by Serbian-backed terrorists in Sarajevo, the capital of the Austrian province of Bosnia, on 28 June 1914. This assassination brought to a head the hatreds which had long poisoned great power relations. In 1914 Europe was divided between two hostile alliance systems: Germany and Austria–Hungary on the one hand, and France, Britain and Russia on the other. In 1904 Britain, increasingly suspicious of Germany's ambitions, had abandoned its policy of 'Splendid Isolation' and had aligned itself with France and, in 1907, with Russia to form the Triple Entente. Any conflict between two rival powers was therefore likely to involve the whole of Europe in a major war. An arms race, together with a series of international crises after 1900, had raised tensions to boiling point.

While Germany was by 1914 the strongest industrial and military power in Europe, it remained restless and insecure. It watched with increasing foreboding the growth of Russia's military power, and its fears for future security were enhanced with encirclement by the Triple Entente, and the growing enfeeblement of its only reliable ally, Austria–Hungary. Serbia was actively conspiring against Austria to bring about its disintegration and the absorption of the South Slavs into a greater Serbia. Serbian complicity in the murder of Francis Ferdinand provided Austria with the opportunity to crush Serbia before it was too late, and Germany urged Austria to act decisively.

Germany hoped that the ensuing conflict could be localized, but its own military and diplomatic strategy made this impossible. Faced by a war on two fronts against France and Russia, its generals had devised a war plan that would enable the main German armies to march through Belgium and defeat France before Russia could mobilize its forces and launch an offensive in the east. Once the French army had been annihilated Germany's main armies would then be switched to crush Russia. This necessitated immediate war with France in the event of a conflict with Russia, since the latter could be allowed no time to complete its laborious mobilization.

When Austria finally declared war on Serbia on 28 July, Russia, acting in defence of fellow Slavs, mobilized on 31 July as a warning to Austria not to go too far. Germany thereupon declared war on Russia on 1 August, and on France on 3 August. Its invasion of Belgium on 4 August brought Britain into the war in defence of Belgian neutrality, and a British force crossed the Channel to fight alongside the French army. All the major powers except Italy, which remained neutral until 1915, were now at war.

The Western Front

Bruges

Ghent

Brussels

BELGIUM

Meuse

Namur

Nieuport

F L A N D E R S

Lys

Passchendaele
July–Oct 1917

Menin

Charleroi

Dinant

Dunkirk

Ypres
29 Oct–11 Nov 1914
22 Apr–24 May 1915

Messines

Lille

Givet

Strait of Dover

Calais

Neuve Chapelle

A R T O I S

La Bassée

Lens

Vimy

Arras

Boulogne

Armentières

Escaut

No military activity –
actual front line indeterminate

Douai

Mons
23 Aug 1914

Maubeuge

Sambre

Mézières

Cambrai
20 Nov–7 Dec 1917

Le Cateau
26 Aug 1914

Bapaume

Flers

The Somme
June–Sept 1916

Albert

P I C A R D Y

Somme

Amiens

Moreuil

Péronne

St. Quentin

Guise

Rethel

Laon

Aisne

C H A M P A G N E

Roye

Oise

Chemin des Dames

Reims

Montdidier

Noyon

Soissons

Maximum German advance
June–July 1918

Marne

Épernay

Compiègne

Villers-Cotterets

Belleau Wood
5–11 June 1918

Château Thierry

F R A N C E

Montmirail

Chantilly

Meaux

The Marne
5–10 Sept 1914

Coulommiers

Paris

Seine

Front lines 1914–1918

5 Sept 1914

Jan 1915

Feb 1916

Aug 1918

Nov 1918

Major battle

| 0 | km | | | 80 |
| 0 | mls | | | 50 |

26

With the outbreak of war in August 1914, powerful German armies thrust through Belgium and into northern France. By 5 September the Germans were 20 miles from Paris on the River Marne. Here the French rallied and forced the Germans to retreat to the River Aisne. After heavy fighting the front stabilized in northern France in November; a continuous line of trenches stretched from the North Sea coast of Belgium to the Swiss border, dividing the two sides. Repeated Franco–British offensives, notably at Ypres in 1915, on the River Somme in 1916 and again at Ypres in 1917, failed to move the front line more than a few miles.

The belligerents attempted to overcome the trench deadlock by using gas, tanks and aeroplanes, but artillery, machine guns and barbed wire remained the predominant weapons in this war of attrition. Attempts by the Allies to find alternative fronts to relieve pressure on the Western front, notably at Gallipoli in 1915, met with little success, and by the end of 1917 the Allied cause in the West had made little progress. Nor did Britain's naval superiority

enable it to defeat Germany at sea. The German navy only ventured out in force once, in May 1916, but the ensuing battle of Jutland was indecisive. In 1917 the Germans, in retaliation for the British blockade of their sea-born commerce, declared unrestricted submarine warfare against British and neutral shipping. The adoption of the convoy system in 1917 saved Britain from starvation, and the submarine campaign also brought the United States into the war against Germany in April 1917.

With the removal of Russia from the war in March 1918, the Germans switched the bulk of their forces to the Western front. By July the Germans had once more reached the River Marne. Heavy German casualties, and increasing shortages of food and raw materials resulting from the Allied blockade, enabled the Allies, reinforced by a million fresh US troops, to launch a counter-offensive in July which by October had driven the Germans back towards the German border. With its armies in retreat and its allies defeated, Germany signed an armistice on 11 November 1918.

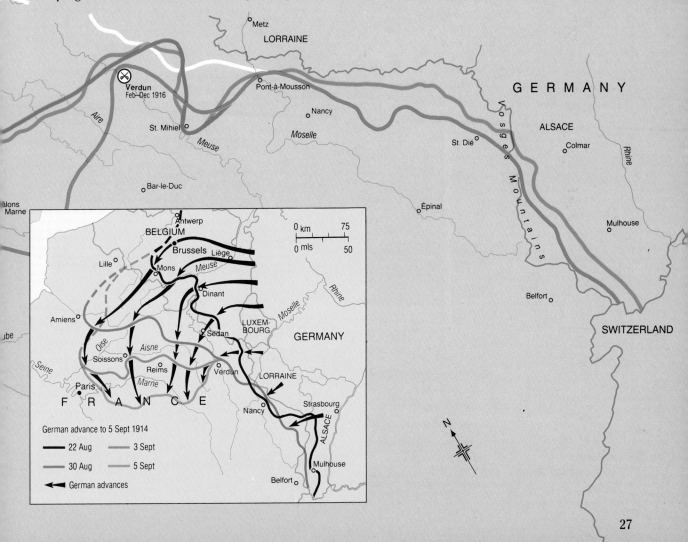

German advance to 5 Sept 1914

— 22 Aug   — 3 Sept

— 30 Aug   — 5 Sept

◄— German advances

World War I: Other Fronts

SWEDEN

BALTIC SEA

DENMARK

Petrograd

Riga
Sept 1917

Dvina

Vitebsk

Orel

Voronezh

Don

RUSSIAN EMPIRE

Memel

Vilnius

Minsk

Gomel

Kharkov

Rostov

Königsberg

Gumbinnen
Aug 1914

Grodno

Augustow

Masurian Lakes
Sept 1914

Baranovichi

Pinsk

Pripet

Pripet Marshes

Kiev

Dnieper

Yekaterinoslav

Tannenberg
Aug 1914

Brest-Litovsk

Thorn

Vistula

Warsaw
Oct–Nov 1914

POLAND

Lutsk

UKRAINE

Berlin

Oder

Lodz

Krasnik

GERMANY

Breslau

Lemberg
(Lvov)

Tarnopol

Odessa

Crimea

Tarnow

GALICIA

Dniester

Krakow

Przemysl
Mar 1915

Czernowitz

Sevastopol

Elbe

Limanowa
Dec 1914

Gorlice

Carpathians

Jassy

BLACK SEA

Prague

Tisza

Sinope

Danube

AUSTRIA-

Vienna

Budapest

HUNGARY

ROMANIA
conquered 1917

Constanta

Munich

Bucharest

Varna

Caporetto
Oct 1917

Belgrade

Danube

BULGARIA

Bosporus

Ankara

SWITZERLAND

Alps

Isonzo
1915–16

Trieste

Constantinople
(Istanbul)

OTT

Vittorio Veneto
Oct 1918

Venice

Sarajevo

Nish
Oct 1918

Sofia

Izmir

Milan

Po

SERBIA
conquered
Nov 1915

Spalato

MONTE-
NEGRO

Skopje

Gallipoli Peninsula
Apr 1915 – Jan 1916

Dardanelles

ITALY

ADRIATIC SEA

Monastir

Salonika
Allied landing
Oct 1915

Limnos

ALBANIA

GREECE

AEGEAN SEA

Athens

MEDITERRANEAN SEA

Alexandria

Legend

Allied Powers

Central Powers

⊗ Major battle

Italian Front
Front line

June 1916

Nov 1917

4 Nov 1918 at Armistice

Lines of advance

→ Central Powers, Oct–Nov 1917

→ Allies, Oct–Nov 1918

Eastern Front

Furthest extent of Russian forces,
Aug 1914

Furthest extent of Romanian forces,
Sept 1916

Front line at Armistice, Dec 1917

Lines of advance

→ Allies

→ Central Powers

→ Brusilov Offensive, Aug 1916

Boundary of Russian territory
occupied by Central Powers after
Treaty of Brest-Litovsk, Mar 1918

28

Given the vast spaces, the fighting in the East was much more fluid than in the West. Russia faced two enemies, Germany and Austria–Hungary. An initial Russian advance into East Prussia was repulsed by the Germans who destroyed the Second Russian Army at Tannenberg in late August 1914. Thereafter, despite inflicting defeats on the Austro–Hungarian armies in Galicia, Russia was steadily pushed out of Poland, while a Russian offensive in 1916 led by General Brusilov failed to regain much ground. The two Russian revolutions of 1917 weakened Russian resolve and led to a cease-fire with Germany and Austria–Hungary in December, in turn leading to the peace treaty of Brest–Litovsk in March 1918, which took Russia out of the War.

At the end of 1914 Turkey declared war on the Allies, and invaded Russian Armenia. Russian appeals for Allied assistance led in 1915 to an Anglo–French attempt to seize Constantinople and force Turkey out of the war. Having failed to take the Dardanelles Straits by naval action in March, the Western Allies landed troops on the Gallipoli Peninsula. The Allied troops were then tied down in trenches in the foot hills facing tenacious Turkish resistance from the high ground above. The expedition was evacuated in January 1916. An Anglo–French–Italian force occupied the Greek city of Salonika in December 1915, but did not break out and defeat Bulgaria until 1918. Italy had joined the Allies in May 1915 but failed to smash the Austro–German front despite a series of offensives along the Isonzo river. Italy suffered a major defeat at Caporetto in late 1917, rallied in 1918 and then defeated the demoralized Austro–Hungarian army at Vittorio Veneto in October.

In the Middle East, British troops attempted to advance from the Persian Gulf and take Baghdad in 1915 but were besieged by the Turks at Kut on the Tigris river and forced to surrender ignominiously early in 1916. Not until 1917, after Lawrence of Arabia had led an Arab guerrilla campaign against the Turks in Arabia, and British expeditions were mounted from Egypt and the Persian Gulf, did the tide turn against the Turks, who were driven out of Mesopotamia and Syria before they surrendered on 30 October 1918. Elsewhere, Britain, Australia, New Zealand, South Africa and Japan occupied Germany's colonies in China, the Pacific and in Africa, although a German force in German East Africa managed to evade the British until the end of the war in November 1918.

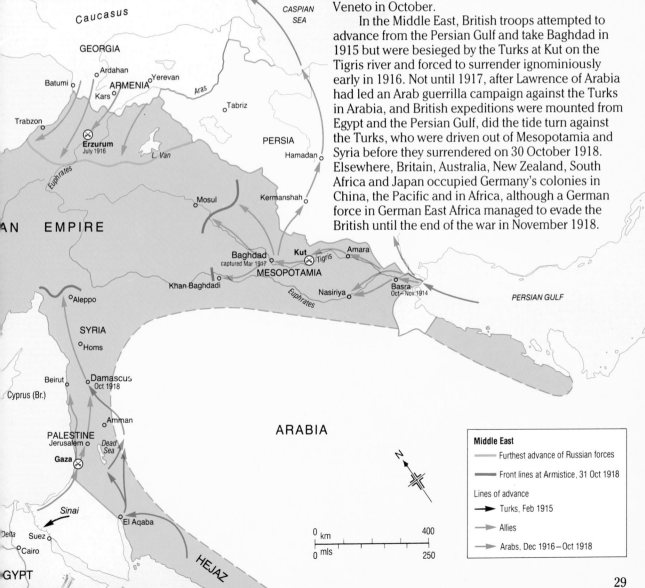

Making Peace

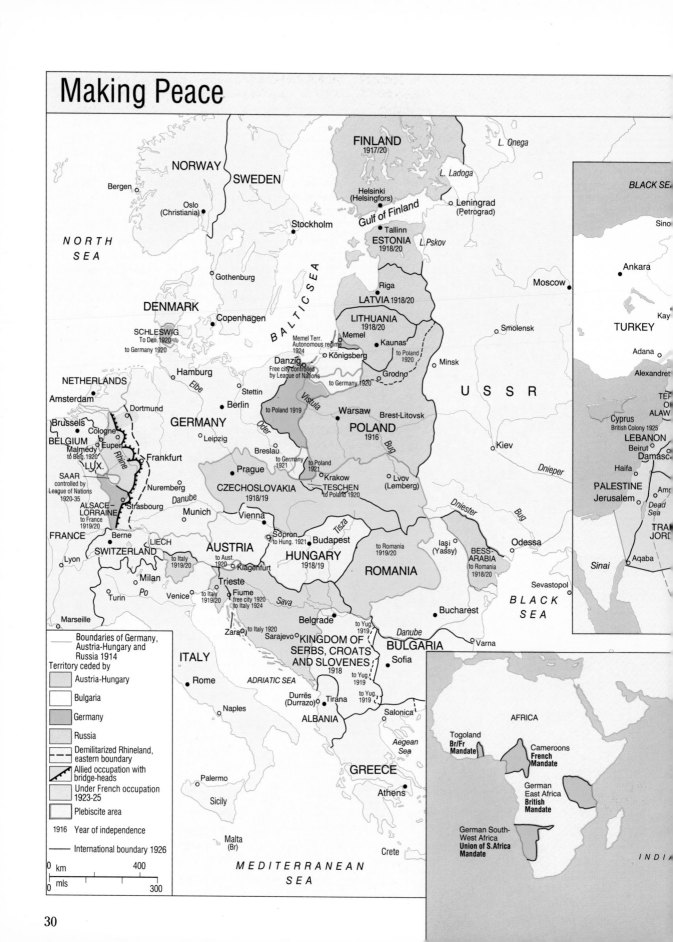

NORWAY

SWEDEN

Bergen

Oslo (Christiania)

Stockholm

NORTH SEA

Gothenburg

DENMARK

Copenhagen

SCHLESWIG
To Den. 1920
to Germany 1920

NETHERLANDS

Amsterdam

Brussels

Dortmund

Cologne

BELGIUM

Malmédy
to Belg. 1920

Eupen

LUX.

Frankfurt

SAAR
controlled by
League of Nations
1920-35

Nuremberg

ALSACE-
LORRAINE
to France
1919/20

Strasbourg

FRANCE

Berne

Lyon

SWITZERLAND

LIECH

Milan

Turin

Marseille

Hamburg

Elbe

Stettin

GERMANY

Berlin

Leipzig

BALTIC SEA

Rhine

Danube

Munich

Vienna

AUSTRIA

to Italy
1919/20

to Aust.
1920

Klagenfurt

Trieste

Fiume
free city 1920
to Italy 1924

to Italy
1919/20

Venice

Po

ITALY

Rome

Naples

ADRIATIC SEA

Zara
to Italy 1920

Durrës
(Durrazo)

Tirana

ALBANIA

Palermo

Sicily

Malta
(Br)

Crete

Breslau

to Germany
1921

Prague

CZECHOSLOVAKIA
1918/19

to Poland
1921

to Poland
1919

Oder

Vistula

Danzig
Free city controlled
by League of Nations

Memel Terr.
Autonomous regime
1924

Memel

Königsberg

to Germany 1920

Warsaw

POLAND
1916

Brest-Litovsk

Bug

Krakow

TESCHEN
to Poland 1920

Lvov
(Lemberg)

Tisza

Sopron
to Hung. 1921

Budapest

HUNGARY
1918/19

to Romania
1919/20

Iaşi
(Yassy)

Dniester

Bug

ROMANIA

Sava

Belgrade

Sarajevo

KINGDOM OF
SERBS, CROATS
AND SLOVENES
1918

to Yug.
1919/
20

to Yug.
1919

Danube

BULGARIA

Sofia

Varna

to Yug.
1919

Aegean Sea

GREECE

Athens

Salonica

FINLAND
1917/20

L. Onega

Helsinki
(Helsingfors)

L. Ladoga

Leningrad
(Petrograd)

Gulf of Finland

Tallinn

ESTONIA
1918/20

L. Pskov

Riga

LATVIA 1918/20

LITHUANIA
1918/20

Kaunas

to Poland
1920

Grodno

Minsk

Moscow

Smolensk

USSR

Kiev

Dnieper

Odessa

BESS-
ARABIA
to Romania
1918/20

Sevastopol

BLACK SEA

Bucharest

Inset (top right)

BLACK SEA

Sino

Ankara

Kay

TURKEY

Adana

Alexandret

Cyprus
British Colony 1925

TER
O
ALAW 1925

LEBANON

Beirut

Damasc

Haifa

PALESTINE

Jerusalem

Amr

Dead Sea

TRA
JOR

Sinai

Aqaba

INDI

Inset (bottom right)

AFRICA

Togoland
Br/Fr
Mandate

Cameroons
French
Mandate

German
East Africa
British
Mandate

German South-
West Africa
Union of S.Africa
Mandate

MEDITERRANEAN SEA

Legend

	Boundaries of Germany, Austria-Hungary and Russia 1914

Territory ceded by

	Austria-Hungary
	Bulgaria
	Germany
	Russia
---	Demilitarized Rhineland, eastern boundary
	Allied occupation with bridge-heads
	Under French occupation 1923-25
	Plebiscite area
1916	Year of independence
—	International boundary 1926

0 km 400

0 mls 300

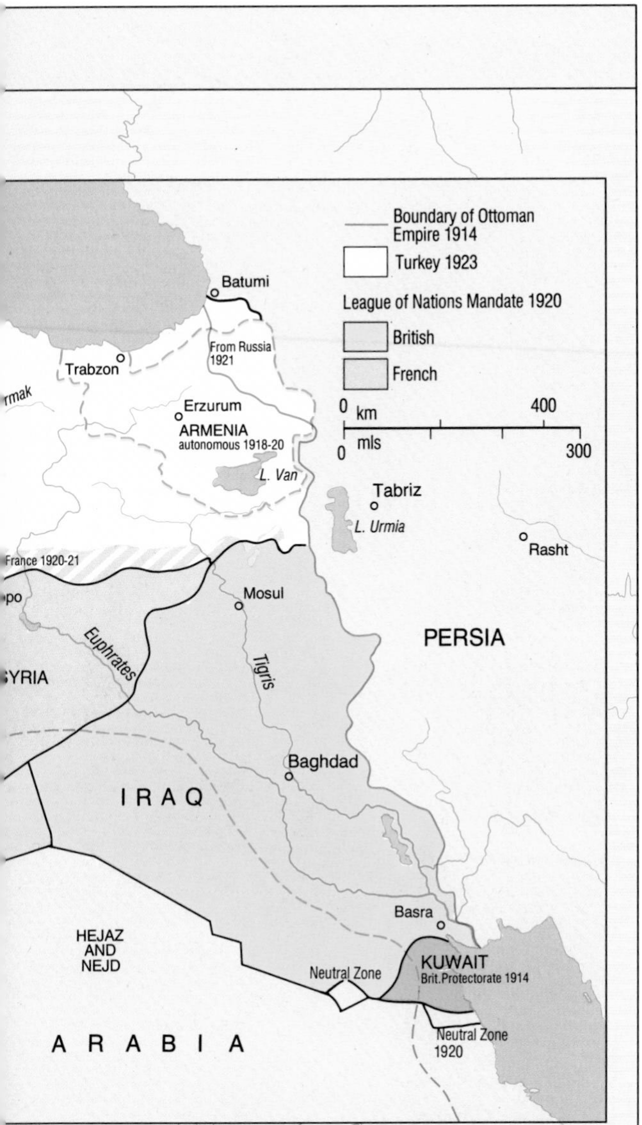
Boundary of Ottoman Empire 1914
Turkey 1923
League of Nations Mandate 1920
British
French
0 km 400
0 mls 300
Batumi
From Russia 1921
Trabzon
Erzurum
ARMENIA autonomous 1918-20
L. Van
Tabriz
L. Urmia
Rasht
France 1920-21
Mosul
Euphrates
Tigris
PERSIA
Baghdad
IRAQ
Basra
HEJAZ AND NEJD
KUWAIT Brit.Protectorate 1914
Neutral Zone
Neutral Zone 1920
ARABIA

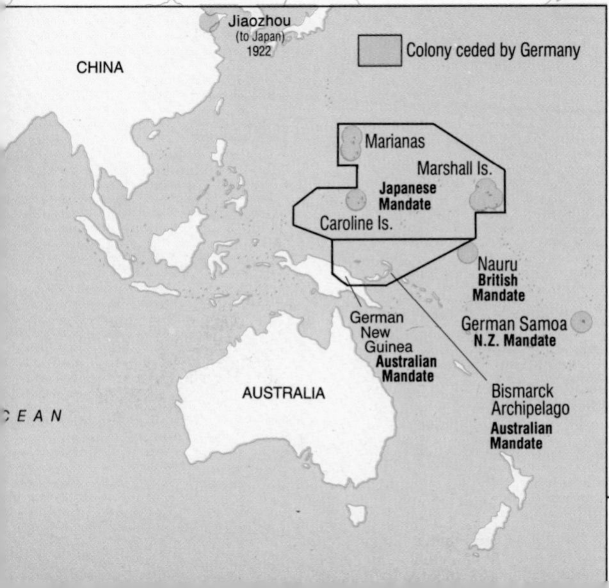
Jiaozhou (to Japan) 1922
Colony ceded by Germany
CHINA
Marianas
Marshall Is.
Japanese Mandate
Caroline Is.
Nauru British Mandate
German New Guinea Australian Mandate
German Samoa N.Z. Mandate
Bismarck Archipelago Australian Mandate
AUSTRALIA

The peace conference which convened in Paris in January 1919 to determine the fate of Germany and its allies was dominated by the five major victor powers – the British Empire, the United States, France, Italy and Japan. The conference was divided from the outset by the rivalry between the peace aims of the US President, Woodrow Wilson, and those of the other great powers. Wilson's post-war policy was based on his Fourteen Points speech of January 1918, which called for a future world order governed by the principles of national self-determination and the prevention of future wars by a world-wide League of Nations. His idealism conflicted with the ambitions of the other four powers, which had made arrangements to annex German and Turkish territories.

French demands, however, caused the most controversy. Conscious of its weakness *vis à vis* Germany, France insisted that the peace settlement should permanently weaken Germany. Britain and the United States successfully resisted the demand for the severance of the Rhineland from Germany, but did agree to a 15-year Allied occupation and permanent demilitarization of the Rhineland and the virtual disarmament of Germany. France also called for the imposition of a reparations bill on Germany to compensate the Allies for damage caused by the war.

Five peace treaties were signed at the end of the war. The main treaty with Germany was signed at the Palace of Versailles, outside Paris, on 28 June 1919. It was followed on 10 September by the Treaty of St Germain with Austria, on 27 November by the Treaty of Neuilly with Bulgaria, on 4 June 1920 by the Treaty of Trianon with Hungary, and finally on 10 August 1920 by the Treaty of Sèvres with Turkey. From these treaties arose the new nations of Poland, Czechoslovakia and Yugoslavia, joining Finland, Estonia, Latvia and Lithuania, which had emerged from the wreckage of the Russian Empire in 1917. Austria and Hungary were divided, Romania was enlarged and Germany was reduced in size. Where disputes arose as to ownership, plebiscites were held by the League of Nations to consult the local populations, although some disputes, notably at Teschen and Fiume, were resolved by force.

Outside Europe, the Allies secured the bulk of their territorial and colonial demands, as German colonies and Turkey's former possessions in the Middle East were handed over to them. Japan took the former German concession of Shandong, amid strong Chinese protests. The entire peace settlement failed to satisfy many nationalist aspirations in Europe and the Middle East, but objections were brushed aside, only to reappear later in new and more threatening guises.

The Costs of the War

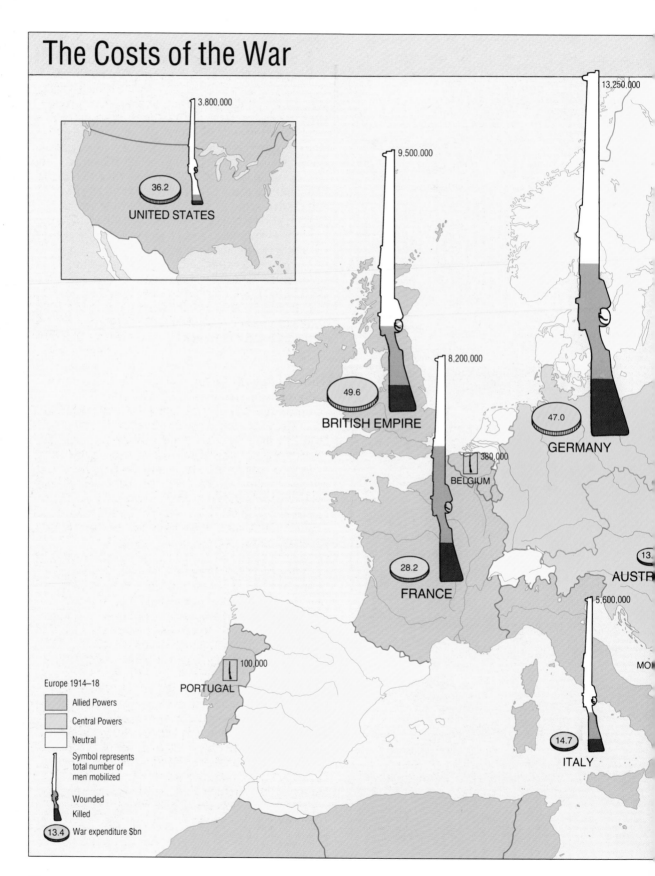

3.800.000

36.2

UNITED STATES

13.250.000

9.500.000

49.6

BRITISH EMPIRE

8.200.000

47.0

GERMANY

380.000

BELGIUM

28.2

FRANCE

13.

AUSTR

5.600.000

MO

100.000

PORTUGAL

14.7

ITALY

Europe 1914–18

Allied Powers

Central Powers

Neutral

Symbol represents
total number of
men mobilized

Wounded

Killed

13.4 War expenditure $bn

32

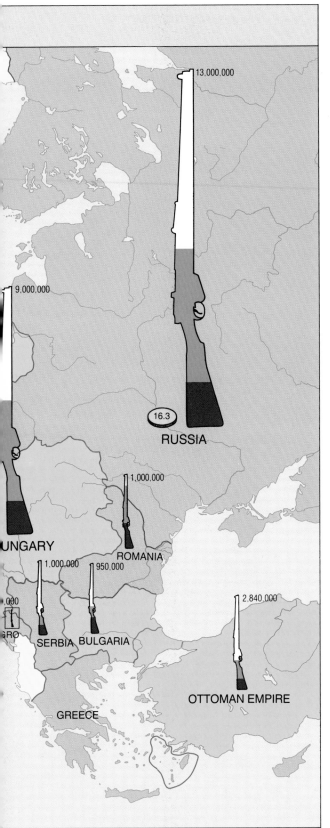

In 1914 millions of young men were conscripted into the armies of the belligerent nations and sent to the front lines. The Allies mobilized about 11 million troops in August 1914 and the Central Powers about eight million. In the long and bloody battles that ensued, in which the results of a half century of advanced military technology were fully employed, the number of casualties suffered on all sides was devastating. Indeed, in the case of Russia it was impossible to calculate a reliable figure. Of the other major powers, French deaths in the field of battle numbered about 1,400,000, German about 1,800,000, Austro–Hungarian some 1,300,000, British and British Empire 900,000, Italian 600,000 and American about 120,000.

In addition the war left behind an enormous legacy of indebtedness. In the Allied countries direct and indirect taxes were raised to unprecedented levels to help pay for the war, while Britain was forced to liquidate many overseas investments, suffering an outflow of gold reserves as it borrowed heavily from New York banks to sustain itself and its Allies in the struggle. By 1919 a complex structure of interlocking loans had been built up. Britain was owed at least $11 billion by other countries, and owed about $4.7 billion to the United States. France owed the United States and Britain a total of $7 billion. The war converted the United States from a debtor into a rich creditor nation, while Britain was now a new debtor whose plight was made worse by the loss of a considerable portion of its pre-war export trade to the United States, Japan and other countries, whose internal economies had not been badly affected by the war. After the war Britain and France pressed the United States to write off their debts as their contribution to the war effort. When the United States refused and turned down a request for reconstruction credits, the Allies sought to recoup their losses from Germany in the form of reparations. The French secured German deliveries of timber and other materials to assist them in the reconstruction of the shattered industries and mines of northern France.

Germany had paid for the war by borrowing heavily from the German people, and from using resources plundered from conquered territories, but by 1918 it, too, was economically exhausted and saddled with a huge internal debt it could not hope to repay. Germany was thus in no mind to pay the massive $32 billion demanded by the Allied Reparation Commission in 1921.

Chronology 1914–1918

EUROPE	AMERICAS

EUROPE

July	• Austria–Hungary declares war on Serbia
July	• Italy declares its neutrality
Aug	• Germany declares war on Russia and France, and invades Luxembourg and Belgium
Aug	• Britain and Belgium declare war on Germany
Aug	• Germans defeat Russians at the Battle of Tannenberg
Aug	• Japan declares war on Germany
Sept	• Trench warfare begins on Aisne salient
Sept	• Allies halt German advance on Paris at the Battle of the Marne
Sept	• Russians invade Hungary
Oct	• (to Nov) Battle of Ypres halts German advance
Nov	• Britain, France and Russia declare war on Turkey

Jan	• Britain announces naval blockade of Germany
Feb	• German submarines begin blockade of Britain
Apr	• Allies land on Gallipoli peninsula, Turkey
Apr	• Germans use poison gas at the Second Battle of Ypres
May	• Sinking of British liner, *Lusitania*, by German U-boat off Irish coast
May	• Italy denounces Triple Alliance and declares war on Austria
Sept	• British–French offensive in Champagne and Flanders fails to break German front
Oct	• Bulgaria joins Central Powers and launches offensive against Serbia with Austria and Germany

Feb	• (to July) German offensive on western front at the Battle of Verdun causes terrible losses
Apr	• Easter Rebellion in Dublin
May	• Battle of Jutland, the only major naval battle in the war between Britain and Germany
June	• Brusilov offensive by Russians in Galicia
July	• (to Nov) Over one million killed at the Battle of the Somme
Aug	• Romania declares war on Germany
Oct	• Greek fleet surrenders to Allies at Athens
Nov	• Central Powers proclaim independence of Poland

Feb	• Revolution in Russia leads to abdication of Tsar (Mar) and establishment of Provisional government
June	• Sinn Féin riots in Dublin
July	• Major Allied offensive at the Third Battle of Ypres (Passchendaele)
Aug	• Revolt in Spain over home rule for Catalonia
Oct	• Italians defeated by Austrians at the Battle of Caporetto
Oct	• Russian Revolution: Bolsheviks led by Lenin seize power

Jan	• Russia proclaimed Union of Soviet Socialist Republic
Mar	• Treaty of Brest–Litovsk: Russia withdraws from the war
Aug	• Allied offensive on western front breaks through Hindenburg line of defences
Oct	• Italian victory at the Battle of Vittorio Veneto: Austria–Hungary surrenders
Oct	• Czechoslovakia proclaimed independent republic
Nov	• German navy mutinies
Nov	• Kaiser Wilhelm II abdicates and Germany is proclaimed a republic
Nov	• Armistice signed between Germany and Allies
Nov	• Poland proclaimed a republic
Dec	• Bolshevik rule in Estonia
Dec	• Serbo-Croat-Slovene Kingdom of Yugoslavia proclaimed

AMERICAS

Aug	• USA proclaims itself neutral
Aug	• Panama Canal opened to commerce
Dec	• British defeat German fleet at Battle of Falklands

Jan	• House of Representatives defeat proposal for women's suffrage in USA
Jan	• Pancho Villa of Mexico signs treaty with USA, halting border conflict
July	• Revolution in Haiti: US troops occupy Haiti to 1934
Sept	• USA loans $500 million to Britain and France

Mar	• US punitive expeditions to Mexico continue
Apr	• Nicaragua grants the USA the right to build trans-isthmian canal
June	• Battle of Carrizal between US and Mexican troops
Nov	• Woodrow Wilson, Democrat, re-elected US President
Nov	• Jeanette Rankin, Montana, becomes first woman member of Congress

Mar	• US marines land at Santiago, Cuba, at request of civil government
Apr	• Following sinking of six US ships, USA, Cuba and all South American states (except Brazil) enter First World War on side of Allies
June	• Brazil revokes its neutrality and seizes German ships
June	• First US troops arrive in France
Dec	• Prohibition in Canada

Jan	• First US oil pipeline begins operation in Wyoming
Jan	• Congress passes law in favour of women's suffrage
May	• Nicaragua and Costa Rica declare war on Central Powers
June	• New York ports close after sinking of nine ships by U-boats off Atlantic coast
Aug	• USA severs relations with Russia

AFRICA, ASIA, AUSTRALASIA

Aug	• British forces capture German Togoland
Aug	• Japan declares war on Germany and seizes German interests in China
Oct	• Boer rebellion under Christiaan de Wet against British in South Africa crushed
Nov	• Anzac (Australian and New Zealand Army Corps) troops occupy Samoa and German New Guinea
Nov	• Indian troops occupy Basra in Persian Gulf
Dec	• Mahatma Gandhi returns to India from South Africa and supports government

Jan	• In response to Japan's '21 demands', China cedes all German interests in southern Manchuria and Inner Mongolia to Japan but rejects Japanese demand for virtual protectorate over China
Jan	• South African troops occupy Swakopmund in German South-West Africa
Feb	• Turks repulsed from Suez Canal
May	• Louis Botha occupies Windhoek, capital of German South-West Africa
July	• German forces in South-West Africa surrender to Botha
Sept	• British forces advance against Turks in Mesopotamia
Nov	• Chinese princes vote for establishment of a monarchy, with Yuan Shikai as emperor

Feb	• British, French and Belgian forces complete conquest of German Cameroons
Apr	• British surrender Kut-el-Amara to Turks
June	• Arab revolt in Hijaz begins as the Grand Sheriff of Mecca revolts against Turkey
June	• T E Lawrence leads Arab forces against the Turks
June	• Jan Smuts captures Wilhelmsthal in German East Africa
Aug	• New British offensive in Mesopotamia
Sept	• British troops take Dar-es-Salaam

Mar	• British capture Baghdad
Aug	• China declares war on Germany and Austria
Oct	• Germans renew offensive in East Africa at Battle of Mahiwa
Nov	• British defeat Turks at Gaza, Jaffa and Jerusalem (Dec)
Nov	• Balfour Declaration promises to establish Jewish 'national home' in Palestine

Feb	• Australians occupy Jericho
Aug	• Japanese advance into Siberia
Sept	• Islamic riots in Calcutta
Oct	• British and Arab forces occupy Damascus
Oct	• Turkey surrenders to Allies
Nov	• German troops surrender in Northern Rhodesia

SCIENCE & CULTURE

- James Joyce *Dubliners*
- Ernest Shackleton leads Antarctic expedition

- Albert Einstein extends his Theory of Relativity
- John Buchan *The Thirty-Nine Steps*
- Virginia Woolf *The Voyage Out*
- Outbreaks of tetanus in trenches controlled by serum injections
- Hugo Junkers makes first all-metal aeroplane
- Alfred Wegener publishes theory of continental drift
- Marcel Duchamp paints first Dada-style picture, *The Bride Stripped Bare*
- D H Lawrence *The Rainbow*
- Gustav Holst *The Planets* suite
- *SS Campania* converted into first aircraft carrier

- First tanks used in Battle of the Somme by British forces
- Typhus disease first isolated
- Refrigeration of blood for transfusion
- Margaret Sanger opens first birth control clinic in USA
- Claude Monet *Water Lilies*
- Dadaist anti-art cult flourishes in Zurich, headed by Tristan Tzara, Hans Arp and Giacomo Balla
- Jazz sweeps USA

- 100-inch telescope built at Mount Wilson in California
- First jazz recording by the Original Dixieland Jazz Band
- T S Eliot *Prufrock and Other Observations*
- The Gotha biplane is the first aircraft specially designed for bombing
- Women in munitions factories cut their hair short as safety measure, and 'bobbed hair' becomes fashionable in Britain and USA

- Béla Bartók *Bluebeard's Castle*
- James Joyce *The Exiles*
- Lytton Strachey *Eminent Victorians*
- Paul Nash exhibits paintings of Western Front Battlefields

THE NEW WORLD ORDER

Nationalist passions increased tension and instability during the inter-war period.

The end of the First World War saw the establishment of a new order across the world. In 1919 the United States and Japan had emerged as leading world powers and, with Britain, France and Italy, were to form the Big Five at the Paris Peace Conference. Russia was torn by revolution and civil war, Austria–Hungary had disappeared from the map of Europe, while Germany was at the mercy of the victorious powers.

The United States was, by 1919 a superpower, her industry and trade having expanded enormously as a result of her relative immunity from the 1914–18 conflict. Britain hoped that the post-war order would be based on Anglo–American collaboration to maintain world peace and stability, but any possibility of this was wrecked when the United States repudiated the Treaty of Versailles and withdrew into isolationism after 1920. The maintenance of the post-Versailles order now depended on Britain and France: Italy, dissatisfied with her gains in 1919, could not be relied upon to support them, and Japan took little interest in European issues.

Britain and France, however, soon quarrelled over the future of Germany. By 1920 the intense war-time anti-German feelings in Britain were subsiding, and a recession and increasing unemployment encouraged the British government to look to the economic recovery of Germany as a means of reviving British industry. France, on the other hand, fearful of the resurgence of Germany's industrial and military power, insisted on Germany's fulfilment of the punitive clauses of the Versailles Treaty, and particularly on the payment in full of its reparations obligations, seen by many French politicians as a means of impeding Germany's economic revival. France and Britain clashed repeatedly in the early 1920s over this and other issues as Britain sought to reduce the reparations burdens on Germany, a course which France rejected. This dispute culminated in a Franco–Belgian occupation of the Ruhr, Germany's main industrial region, when Germany defaulted on its reparations payments in 1923.

The new balance of power was thus inherently unstable, with the United States, the only power capable of mediating between Britain and France, remaining aloof. A shaky compromise was patched together between the two European powers in 1924 and 1925, when France was persuaded to reduce its reparations demands and withdraw from the Ruhr, while a series of multilateral treaties signed at Locarno guaranteed the western frontiers of France, Germany and Belgium. Germany then re-entered the concert of powers and for the remainder of the decade Europe remained relatively peaceful.

Outside Europe, the new world order faced a different set of problems, for while the First World War had led to the success of nationalist particularism in Europe, it had also generated intense

The Exploited Continent

▲ Crowds gather during the Irish Free State elections in August 1923 in which de Valera's wing of Sinn Féin sought complete independence from Britain.

Although South America was composed of independent republics, its resources had always been developed with outside capital. Most South American economies were controlled by overseas entrepreneurs, who helped between the wars to develop new industries based on the exploitation of tin, oil, copper, rubber and guano. Cattle, grain, coffee and bananas were also produced in abundance, mostly on large estates, but there was no developed peasant agriculture and the Indian tribes were pushed further into the hinterland.

After 1920 relations between the separate states of Latin America remained generally peaceful, although there was intermittent conflict between Bolivia and Paraguay over a border dispute after 1928, Bolivia being defeated in 1935. The Pan-American Congress, set up in 1889, was dominated by the United States, which intervened in Central America seven times between the wars to protect its trade and investment, notably in Nicaragua and Cuba. The Congress met every five years, but United States domination was resented in South America, and many South American states joined the League of Nations in the vain hope that it would provide a counterweight to the United States. The Congress organized binding arbitration in the case of border disputes in 1936, and in 1928, 21 American states signed a peace pact. South America remained neutral in the developing world tension after 1931, but the United States became concerned about the growth of fascist influence in the German communities in Argentina and Brazil.

nationalist feelings in the overseas empires of the victorious Western European powers.

The British Empire emerged from the war greatly enlarged as a result of its seizure of Germany's former colonies and its occupation of Mesopotamia and Palestine after the collapse of the Ottoman Empire. However, this outwardly imposing structure concealed serious weaknesses which were ultimately to destroy it. The cost of policing and administering the diverse and increasingly restive populations of the Empire was to become an ever increasing burden on an already strained exchequer. Furthermore, the extended nature of the Empire, dependent on the sea for its protection and commerce, posed equally expensive problems for its defence during the 1930s against hostile Japan and Italy. French and Dutch colonies in the Far East were to face similar problems including those of internal security and external defence during the period.

While paying lip service to Woodrow Wilson's principle of national self-determination in 1919, British, French and Italian politicians had no intention of applying this to their existing colonies or to their newly acquired territories; although they agreed to administer the latter under League of Nations mandates to create an illusion of international surveillance, the League's powers were minimal. Supplicants from Ireland and other disaffected nationalities in the British Empire were refused a hearing at the Paris Peace Conference.

The 'white' British dominions – Canada, Australia, New Zealand and South Africa – had already achieved self-government and autonomy from close Whitehall control, and the 1931 Statute of Westminster gave their independence legal validity. After a bitter struggle with Britain, southern Ireland achieved dominion status and virtual independence in 1921. However, for the most part the Western powers did not believe that colonial peoples were yet ready for self-government and even the governments of the Arab countries in the Middle East which had emerged after the war were deemed to require considerable European vigilance and the presence of European army and air bases to ensure their good behaviour. It was felt that the education of the indigenous inhabitants of colonial territories in the intricate arts of democratic government and administration would entail a long process of instruction.

The Far East

After 1914 Japan took advantage of the preoccupation with the war in Europe of its rivals in the Far East and seized Germany's Chinese concession in Shandong and its islands in the north Pacific. Japan also sought to increase its influence over the Chinese government by presenting 21 demands to Beijing in March 1915, which not only called for Chinese recognition of Japan's concessions in Manchuria and Shandong but would also have placed the whole of China under a virtual Japanese protectorate. Anglo–American pressure forced Japan to abandon the more far-reaching demands, but Japanese ambitions in China were to resurface in the 1930s. Japan also took the opportunity afforded by the Bolshevik revolution in Russia to occupy Vladivostock and eastern Siberia temporarily.

At the Paris Peace Conference, despite US protests, Japan retained Germany's former economic concession in Shandong – the United States had wanted the province to be restored to China in its entirety. In 1921 American and Canadian pressure forced Britain to abandon the 1902 alliance with Japan in return for US agreement to limit its naval building, with which Britain was finding it financially difficult to compete. The agreement provided for a 5 : 5 : 3 ratio in battleship strengths between Britain, the United States and Japan, which left Japan (with no global naval responsibilities)

◄ A song sheet illustrates the elegance and daring of the 'Roaring Twenties'.

▼ With the collapse of the German economy in 1923, disorder spread throughout the country. Socialists and communists formed governments and set up Red or republican militias in defence against the Right.

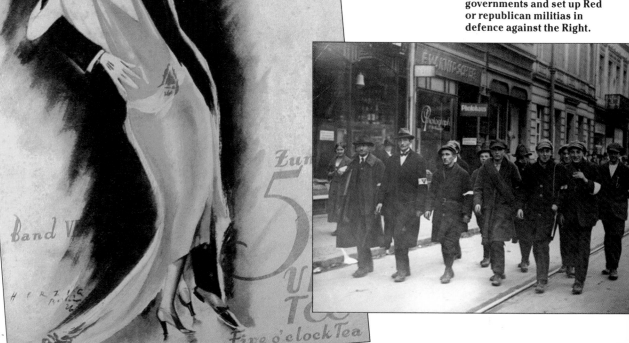

supreme in Far Eastern waters. The Anglo–Japanese alliance was replaced by innocuous multilateral treaties providing for cooperation between the great powers in the Pacific area in the event of problems arising there, and a pledge that they would respect China's integrity. Japan also withdrew its troops from Siberia. The result of the loss of the alliance was that Japan no longer needed to respect Britain's views about its activities in China. Both Australia and New Zealand had pressed Britain to maintain the alliance, since they, like many British politicians, had little confidence in American willingness to join with the other powers in deterring any future Japanese advances in the Far East. In the last resort Britain, anxious to avoid a major breach with the United States, and conscious of America's financial strength, gave way to American pressure. However, until 1931, the civilian government in Tokyo was in full control of the Japanese military and pursued a relatively peaceful policy towards China, despite frequent Chinese nationalist interference with Japan's commerce and concessions in China. After 1931 the situation changed dramatically as Japan launched an all-out assault on China's territorial integrity while the other powers looked on helplessly.

▶ **Hirohito became Emperor of Japan in 1926.**

The Western powers were faced with the greatest challenge to their domination in the Far East, where Moscow-backed communist parties and Japanese-financed propaganda in India, China, Indo-China and Indonesia sought to undermine the loyalty of the inhabitants to their European rulers. The nationalist parties were led by Western-educated middle-class intellectuals, who saw themselves as the natural liberators of their countries from foreign control and who demanded independence on the basis of those very democratic principles which the 1919 peace-makers extolled. Britain evolved a policy of granting limited self-rule to Indian assemblies, but nationalist discontent during Gandhi's non-violent civil disobedience campaigns, and the reluctance of many moderate nationalists to compromise themselves in the eyes of their supporters by associating with 'puppet' governments, enabled the British to delay any real transfer of power in India until 1947. In Palestine the situation was complicated by the influx of Jewish refugees from Europe, enticed there by Britain's 1917 promise of a 'National Homeland' for the Jews in Palestine. Their arrival was bitterly resented by the resident Arab population, and this resulted in increasing anti-Jewish violence during the 1930s which necessitated the despatch of strong British troop reinforcements to maintain order.

Nationalist passions created increasing tension and instability in Europe during the inter-war period.

In Germany resentment at the allegedly harsh and vindictive Versailles Treaty exploded in the 1930s into the extremism and excesses of Hitler's national socialism, which was determined to overthrow the entire European status quo in Germany's favour. In Eastern and Central Europe, Yugoslavia and Czechoslovakia struggled, and ultimately failed, to create unified states out of their ethnically diverse peoples. Poland, which had absorbed Ukrainians, Lithuanians and Germans during and after 1919, sought to maintain its integrity in the face of the demands of a resurgent Germany and an increasingly powerful Soviet Russia during the late 1930s for the incorporation of their fellow nationals into their own countries. After Stalin's rise to power, the non-Russian peoples of the Soviet Union, who had achieved a degree of autonomy in the early 1920s, were gradually brought under Moscow's control and cultural and linguistic separatism was suppressed.

In Turkey the nationalists, led by Mustapha Kemal, sought to modernize and secularize the country after its humiliating defeat in 1918. The attempt to reconstruct a solely Turkish Republic as a cohesive state brought the nationalists into bitter conflict with Greece in Smyrna and Thrace and a near war with Britain in 1922 at Chanak. Eventually Turkey succeeded in its endeavour: it was the only country in south-eastern Europe to preserve its independence and unity during the Second World War.

The League of Nations

GREENLAND
(Denmark)

NORWAY

SWEDEN

FINLA
1920

ICELAND

UNITED
KINGDOM

DENMARK

EIRE
1923

Danzig

GERMANY
1926 **1933**

POLAND

CZECH.

FRANCE

ITALY
1937

ROMA

BUL

SPAIN
1939

GREECE

PORTUGAL

GREENLAND

CANADA

UNITED STATES

1	NETHERLANDS	
2	BELGIUM	
3	LUXEMBOURG	1929
4	SWITZERLAND	
5	AUSTRIA	1920
6	HUNGARY	1922
7	YUGOSLAVIA	
8	ALBANIA	

MEXICO
1931

CUBA

DOMINICAN
REPUBLIC
1924

HAITI

HONDURAS **1936**

GUATEMALA **1936**
EL SALVADOR 1924 **1937**

NICARAGUA **1936**

COSTA RICA 1924

VENEZUELA
1938

PANAMA

COLOMBIA

ECUADOR
1934

BRAZIL
1926

PERU
1939

BOLIVIA

PARAGUAY
1935

CHILE
1938

ARGENTINA

URUGUAY

LIBERIA

(Br and Fr)

(Br and Fr)

(S.Afr)

SOUTH
AFRICA

EGY
19

Founder member

State admitted in 1920 by invitation

State subsequently admitted

Colony of member state

Mandated territory

Non-member

1924 Date of joining

1937 Date of leaving

40

The United States repudiation of the Covenant of the League of Nations in 1920 was a major blow to the effectiveness of the League as an international organization. Given America's isolationism and Japan's lack of interest in events outside China and the Pacific, Britain and France were the only powers concerned with upholding the League as a peace-keeping organization.

During the early 1920s the League – which had its headquarters in Geneva – attempted to formulate arms limitation and collective security agreements as required by the Covenant, but these efforts foundered on the mutual suspicions and hostilities of the powers. The Disarmament Conference, convened in 1932, collapsed in 1934, chiefly as a result of Germany's demand for parity in armaments with the other powers and France's refusal to agree to this unless it received further guarantees of its security.

The League, which supervised the system of mandates and controlled the Free City of Danzig (Gdansk) in what is now Poland was presented with a first major challenge in 1931–2 when China appealed to the League against Japan's invasion of Manchuria. The United States refused to apply sanctions and Britain did not wish to become involved in war with Japan. As a result, the resolutions passed by the League failed to deter Japan's takeover of Manchuria. The impotence of the League was demonstrated in 1935, when despite the imposition of sanctions, it failed to prevent Italy's conquest of Abyssinia. The British government, caught between its unwillingness to fight and public indignation at Italy's aggression, adopted a pusillanimous policy which destroyed the League's effectiveness.

Japan and Germany left the League in 1933, and Italy in 1937, losses balanced to some extent by the accession of the Soviet Union in 1934. But its final act before it was overwhelmed by the Second World War, was to expel the Soviet Union following the latter's invasion of Finland in 1939.

China in Turmoil

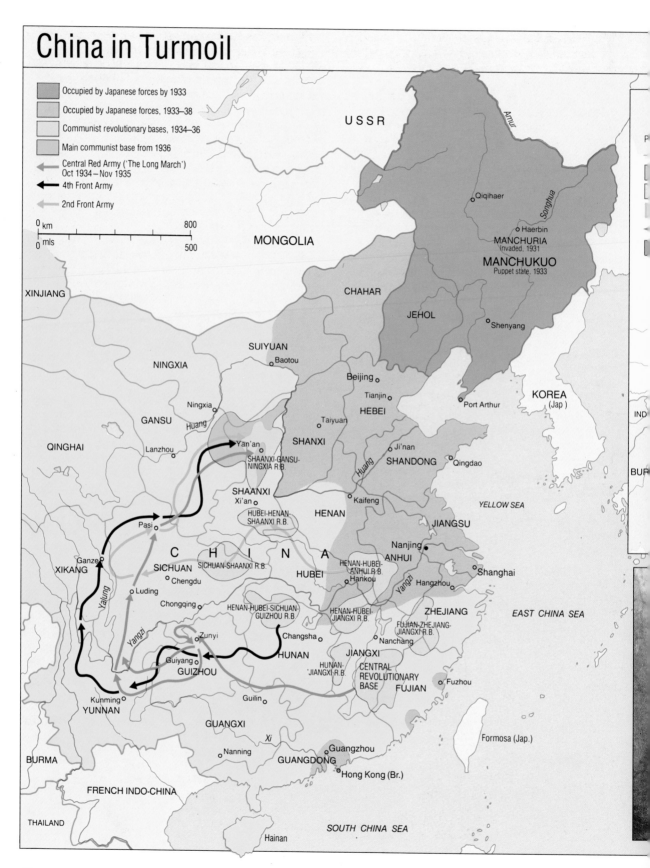

Occupied by Japanese forces by 1933
Occupied by Japanese forces, 1933–38
Communist revolutionary bases, 1934–36
Main communist base from 1936
Central Red Army ('The Long March') Oct 1934 – Nov 1935
4th Front Army
2nd Front Army

0 km _____ 800
0 mls _____ 500

USSR

MONGOLIA

XINJIANG

MANCHURIA
Invaded, 1931
MANCHUKUO
Puppet state, 1933

o Qiqihaer

o Haerbin

CHAHAR

JEHOL

o Shenyang

KOREA
(Jap)

IND

BUR

SUIYUAN
o Baotou

NINGXIA

Beijing o

o Tianjin
HEBEI

o Port Arthur

Ningxia o

GANSU
Huang

o Taiyuan

o Lanzhou

Yan'an o
SHAANXI-GANSU-
NINGXIA R.B.

SHANXI

o Ji'nan

SHANDONG
o Qingdao

Huang

YELLOW SEA

QINGHAI

SHAANXI
Xi'an o

HUBEI-HENAN-
SHAANXI R.B.

HENAN

o Kaifeng

JIANGSU

Pasi o

C H I N A

SICHUAN-SHAANXI R.B.

Nanjing •

Ganze o
XIKANG

SICHUAN
o Chengdu

HUBEI

HENAN-HUBEI-
ANHUI R.B.

ANHUI

o Shanghai

o Luding

Yalung

o Chongqing

HENAN-HUBEI-SICHUAN-
GUIZHOU R.B.

Hankou o

Yangzi

o Hangzhou

ZHEJIANG

EAST CHINA SEA

HENAN-HUBEI-
JIANGXI R.B.

FUJIAN-ZHEJIANG-
JIANGXI R.B.

Yangzi

Zunyi o

o Changsha

o Nanchang

Guiyang o
GUIZHOU

HUNAN

JIANGXI

CENTRAL
REVOLUTIONARY
BASE

o Fuzhou

HUNAN-
JIANGXI R.B.

Kunming o
YUNNAN

o Guilin

FUJIAN

GUANGXI

Xi

o Nanning

GUANGDONG

o Guangzhou

Formosa (Jap.)

o Hong Kong (Br.)

BURMA

FRENCH INDO-CHINA

THAILAND

SOUTH CHINA SEA

Hainan

Map legend (partial, left margin)

Rise of the Guomindang
1932

...lords, 1926

...ndary of Warlord area, 1926

...a controlled by Guomindang, 1926

...a coming under effective Guomindang
...trol at date shown

...a coming under nominal Guomindang
...trol at date shown

...thern expedition, 1926–27

...cupied by Japan, 1931

Map labels

USSR

Amur

Haerbin

MANCHURIA

ZHANG ZUOLIN
1928

Shenyang

FENG YUXIANG

Beijing

Port Arthur

KOREA (Jap.)

YAN XISHAN

SHANDONG
1930

Qingdao
under Japanese control,
1927–29
subsequently
HAN FUZHU

Huang

Xi'an
1930

Kaifeng

C H I N A

Nanjing

Shanghai

Hankou
1929
1926–27

Hangzhou

8 SICHUAN WARLORDS

Yangzi

Chongqing

WU PEIFU

SUN CHUANFANG

Changsha

Fuzhou
1929

TANG JIYAO

Kunming

GUANGXI CLIQUE

Formosa (Jap.)

FRENCH INDO-CHINA

GUOMINDANG

Guangzhou

Hong Kong (Br.)

subsequently
ZHEN JIDANG
1929

km 750

mls 500

After the 1911 revolution that overthrew the Qing dynasty, and the disappearance of the unifying Manchu bureaucracy, China sank into chaos. A semi-parliamentary government at Nanjing was established by the Nationalist party, or Guomindang, led by a Western-educated intellectual, Sun Yixian (Sun Yat-sen). It was opposed by a conservative regime at Beijing in the north led by General Yuan Shikai. After Yuan's death in 1916 the north–south divide became even more pronounced. In 1921–2 civil war broke out in the north between various warlords, while in Guangzhou (Canton) Sun Yixian secured Soviet assistance in strengthening his military forces and in reorganizing the Guomindang. His death in 1925 opened the way for increasing Chinese Communist party and Soviet influence on the Guomindang movement, which manifested itself in anti-foreign strikes and riots, a boycott of foreign goods and a campaign for the abolition of the privileges which foreign powers had extracted from China in the 19th century. At the same time the Guomindang army, led by Jiang Jieshi (Chiang Kai-shek), who had served in the Japanese army and had trained with the Red Army in Moscow, marched against the northern warlords, capturing Hankou, Nanjing and Shanghai by 1927, and simultaneously thwarting a communist take-over of the Guomindang.

By 1928 the Guomindang armies had defeated all the northern warlords and entered Beijing. A national government was set up and the nationalists were in control of much of China. By 1930 Jiang had become the real power in the Nationalist party. However, the new government's writ was a tenuous one. The Japanese had reacted violently to nationalist encroachments on their concessions in Shanghai, Manchuria and Shandong, and this boded ill for the future. Widespread banditry occurred after the disbandment of soldiers from the various civil war armies, famine was endemic, and a Communist government had established itself in Jiangxi in the south.

In 1934 Jiang's forces drove the communists out of Jiangxi. Mao Zedong (Mao Tse-tung) and more than 100,000 men and their dependents trekked 8,000 miles on the Long March north-west to Yan'an in Shaanxi province, 6,000 survivors arriving in October 1935, to set up a guerrilla regime there. The nationalist hope for a peaceful and modernized China with a strong central government eventually succumbed to the twin impacts of Japanese aggression and communist penetration of the Chinese interior. The invasion by Japanese forces, however, led to a truce between the Guomindang and the communists as they joined forces in the fight against Japan in 1937.

**General
Jiang Jieshi
(Chiang Kai-shek).**

THE CONFLICT OF IDEOLOGIES

Both fascism and communism weakened the will-power of bourgeois governments.

The length and destructiveness of the First World War was largely responsible for the rise of both communism and national socialism in Europe. The chaos the war caused in Russia enabled the Bolsheviks to seize power in November 1917, with Lenin as Chairman of the Council of People's Commissars. The Bolsheviks appreciated as much as the fascists that they needed at least the tacit support of the masses to succeed, and Lenin's slogan 'bread, land and peace' appealed to Russian peasants, workers and soldiers alike. All the resources of the Bolshevik state were employed to consolidate the revolution at home and propagate it abroad – the Red Army, the secret police, political agitation, propaganda, subversion, diplomacy, and financial and political aid and advice to dissident elements abroad. Compromises with the capitalist enemy were regarded as tactical manoeuvres, designed to keep capitalism off-guard until such time as the onward march of the revolution could be resumed. Force and violence, both in word and deed, were the prime methods by which communism defended itself, and all anti-Bolshevik parties in Russia were ruthlessly crushed. The Soviet Union was a one-party state, and party membership was small and tightly controlled. Yet, while its revolutionary propaganda overseas alarmed the ruling classes, communism posed no real threat to the status quo in Europe between 1918 and 1939, and after the collapse of short-lived communist regimes in Hungary and Bavaria in 1919, no country became communist. However, the bitter division between the socialists and communists in Germany in the 1920s helped ease Hitler to power.

Fascism was also a product of the war's violence, although it also drew much of its inspiration from pre-war ideologies and insecurities, which manifested themselves in violent nationalism and anti-Semitism. Fascism capitalized on the dissatisfaction and unrest of demobilized ex-servicemen, of lower-middle classes made even more insecure by war-induced changes in society, and of ultra-nationalists and others who were bitterly opposed to the peace settlements. Since it was based essentially on the state, its ideology was not uniform throughout Europe, although it was anti-communist, anti-Semitic (except in Italy where there were few

Jews), anti-liberal and anti-parliamentarian. It demanded the dissolution of the allegedly corrupt and inefficient existing order and its replacement by a new, vigorous and disciplined system which in its corporate aspects would control both capital and labour for the benefit of the nation. The very dynamism of fascism had widespread appeal since it promised renewal and revival after the post-1918 disillusionment. In Germany and Hungary, fascism

Inflation in the 1920s

capitalized on the bitterness of defeat and the harshness of the peace treaties, in Italy on the dissatisfaction with Italy's meagre territorial gains. In every country it harked back to a supposed former greatness. By 1939 it had captured Italy and Germany, but fascist parties in France, Belgium, Holland and Britain, the Falange in Spain, and the Iron Guard in Romania did not survive.

Both fascism and communism sowed dissension and discord, undermining the existing order, and helping to weaken further the will-power of bourgeois governments, particularly in France, to resist Hitler. During the 1930s, Stalin sought to forge a united front of the left to resist fascism and encouraged the formation of Popular Front governments in France and Spain for this purpose. But the suspicions of communism which had been aroused in the middle classes during the 1920s worked against the success of such experiments, while Hitler played on their fears for his own purposes.

Although both Britain and France suffered inflationary pressures after the war, it was Germany, Russia and Central and Eastern Europe that suffered the most. In these states inflation had a catastrophic effect. Russia's banknote issue increased fivefold during the war, but the value of the rouble was maintained by Allied credits and by making exporters take roubles rather than foreign currency. The Provisional government increased the money supply by five and a half times in six months in 1917, but following the October revolution economic activity came to a halt during the civil war and as a result of communist seizure of property and industries. The expropriation of foreign investments meant that the Soviet government was refused foreign credits. By June 1919, ninety per cent of Soviet expenditure was met by printing banknotes: inflation became uncontrollable.

The Weimar Republic, forced to pay reparations and committed to welfare schemes, began to print money to meet the cost. The Franco–Belgian occupation of the Ruhr, Germany's main industrial region, resulted in the Ruhr workers refusing to work the mines and factories from 1923–25, and output collapsed. The Berlin government resorted to the printing press to pay for essential services, and eventually the currency collapsed completely. By November 1923 the mark was worth one-trillionth of its 1914 value, and workers were paid daily, only to find that the mark had depreciated further by the time they came to spend it. Pensions and savings became worthless and businesses were wiped out. Although the currency was stabilized after 1925, the middle and lower-middle classes, who had suffered so much from this hyper-inflation, turned to the national socialists in large numbers when depression led them to fear renewed inflation in 1930.

Italy: the First Fascist State

Benito Mussolini was a journalist and former anti-war socialist, who had, during the First World War, become a fervent supporter of Italy's intervention on the side of the Entente. He owed his political triumph in Italy to his clever manipulation of Italy's disappointment at the meagre territorial gains in 1919 and of the distress which resulted from the post-war economic crisis in Italy. He set up the *Fasci di Combattimento* in Milan in 1919, a semi-military organization calling for the satisfaction of Italy's imperialist claims and for numerous internal reforms. After the war anarchy had spread across Italy as peasants seized land and workers occupied factories. Communist encouragement of these outrages alarmed the middle classes, who feared that the country was on the brink of a Bolshevik takeover. The fascists played on these fears, securing subsidies from industrialists and landowners and arms from a sympathetic Italian army. In October 1922 the fascists organized their forces for a march on Rome to overthrow the government, while Mussolini took advantage of the rising tension to bully the king into appointing him Prime Minister. Over the next four years he gradually consolidated his power by absorbing nationalists into the Fascist party. He secured centre party support for changes in the electoral law in 1923 which enabled the fascists to gain sweeping victories in the 1924 elections, and then took advantage of the uproar resulting from the murder by fascist thugs of the socialist Giacomo Matteotti to impose a fascist totalitarian regime. All other political parties were then banned.

The Russian Civil War

SWEDEN

FINLAND

Stockholm

Helsinki

Tallinn (Reval)

ESTONIA
Dorpat

Narva

Valka

Riga

LATVIA

LITHUANIA

Königsberg

EAST
PRUSSIA

Kaunas

Vilna

BALTIC
SEA

Vyborg

Kronstadt

Petrograd

Yudenich
1919

Novgorod

Pskov

Vitebsk

Dvinsk

Dvina

L. Onega

L. Ladoga

Petrozavodsk

Maloya Vishera

Vologda

BOLSHEVIK

Vyatka

Archangel

Entente forces
1918

Feb 1920

Shenkursk

Glazov

Kolchak
1918–19

Per

Izhevsk

Warsaw

POLAND

Brest-Litovsk

Vistula

Aug 1920

Pripet
Poles
1920

Minsk

Mogilev

Smolensk

Gomel

Moscow

RUSSIA

Kaluga

Tver

Volga

Yaroslavl

Ivanovo

Kostroma

Nizhniy Novgorod

Kazan

Volga

Simbirsk

Oct 1919

Penza

Samara

Orenbu

Lvov

Zhitomir

Aug 1920

Kiev

UKRAINE

Oct
1919

Kursk

Denikin
1919–20

Kharkov

Poltava

Dnieper

Bug

Orel

Tula

Voronezh

Tambov

Saratov

Ural

ROMANIA

BESSARABIA

Dniester

Kishinev

Odessa

Nikolayev

Wrangel
1920

Yekaterinoslav

Mariupol

Nov 1920

Jan 1920

Don

Novocherkassk

Rostov

Mar
1920

Tsaritsyn

Volga

Cossacks
1918–20

Astrakhan

Bucharest

Danube

BULGARIA

Crimea

Sevastopol

Simferopol

BLACK SEA

Entente forces

Constantinople

Novorossiysk

Sochi

Cossacks
1917–19

Piatigorsk

Grozny

Vladikavkaz

Feb
1921

Caucasus

CASPIAN
SEA

TURKEY

Batumi

Kars

Tiflis

Apr
1920

Baku

Entente
forces

Krasnovo

46

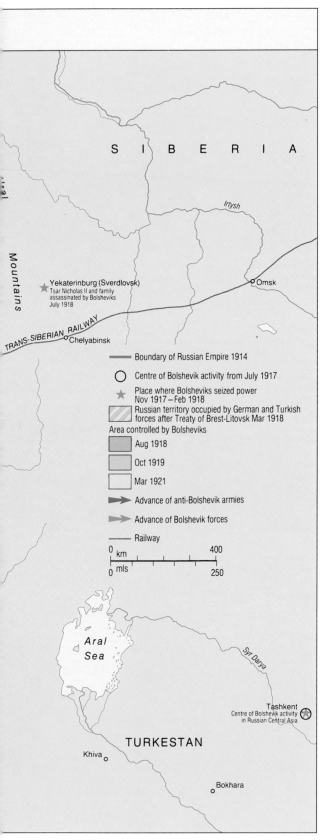

S I B E R I A

Irtysh

Yekaterinburg (Sverdlovsk)
Tsar Nicholas II and family
assassinated by Bolsheviks
July 1918

Omsk

Mountains

TRANS-SIBERIAN RAILWAY
Chelyabinsk

——— Boundary of Russian Empire 1914

○ Centre of Bolshevik activity from July 1917

★ Place where Bolsheviks seized power
Nov 1917–Feb 1918

Russian territory occupied by German and Turkish
forces after Treaty of Brest-Litovsk Mar 1918

Area controlled by Bolsheviks

Aug 1918

Oct 1919

Mar 1921

➤ Advance of anti-Bolshevik armies

➤ Advance of Bolshevik forces

——— Railway

0 km   400
0 mls   250

*Aral
Sea*

Syr Darya

Tashkent
Centre of Bolshevik activity
in Russian Central Asia

TURKESTAN

Khiva ○

○ Bokhara

The Russian civil war began in May 1918 when the Czechoslovak Corps (ex-prisoners of war who were travelling on the Trans-Siberian railway towards Vladivostok and evacuation) clashed with Soviet troops in the Urals and proceeded to occupy the railway. This occupation enabled counter-revolutionary forces (or Whites) to organize anti-Bolshevik armies in western Siberia. White forces also began to establish themselves in those areas of European Russia which the Germans occupied in March 1918. Although, during 1918, a small detachment of British troops landed at Archangel, Murmansk and in the Transcaucasus in support of the Whites, and French troops occupied Odessa, Allied intervention was at most half-hearted. By the end of 1919 they had evacuated their troops from Russia.

The Bolsheviks were threatened from all sides. In the Ukraine the Germans set up a Ukrainian separatist government, while in the south, a former Tsarist general, Denikin, formed a volunteer army consisting mainly of Cossacks and drove the Reds out of the Caucasus. In the Urals and Siberia, an ex-Tsarist admiral, A.V. Kolchak, raised an army and proclaimed himself Supreme Ruler of Russia in November 1918. Both these White armies met with initial successes in 1919. In the spring Kolchak nearly reached the Volga while Denikin's forces had advanced to within 240 miles of Moscow by October 1919. However, Red Army counter-offensives in the autumn drove Kolchak's forces back into Siberia and by March 1920 his army was crushed. The same fate was suffered by Denikin's Volunteer Army by the spring of 1920 and by his successor, General Wrangel, in the Crimea. A White army under former Tsarist general, Yudenich, which had begun advancing from Estonia towards Petrograd during the summer of 1919 was also defeated. The last major threat was Poland's invasion of the Ukraine in April 1920. This was repulsed by the Red Army, which drove the Poles back to the Vistula. Warsaw was saved by spirited Polish resistance. In October the two sides signed an armistice.

With the defeat of the Whites, the Bolsheviks were able to establish their control over other regions of Russia which had broken away after the revolution. The last outpost of resistance, Vladivostok, was recovered when a Japanese garrison, which had occupied the port in 1918, departed in October 1922.

The victory of the Bolsheviks was the product of a number of factors: the organizing abilities of the Commissar for War, Leon Trotsky, who recruited former Tsarist officers and built up the Red Army into a formidable fighting force; their control of the central Russian war industries; and the flexibility which Moscow's radial communications gave their forces.

Soviet Foreign Policy

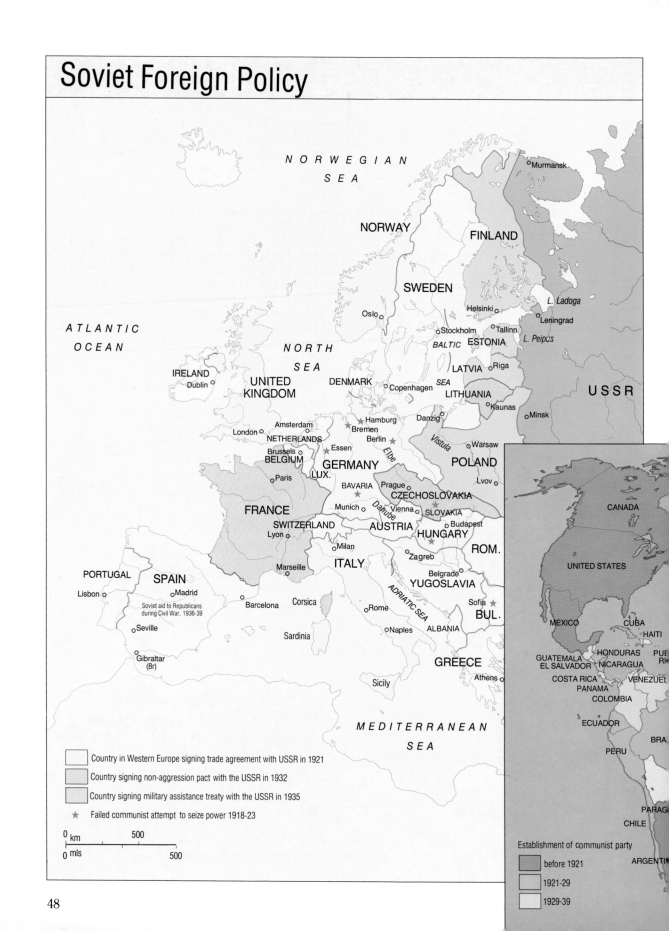

NORWEGIAN SEA

NORWAY

FINLAND

SWEDEN

o Murmansk

ATLANTIC OCEAN

Oslo o

Helsinki o

o Stockholm

L. Ladoga

Leningrad o

NORTH SEA

o Tallinn

BALTIC ESTONIA

L. Peipus

IRELAND
Dublin o

UNITED KINGDOM

DENMARK

LATVIA o Riga

SEA

o Copenhagen

LITHUANIA

USSR

London o

Amsterdam
NETHERLANDS

Brussels o
BELGIUM

o Paris

* Hamburg
* Bremen
Berlin *

Danzig

o Kaunas

o Minsk

Vistula

o Warsaw

Essen *

Elbe

LUX.

GERMANY

BAVARIA
*

Prague *
CZECHOSLOVAKIA

POLAND

Lvov o

FRANCE

SWITZERLAND
Lyon o

Munich o

Danube

Vienna o
AUSTRIA

SLOVAKIA *

o Milan

Budapest

HUNGARY *

ROM.

PORTUGAL
Lisbon o

SPAIN
o Madrid

Soviet aid to Republicans
during Civil War, 1936-39

Barcelona o

Corsica

Marseille o

ITALY

o Seville

Sardinia

o Rome

ADRIATIC SEA

o Naples

Zagreb o

Belgrade o
YUGOSLAVIA

ALBANIA

Sofia *
BUL.

o Gibraltar
(Br)

GREECE

Athens o

Sicily

MEDITERRANEAN SEA

Country in Western Europe signing trade agreement with USSR in 1921

Country signing non-aggression pact with the USSR in 1932

Country signing military assistance treaty with the USSR in 1935

★ Failed communist attempt to seize power 1918-23

0 km   500

0 mls   500

CANADA

UNITED STATES

MEXICO

CUBA

HAITI

GUATEMALA
EL SALVADOR

HONDURAS

NICARAGUA

PUE
RIC

COSTA RICA
PANAMA

VENEZUEL

COLOMBIA

ECUADOR

BRA

PERU

PARAG

CHILE

Establishment of communist party

before 1921

1921-29

1929-39

ARGENTI

48

The Bolshevik victory in the Russian civil war in 1921 left the new regime ostracized by the outside world. The 1921 famine led the Bolsheviks to seek to restore trade links with the West. However, the results of these efforts were negligible. The Soviets refused to repay the Allied loans to the Tsarist regime which had been sequestrated after the revolution and so further Allied investment was not forthcoming. The activities of the Moscow-controlled Third Communist International or 'Comintern', which had been set up as an agency to spread revolutionary propaganda, further alienated the West. It fostered working class unrest in Western Europe and nationalist outbreaks in India, China and elsewhere in Asia as well as setting up and supporting communist parties around the world. The West would not accept the communist fiction that the Comintern was independent of the Soviet government. However, the failure of Comintern-inspired revolutions in Germany in 1923 discredited it in the eyes of Soviet leaders, and with Stalin's rise to power after 1924, the Comintern was brought more closely under party control. After 1927 Stalin launched an industrialization programme and the Soviet Union began to pay less attention to external revolutionary activity. A more peaceful Soviet Union

was then able to sign non-aggression and trade pacts with many of its neighbours.

After 1933, alarmed by the threats posed by resurgent Germany and Japan, Stalin became a leading exponent of collective security against fascist aggression. The Soviet Union joined the League of Nations in 1934 and signed an alliance with France the following year. Britain remained aloof, its hostility increased by Soviet aid to the Spanish republicans during the civil war, which led to fears in London of a Bolshevik Spain. Stalin's purges of the Red Army High Command in the mid-1930s convinced many in the West that the effectiveness of that army had been gravely weakened. Britain preferred to conciliate Germany, and when Moscow was not consulted in 1938 over the fate of Czechoslovakia, with whom the Soviet Union had an alliance, Stalin began to despair of his efforts to build up an anti-fascist front. In August 1939 Stalin signed a non-aggression pact with Germany, which in return for Russia's neutrality promised it eastern Poland. Stalin had achieved his ambition of keeping the Soviet Union out of war, but the cost was to be a heavy one for his country.

1 DENMARK
2 NETHERLANDS
3 BELGIUM
4 GERMANY
5 SWITZERLAND
6 ITALY
7 AUSTRIA
8 CZECHOSLOVAKIA
9 HUNGARY
10 YUGOSLAVIA
11 BULGARIA
12 GREECE

Russia under Stalin

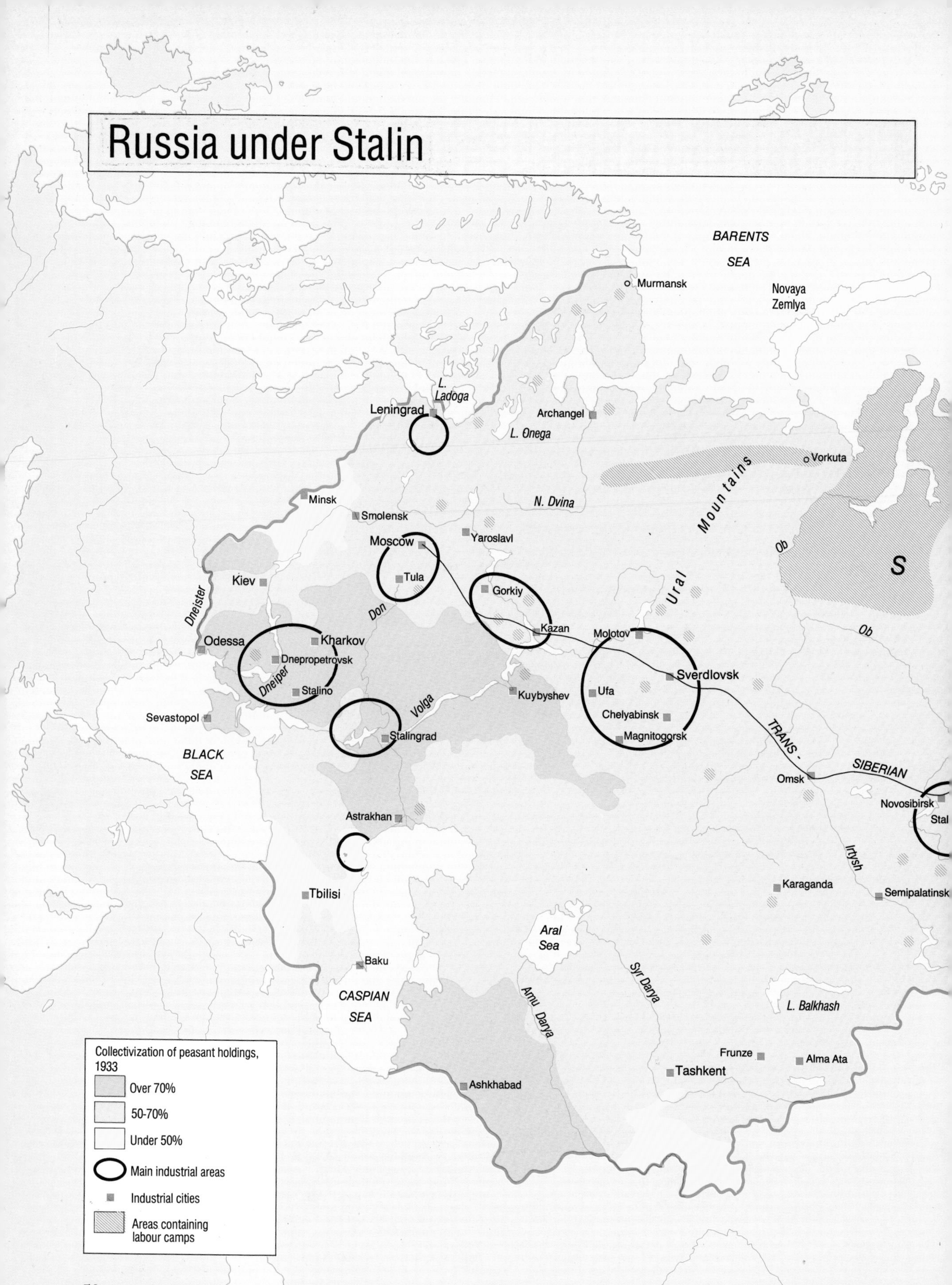

BARENTS
SEA

o Murmansk

Novaya
Zemlya

L. Ladoga

Leningrad

Archangel

o Vorkuta

L. Onega

Minsk

Smolensk

N. Dvina

Moscow

Yaroslavl

Ural

S

Kiev

Tula

Gorkiy

Kazan

Molotov

Ob

Dniester

Don

Sverdlovsk

Odessa

Kharkov

Dnepropetrovsk

Ob

Dnieper

Stalino

Volga

Kuybyshev

Ufa

Chelyabinsk

Mountains

Sevastopol

Stalingrad

Magnitogorsk

TRANS-

SIBERIAN

BLACK
SEA

Omsk

Astrakhan

Novosibirsk

Stal

Tbilisi

Karaganda

Irtysh

Semipalatinsk

Aral
Sea

Baku

Amu Darya

Syr Darya

L. Balkhash

CASPIAN
SEA

Frunze

Alma Ata

Tashkent

Ashkhabad

Collectivization of peasant holdings,
1933

Over 70%

50-70%

Under 50%

Main industrial areas

Industrial cities

Areas containing
labour camps

ARCTIC OCEAN

Kolymskaya

Kolym

Indigirka

Magadan

Lena

Igarka

SEA OF
OKHOTSK

S   B   E   R   I   A

Lower Tunguska

Upper Tunguska

Yakutsk

enisey

Angara

Lena

Amur

ILWAY

Krasnoyarsk

L. Baykal

Blagoveshchensk

Khabarovsk

Chita

Irkutsk

Ulan Ude

Vladivostok

The 1921 famine in Russia led the Communist party to allow the re-emergence of free enterprise in the agricultural sector. Lenin's New Economic Policy enabled the peasantry to market their produce and retain any profits that accrued. As a result, agricultural production increased significantly during the 1920s.

After Lenin's death in January 1924, Josef Stalin triumphed over Leon Trotsky in the struggle for Soviet leadership. Stalin then sought to strengthen the Soviet Union as the bastion of communism by a vigorous programme of industrialization and modernization under the slogan 'Socialism in One Country'. This was inaugurated in 1928 by the first Five Year Plan. Short

of capital and overseas credits the plan could only be successful through ruthless exploitation of the peasantry. After 1928 the peasants were forced to sell their produce to the state at controlled prices. They were herded into collective farms, and the richer peasants were deported to forced labour camps. Detachments of secret police enforced obedience to the system and, as a result, agricultural production collapsed and a terrible famine gripped the Soviet Union in 1932. Industrialization and urbanization, on the other hand, proceeded rapidly during the 1930s, and both output and gross national product doubled as new industrial areas were opened in the mineral-rich Urals and western Siberia.

The Rise of Nazism

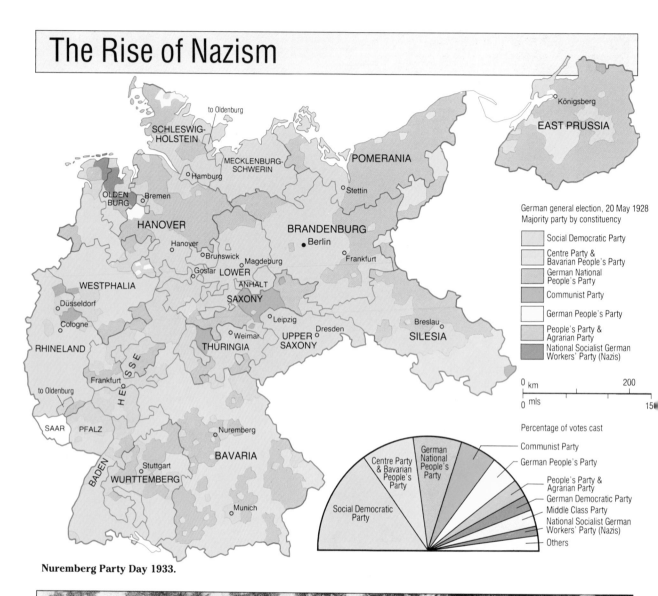

to Oldenburg

SCHLESWIG-
HOLSTEIN

MECKLENBURG-
SCHWERIN

POMERANIA

Hamburg

OLDEN-
BURG   Bremen

HANOVER

Hanover

Brunswick

LOWER
SAXONY

Magdeburg

ANHALT

WESTPHALIA

Düsseldorf

Cologne

RHINELAND

HESSE

Frankfurt

to Oldenburg

SAAR   PFALZ

BADEN

WÜRTTEMBERG   Stuttgart

Weimar

THÜRINGIA

Leipzig

UPPER
SAXONY

Dresden

Nuremberg

BAVARIA

Munich

BRANDENBURG

Berlin

Frankfurt

Stettin

Breslau

SILESIA

Goslar

KÖNIGSBERG

EAST PRUSSIA

German general election, 20 May 1928
Majority party by constituency

- Social Democratic Party
- Centre Party & Bavarian People's Party
- German National People's Party
- Communist Party
- German People's Party
- People's Party & Agrarian Party
- National Socialist German Workers' Party (Nazis)

0 km   200
0 mls   150

Percentage of votes cast

- Communist Party
- German People's Party
- People's Party & Agrarian Party
- German Democratic Party
- Middle Class Party
- National Socialist German Workers' Party (Nazis)
- Others

Centre Party & Bavarian People's Party

German National People's Party

Social Democratic Party

Nuremberg Party Day 1933.

The National Socialist German Workers' (Nazi) Party was marked by its virulent anti-Semitism and anti-communism. It was led by Adolf Hitler, an Austrian malcontent who had joined the German army in 1914. As a leader Hitler had charisma and was a compelling orator. After an unsuccessful Nazi coup against the Bavarian government in 1923, for which Hitler was subsequently imprisoned, his movement remained insignificant during the post-1925 years of economic recovery in Germany. It was given a new lease of life by the onset of the depression in 1930. The Nazis capitalized on the widespread unemployment that ensued – it reached five million in September – by promising to restore the economy and create full employment. It also drew on German feelings of superiority – the myth of the 'master race' – and dissatisfaction with the punitive

terms of the Treaty of Versailles in order to increase its strength. At the general election of 14 September 1930 the Nazi party increased its share of votes from 810,000 in 1928 to 6.4 million, rising from 12 seats to 107 in the Reichstag, more than the Socialist and Communist parties combined, although no party possessed an overall majority. The Conservative and Nationalist politicians who surrounded the ageing President Hindenburg sought to use the Nazis for their own ends. Despite a set-back in the November 1932 elections, when the Nazis lost 34 of the 230 Reichstag seats won in July, former Chancellor Franz von Papen persuaded Hindenburg to appoint Hitler as Chancellor of a coalition government of National Socialists, Conservatives and Nationalists, with von Papen as Vice-Chancellor, on 30 January 1933. The Third Reich had begun.

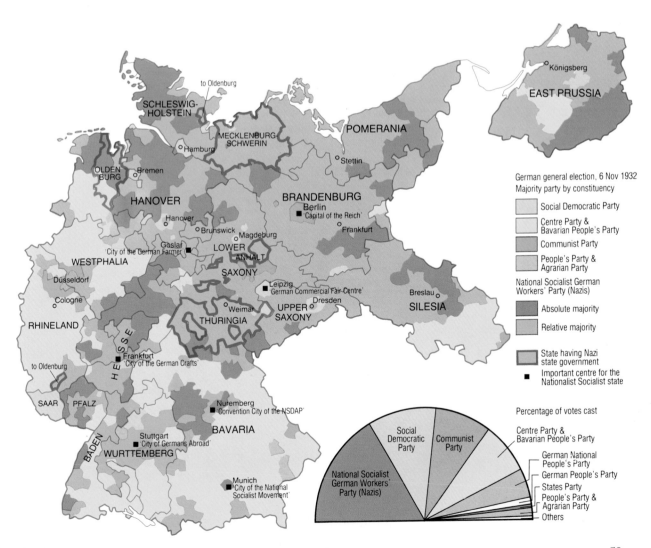

THE CRISIS YEARS

Membership of fascist parties escalated as the poverty-stricken flocked to their ranks.

During the 1930s the world order created in 1919 gradually collapsed under the impact of economic crisis and political extremism. The Depression, which began in the United States in 1929, and spread to Europe in the following year, created heavy unemployment and immense distress as banks closed, industrial production slumped and markets for agricultural products and raw materials collapsed. The imposition of high tariff walls by the United States and Britain made the situation even worse. The disaffected elements which had emerged in every society after the First World War, especially in Germany, Italy and Japan, but which had been contained by a measure of economic prosperity and political stability after 1925, became active once more during the Depression. Membership of fascist and crypto-fascist parties escalated as the unemployed and the poverty-stricken lower-middle classes flocked to their ranks. Ultimately the impotence of the German government in the face of the Depression and the electoral strength of the National Socialist party propelled Hitler to power in 1933. After 1930 fascist Italy emerged as a threat to the status quo in the Adriatic and Mediterranean. Japan was hard hit by the Depression, especially as much of the trade vital to its survival was shut out of the American market by tariffs. The only outlet for Japanese trade and investment lay in Manchuria and north China, rich in agriculture and minerals, and it was in this area, weakened by civil war and revolution, that younger officers in the Japanese army saw Japan's economic salvation. They were behind the seizure of Manchuria in 1931 in defiance of their own government and the League of Nations. By 1934 the Japanese were encroaching on the rest of northern China and in 1937 full scale war broke out between Japan and China.

Nazi Germany also embarked on an aggressive foreign policy. On coming to power Hitler had inaugurated a massive rearmament programme, which he confirmed publicly in 1935, when Germany denounced the disarmament clauses of the Versailles Treaty. He took advantage of the breach between France and Britain on the one hand and Italy on the other over the latter's seizure of Abyssinia in 1935, to draw Italy into close alignment with Germany. The British Prime Minister, Neville Chamberlain, believed that if Germany's grievances could be rectified, it would become stable and peaceful. Britain and

◄ Sacred cows form the vanguard of a peaceful demonstration in Delhi. Between the wars, Britain also faced problems in India. The Indian National Congress campaigned for Indian independence throughout the 1920s, led by Mahatma Gandhi who adopted a policy of civil disobedience. During 1930 and 1931 the British met with Congress and Indian minority groups but no agreement was reached and, in 1932, Gandhi was arrested and Congress banned. Congress later agreed to cooperate with Britain's Government of India Act in 1935 which established Indian provincial administrations and a federal parliament.

► Nazi propaganda celebrates the Third Reich and Austria's union with Germany.

13.·MÄRZ 1938
EIN VOLK EIN REICH
EIN FÜHRER

►► Crowds mass in Lustgarten, Berlin, in 1936 to hear Hitler give his May Day address.

France did nothing to hinder Germany's remilitarization of the Rhineland in 1936 or its seizure of Austria early in 1938. Indeed, later in the same year Chamberlain supported Hitler's demand for the annexation of German Sudetenland, on the grounds of self-determination, thus destroying Czechoslovakia as a viable military and economic power.

Britain and France were also badly hit by the Depression. The weak Labour government in Britain collapsed in 1931 and was replaced by a Conservative-dominated coalition. This government, concerned at the fragility of Britain's economy during the 1930s, and conscious of its military weakness, pursued a cautious policy at home and abroad, hoping to avoid any collision that would bring it into conflict with a possible combination of Germany, Italy and Japan, which Britain could not hope to defeat. France, even more timid in dealing with Hitler, was bitterly divided politically and threatened internally by a combination of right-wing extremists and fascists who nearly brought down the Third Republic in 1933. However, democracy survived, as it did in the United States, despite the devastating effects of the Depression on that country's economy. Franklin Delano Roosevelt's election to the presidency in 1932 resulted in a vigorous assault on unemployment and economic distress – the New Deal – which, while only partly successful, saved the country from extremism. The Depression made the United States even more determined to remain free of international entanglements so it avoided any involvement in the dramatic events that were unfolding in Europe.

The Soviet Union was unaffected by the Depression. Stalin's alarm at the threatening behaviour of Nazi Germany and Japan in the 1930s led him to approach Britain and France to join the Soviet Union in an anti-fascist coalition. Western distrust of Soviet Russia was too strong to allow this, and Moscow was not consulted about the fate of Czechoslovakia in 1938. As a result Stalin, in disgust, turned to Germany in 1939 as a means of avoiding war, while Hitler sought further gains at the expense of Czechoslovakia and Poland. The stage was set for the Second World War, the conclusion, in W. H. Auden's words, of 'a low dishonest decade'.

The Third Reich

When Hitler became Chancellor of Germany in 1933 he began to consolidate all power in the hands of the National Socialist (Nazi) party. After the Reichstag fire on 27 February 1933 emergency decrees led to the arrest of communists, socialists and other opponents of the regime and their incarceration in concentration camps. The National Socialists gained a 52 per cent majority in the Reichstag elections of 5 March, and immediately passed an act enabling the government to rule for four years without calling parliament. Thereafter the freedom of the press was abolished, Jews were deprived of their employment, and the trade union movement and all other political parties were banned. When the Brownshirts, the paramilitary wing of the Nazi party, became critical of the slow progress of the Nazi revolution and demanded their incorporation into the army, Hitler acted on 30 June 1934 – 'the night of the long knives'. Brownshirt leaders were rounded up and shot, while a number of other opponents of the regime were also eliminated. When President Hindenburg died on 2 August 1934, Hitler took over the powers of the presidency, including that of Commander-in-Chief of the army, and he made the German army swear an oath of allegiance to himself as *Führer* or leader.

By 1937 many in the army leadership had become alarmed over Hitler's rash foreign policy. In January 1938 Hitler sacked the Army chief of staff and the Defence Minister, purged the High Command of anti-Nazi officers and replaced the remaining conservatives in his government with Nazis. He also became Supreme Commander of the Armed Forces and abolished the War Ministry.

Europe between the Wars

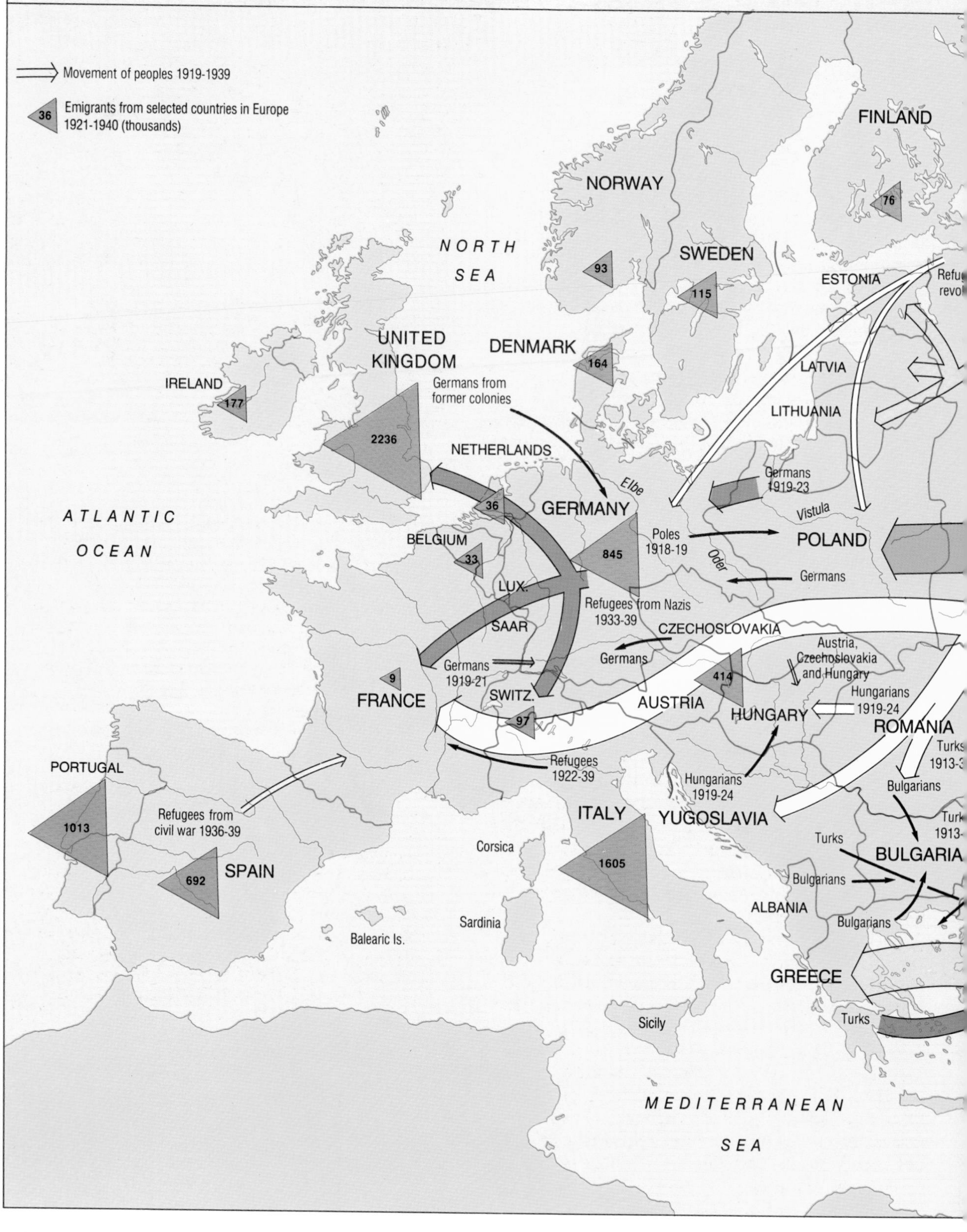

Movement of peoples 1919-1939

36 Emigrants from selected countries in Europe
1921-1940 (thousands)

FINLAND

NORWAY

NORTH SEA

SWEDEN

76

ESTONIA

Refu
revol

93

115

UNITED
KINGDOM

DENMARK

LATVIA

IRELAND

164

LITHUANIA

177

2236

Germans from
former colonies

NETHERLANDS

Elbe

GERMANY

Germans
1919-23

Vistula

*ATLANTIC
OCEAN*

36

BELGIUM

845

Poles
1918-19

POLAND

33

LUX.

Oder

Germans

SAAR

Refugees from Nazis
1933-39

CZECHOSLOVAKIA

Austria,
Czechoslovakia
and Hungary

9

Germans
1919-21

Germans

FRANCE

SWITZ.

AUSTRIA

414

HUNGARY

Hungarians
1919-24

ROMANIA

97

Turks
1913-3

Refugees
1922-39

Hungarians
1919-24

Bulgarians

PORTUGAL

Refugees from
civil war 1936-39

ITALY

YUGOSLAVIA

Turk
1913

1013

Turks

BULGARIA

692

SPAIN

Corsica

1605

Bulgarians

ALBANIA

Bulgarians

Sardinia

Balearic Is.

GREECE

Sicily

Turks

*MEDITERRANEAN
SEA*

It took several years after 1919 before Europe began to recover from the devastating economic effects of the Great War. For a short period, between 1925 and 1929, the European economy recovered as international trade expanded and American investment began to pour into Europe. It is impossible to establish a definite connection between the economic wellbeing of communities and emigration, but during the 1920s emigration from Europe to the United States and Britain's White Dominions increased rapidly. On the other hand it fell markedly during the depressed 1930s. Following the treaties made after the First World War there was a great movement of people within Europe itself. With the drawing of new boundaries many people found themselves living under alien rule and vast numbers of refugees moved to escape from foreign powers and fascist and Bolshevik leaders.

With the October 1929 New York stock market crash, the post-1925 recovery was abruptly thrown into reverse and the capitalist economies of Europe suffered severely. As a means of overcoming the crisis they sought balanced budgets, deflation and public expenditure cuts which worsened the situation by further reducing purchasing power. Most European powers raised tariffs as a means of excluding foreign competition. Britain's system of imperial preference enabled an expansion of trade with the Dominions, while Germany arranged barter deals with Eastern Europe whereby she purchased their agricultural produce in return for manufactured goods. Unemployment levels in Germany remained relatively low partly as a result of the exodus of foreign workers after 1933. Everywhere, emigration fell markedly after 1930.

Unemployed workers in 1939 in Britain.

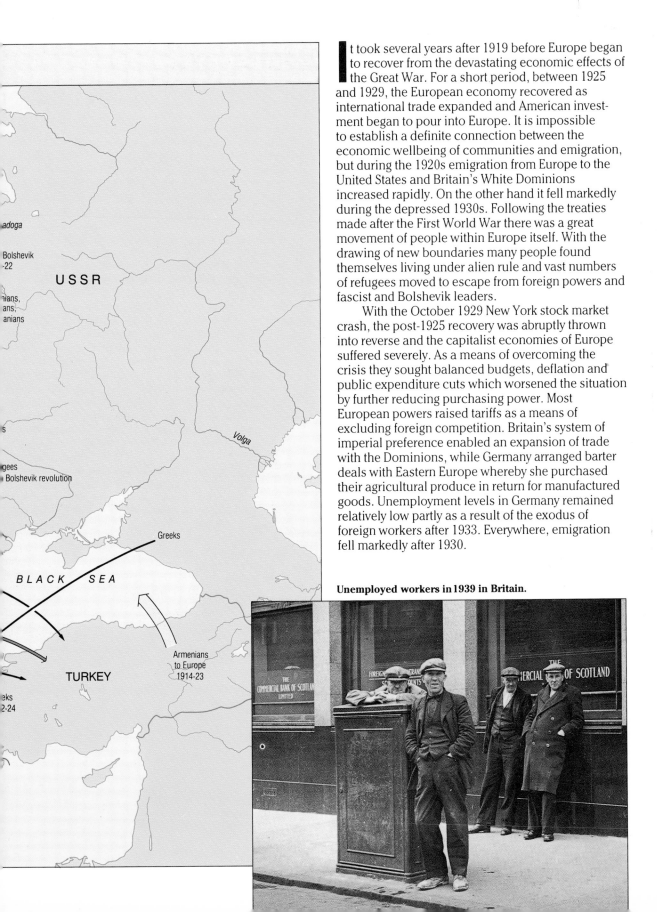

USSR

Volga

Greeks

BLACK SEA

Armenians
to Europe
1914-23

TURKEY

adoga

Bolshevik
-22

nians,
ans,
anians

s

gees
Bolshevik revolution

eks
2-24

United States: The Great Depression

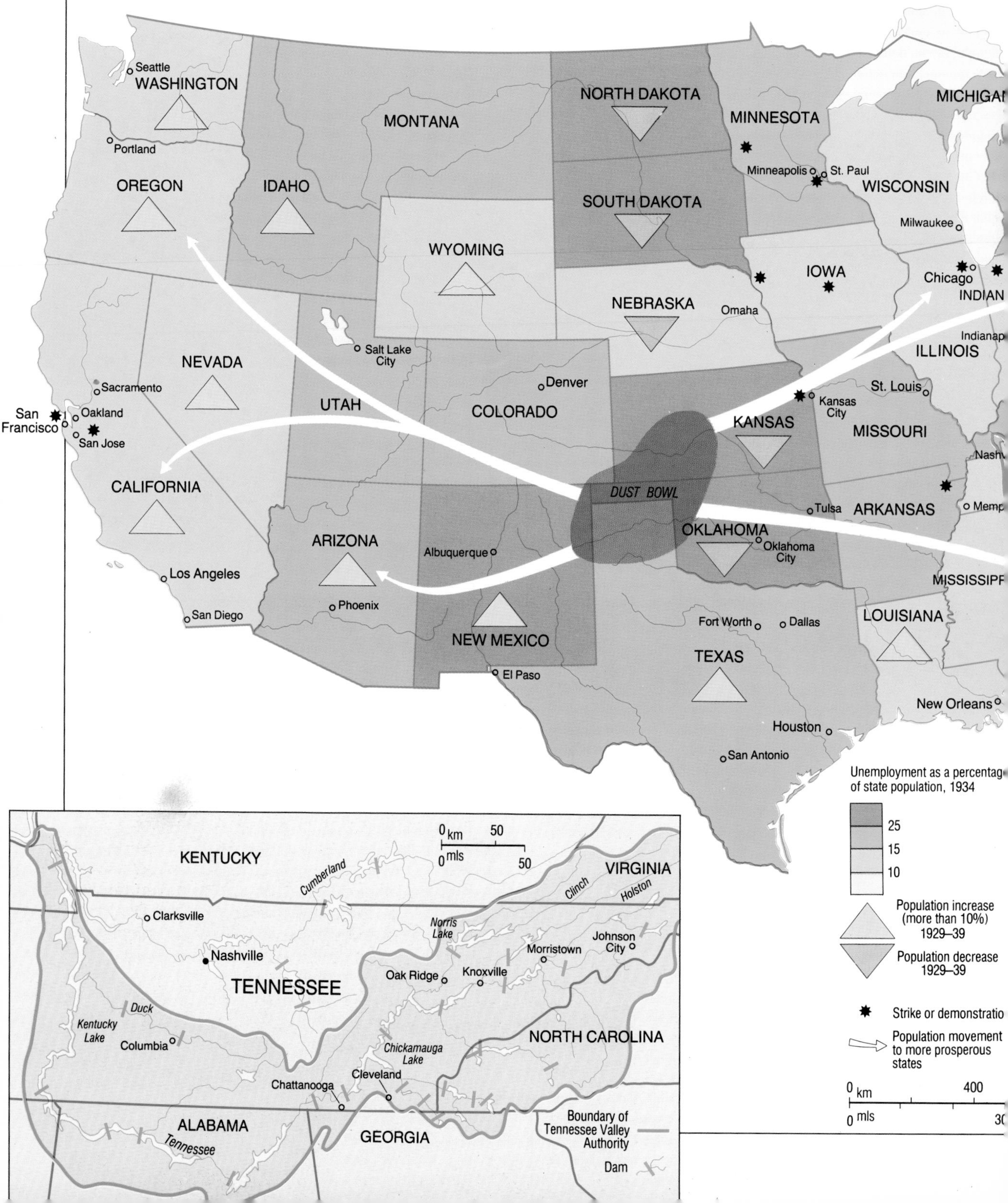

WASHINGTON
Seattle
Portland
OREGON
IDAHO
MONTANA
NORTH DAKOTA
MINNESOTA
Minneapolis
St. Paul
WISCONSIN
MICHIGAN
Milwaukee
SOUTH DAKOTA
WYOMING
IOWA
Chicago
INDIAN
NEBRASKA
Omaha
Indianap
ILLINOIS
NEVADA
Salt Lake City
UTAH
Denver
COLORADO
KANSAS
Kansas City
St. Louis
MISSOURI
Nash
Sacramento
San Francisco
Oakland
San Jose
DUST BOWL
Tulsa
ARKANSAS
Memp
CALIFORNIA
Los Angeles
San Diego
ARIZONA
Phoenix
Albuquerque
OKLAHOMA
Oklahoma City
MISSISSIPP
NEW MEXICO
El Paso
Fort Worth
Dallas
LOUISIANA
TEXAS
New Orleans
Houston
San Antonio

Unemployment as a percentage of state population, 1934

	25
	15
	10

Population increase (more than 10%) 1929–39

Population decrease 1929–39

Strike or demonstratio

Population movement to more prosperous states

0 km   400
0 mls   30

Inset map

0 km   50
0 mls   50

KENTUCKY
Cumberland
VIRGINIA
Clinch
Holston
Clarksville
Norris Lake
Morristown
Johnson City
Nashville
Oak Ridge
Knoxville
TENNESSEE
Duck
Kentucky Lake
Columbia
Chickamauga Lake
NORTH CAROLINA
Chattanooga
Cleveland
ALABAMA
GEORGIA
Tennessee

Boundary of Tennessee Valley Authority

Dam

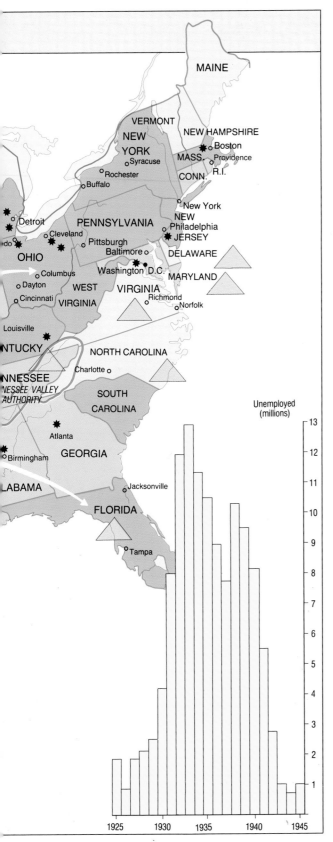

Unemployed
(millions)

The beginning of the Great Depression is associated with the New York stock market crash (the 'Wall Street Crash') of October 1929. The immediate effects of the Wall Street Crash were a collapse in share prices, a withdrawal of credit, rising unemployment and the closure of many banks. At first, the US government appeared powerless in the face of such economic calamity. But the election of a new president in 1932 marked a new era in economic management.

President Franklin Delano Roosevelt's 'New Deal' involved intervention in the economy on an unprecedented scale and directly challenged the American tradition of orthodox budgetary management and free enterprise. During the so-called 'Hundred Days', from March to June 1933, he secured Congressional enactment of 75 laws, all of which sought to reinvigorate the economy. He restored confidence in the banking system, guaranteed farm prices, and tried to freeze agricultural production by paying farmers a subsidy for not planting their land. Attention was also paid to the problems of farmers affected by the creation of a Dust Bowl in the Prairie States after 1934 caused by overfarming of the arid soil. The Tennessee Valley Authority, intended to build dams to provide cheap hydro-electricity and to develop the resources of impoverished Tennessee and neighbouring states, was created in 1933. The National Recovery Administration was set up to aid businessmen, raise wages and cut hours. Later, unemployment benefit and old age pensions were introduced.

Industrial production rose steadily after 1935 and by early 1937 production was back to 1929 levels. High unemployment and unrest persisted however, as did the social dislocation caused by mass migration out of the Dust Bowl and other poor States to California and elsewhere in search of work, and many of Roosevelt's measures were declared unconstitutional by the Supreme Court. In 1937, concerned about budget deficits, he cut expenditure sharply. This resulted in a new recession in mid-1937, with two million being added to the unemployment totals. His policies were running into increasing opposition from businessmen and conservatives who were reacting against excessive state intervention and higher taxes on the rich. However, the 'New Deal' stablized the country politically and economically and provided work and basic security for many employees, farmers and home owners. The unemployment problem was not, however, finally solved until the United States began to rearm in 1940.

Democracies in Danger

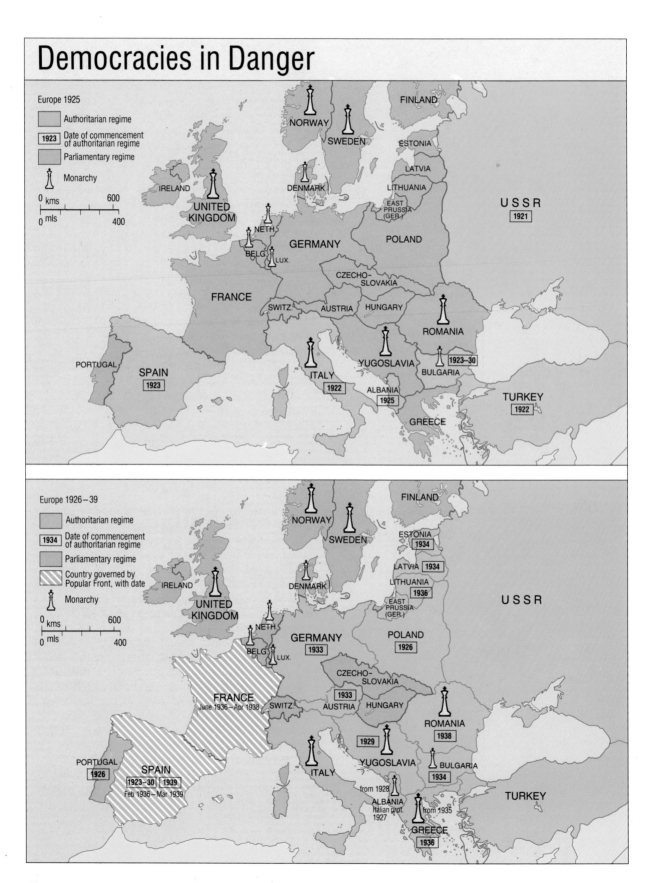

Europe 1925

Authoritarian regime

1923 — Date of commencement of authoritarian regime

Parliamentary regime

Monarchy

0 kms 600
0 mls 400

FINLAND

NORWAY

SWEDEN

ESTONIA

LATVIA

LITHUANIA

EAST PRUSSIA (GER.)

USSR
1921

IRELAND

UNITED KINGDOM

DENMARK

GERMANY

POLAND

NETH.

BELG. LUX.

FRANCE

SWITZ.

AUSTRIA

CZECHO-SLOVAKIA

HUNGARY

ROMANIA

PORTUGAL

SPAIN
1923

ITALY
1922

YUGOSLAVIA

BULGARIA
1923–30

ALBANIA
1925

GREECE

TURKEY
1922

Europe 1926–39

Authoritarian regime

1934 — Date of commencement of authoritarian regime

Parliamentary regime

Country governed by Popular Front, with date

Monarchy

0 kms 600
0 mls 400

FINLAND

NORWAY

SWEDEN

ESTONIA
1934

LATVIA 1934

LITHUANIA
1936

EAST PRUSSIA (GER.)

USSR

IRELAND

UNITED KINGDOM

DENMARK

GERMANY
1933

POLAND
1926

NETH.

BELG. LUX.

FRANCE
June 1936 – Apr 1938

SWITZ.

AUSTRIA

CZECHO-SLOVAKIA
1933

HUNGARY
1929

ROMANIA
1938

PORTUGAL
1926

SPAIN
1923–30 1939
Feb 1936 – Mar 1939

ITALY

YUGOSLAVIA

BULGARIA
1934

ALBANIA
Italian prot.
1927

from 1928

from 1935

GREECE
1936

TURKEY

60

In the 1920s the economic weakness of many of the newly independent Central and Eastern European states bred political instability, and in Poland, Romania, Hungary, Yugoslavia and Bulgaria conservative authoritarian regimes soon replaced the fragile democracies that had been established in 1919. Czechoslovakia was an exception in that it maintained its democratic constitution until 1939, but the country was much more economically and industrially advanced than any of the others. Austria depended on foreign loans for its very survival during the 1920s but its democratic system fell apart in the early 1930s. Romania, Czechoslovakia and Yugoslavia were reluctantly forced into a degree of political cooperation by the threat of a Habsburg restoration in Hungary in 1921, but they had few other interests in common: Czechoslovakia feared the revival of Germany, Romania of Russia and Bulgaria, while Yugoslavia was apprehensive of Italian ambitions along the Dalmatian coast. Poland remained apart: it had serious boundary disputes with Czechoslovakia and Lithuania, and dreaded the resurgence of Russia and Germany.

The weaknesses and divisions of these four states made them tempting targets for German economic and political penetration during the 1920s and 1930s. Faced with threats of a resurgent Germany and a communist Soviet Union, the four states allied themselves with Germany's traditional enemy, France. During the 1920s, Poland, Czechoslovakia, Yugoslavia and Romania all signed treaties with France which were designed both to secure the Versailles settlement and to enhance French security against Germany. France, however, was a far from stable partner in these alliances.

Between 1918 and 1940 the Third Republic in France saw more than 40 governments. However, the threat to French democracy was more apparent than real, since the Radical Socialist party was the mainstay of most French cabinets during the period, its ministers merely exchanging offices when governments changed. The French civil service provided the state with administrative continuity, while the French army was loyal to the Republic. The Republic's existence was only seriously challenged in 1934, when the suicide of Serge Stavisky, a fraudulent Jewish businessman, exposed a major financial scandal, the latest in a long series, in which many cabinet ministers and parliamentary deputies were implicated. This scandal coincided with the worst effects of the depression on France. As a result a number of extreme right-wing groups and the communists joined together to assault the discredited democratic system, and in so doing aroused considerable anti-Semitic feeling. After demonstrations in Paris on 6 February, a large crowd of rioters attempted to storm the Chamber of Deputies, but were eventually dispersed by the police. While there was much support for the extremists, the various right-wing leagues lacked a single leader or a unifying ideology: they were variously fascist, monarchist or Catholic. The election of a Popular Front government, which had communist support in 1936 alarmed the bourgeoisie but it collapsed in April 1938, and was succeeded by a Radical Socialist cabinet which remained in power until May 1940, when the Republic finally collapsed amid German conquest.

Percentage of votes cast for the
Popular Front in France, 26 April 1936
(by department)

60   52·5   45   37·5   30   22·5

The Spanish Civil War

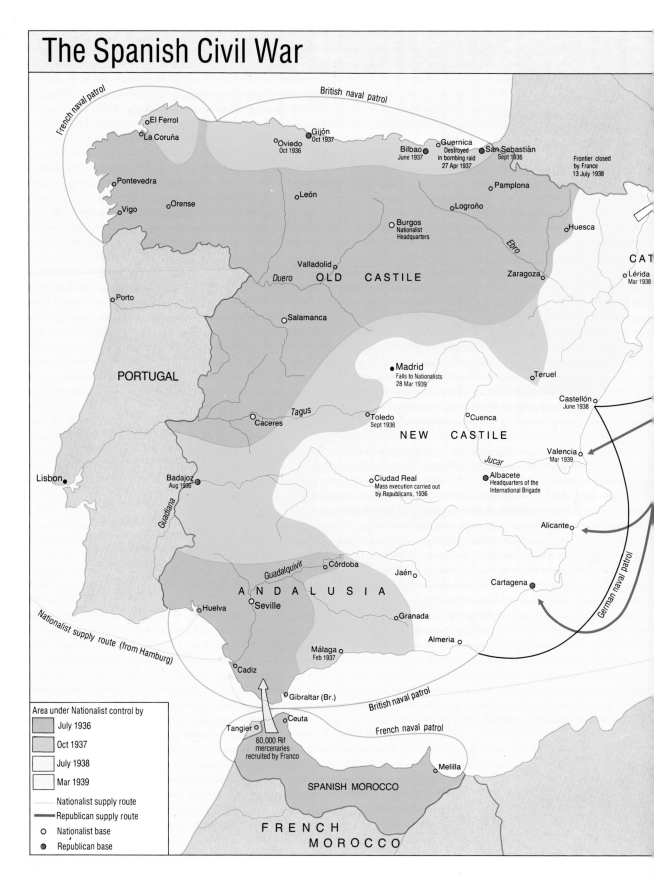

French naval patrol

British naval patrol

El Ferrol ○
La Coruña ○

Gijón ●
Oct 1937

Oviedo ○
Oct 1936

Guernica
Destroyed
in bombing raid
27 Apr 1937

Bilbao ●
June 1937

San Sebastián ●
Sept 1936

Frontier closed
by France
13 July 1938

Pontevedra ○

Orense ○

León ○

Pamplona ○

Logroño ○

Huesca ○

Vigo ○

Burgos ●
Nationalist
Headquarters

Ebro

C A T

Porto ○

Valladolid ○

Duero

O L D   C A S T I L E

Zaragoza ○

Lérida ○
Mar 1938

Salamanca ○

PORTUGAL

Madrid ●
Falls to Nationalists
28 Mar 1939

Teruel ○

Castellón ○
June 1938

Cáceres ○

Tagus

Toledo ○
Sept 1936

Cuenca ○

N E W   C A S T I L E

Júcar

Valencia ○
Mar 1939

Lisbon ●

Badajoz ●
Aug 1936

Guadiana

Ciudad Real ○
Mass execution carried out
by Republicans, 1936

Albacete ●
Headquarters of the
International Brigade

Alicante ○

Córdoba ○

German naval patrol

Guadalquivir

Jaén ○

Cartagena ●

Huelva ○

A N D A L U S I A

Seville ●

Granada ○

Almería ○

Nationalist supply route (from Hamburg)

Málaga ○
Feb 1937

Cadiz ○

Gibraltar (Br.) ○

British naval patrol

Tangier ○

Ceuta ○

French naval patrol

60,000 Rif
mercenaries
recruited by Franco

Melilla ○

SPANISH MOROCCO

F R E N C H
M O R O C C O

Area under Nationalist control by

	July 1936
	Oct 1937
	July 1938
	Mar 1939

— Nationalist supply route

— Republican supply route

○ Nationalist base

● Republican base

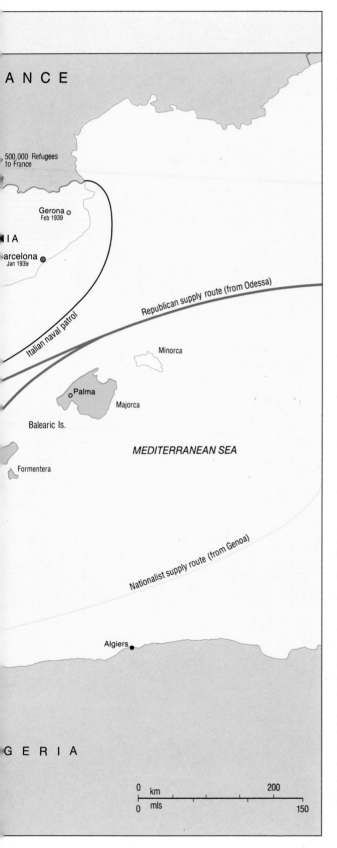

F R A N C E

500,000 Refugees
to France

Gerona o
Feb 1939

I A

arcelona ●
Jan 1939

Republican supply route (from Odessa)

Italian naval patrol

Minorca

o Palma

Majorca

Balearic Is.

MEDITERRANEAN SEA

Formentera

Nationalist supply route (from Genoa)

Algiers ●

G E R I A

0   km   200
0   mls   150

In the 1930s Republican Spain was polarized not only between Left and Right, but between monarchists and republicans, fascists and communists, traditionalists and modernists, anarchists and conservatives. Violence and disorder were endemic. The elections of February 1936 resulted in a Popular Front government, led by Manuel Azana, consisting of liberals, socialists, communists and anarchists. Many people feared either a right-wing coup or a bloody revolution. The middle classes and landowners in particular feared that the new government would expropriate their property, while the government itself seemed unable or unwilling to stem the general disorder which spread across the country. On 17 July 1936 the Spanish army, led by General Francisco Franco, intervened, bringing troops over from Spanish Morocco to crush the government. Franco had no clear programme beyond overthrowing the Republic, but by 1937 he had brought the other right-wing parties, including the Falange, under army control and into an amorphous Nationalist movement.

The civil war was marked by fearful violence and atrocities on both sides. On the Republican side, especially in the early days, violence was spontaneous and personal. Large numbers of priests were tortured and murdered, 'class enemies' were shot out of hand. Nationalist violence consisted of more organized massacres of prisoners and political opponents. Public opinion outside Spain was, initially, largely against the Republicans, and many saw the situation as another Bolshevik revolution. Britain and France adopted a policy of non-intervention, fearing that great power involvement might result in a major war. However, Italy sent military assistance to Franco, while Germany provided his forces with tanks, aircraft and advisers. The Soviet Union provided aid to the Republicans, and thousands of volunteers joined 'International Brigades' to fight on the Republican side. The war became a great ideological crusade for the Left.

At the outset the Spanish government controlled the east and centre of Spain and the Basque country in the north. The war lasted three years, with Franco's forces gradually getting the upper hand. The Nationalist victory, in March 1939, was based on its superior resources and unity of command. The Republicans suffered from deep divisions within their ranks, and inadequate supplies; by the end of the war their centres of power had been isolated by the Nationalists. The legacy of the civil war was oppression, bitterness or exile. Nationalist reprisals after the war were severe, but Franco established an uneasy peace and by keeping Spain out of the Second World War laid the foundations for gradual recovery.

The Path to War

SWEDEN

DENMARK

NORTH SEA

BALTIC SEA

• Copenhagen

Königsb

• Kiel

Danzi

UNITED
KINGDOM

Hamburg

Stettin

• Bydgoszcz

Amsterdam

Ems

Hanover

Berlin

• Poznan

Vistula

• London

NETHERLANDS

Brunswick

Magdeburg

Lodz

• Essen

Kassel

GERMANY

Oder

• Brussels

Cologne

Leipzig

Breslau

BELGIUM

Rhine

Dresden

Kato

LUXEMBOURG

Demilitarized
Rhineland
occupied Mar 1936

Frankfurt

Ceded to Germany by Czechoslovakia
at Munich agreement Oct 1938

Elbe

SUDETENLAND

SUDETEN-
LAND

Krak
to Poland
Czechosl
Sept 1

• Paris

Würzburg

Pilsen

Prague

Nuremberg

BOHEMIA-
MORAVIA
Invaded Mar 1939

Saarbrücken
SAAR
to Germany
by plebiscite
Mar 1935

Karlsruhe

• Brno

FRANCE

Stuttgart

Danube

SLOVAK
Satellite, Mar 1

Rhine

Augsburg

Linz

Vienna

Bratislava
Oct 1938

Munich

AUSTRIA
Annexed Mar 1938

Budapest

• Berne

Salzburg

SWITZERLAND

Innsbruck

Graz

HUNGA

Tisza

Drava

Drava

Subot

Milan

Zagreb

Trieste

Venice

Sava

ITALY

YUGOSLAVIA

Florence

Legend

Nazi Germany, 1933-35

Territory gained

1935-36

1938

1939

Boundary of Germany
1 Sept 1939

Other international boundaries,
1 Sept 1939

Autobahns 1939

Constructed

planned

Under the impact of Hitler's moves in Europe, Mussolini's seizure of Abyssinia in 1935–6 and Albania in 1939, and Japan's advance into China after 1931, the 1930s witnessed the gradual disintegration of the world order established in 1919. The first major blow to the Versailles system was Germany's remilitarization of the Rhineland on 7 March 1936. Beyond making diplomatic protests, Britain and France did nothing to resist Hitler's move. Indeed, when Neville Chamberlain became British Prime Minister in 1937, he adopted a policy of conciliating or appeasing Hitler in the hope that if the Western democracies satisfied Germany's legitimate demands for territorial revision it might settle down to become a peaceful member of the European community. In this policy Chamberlain gravely miscalculated, since Hitler was not interested merely in alterations to the status quo in Europe: he wanted to overthrow it altogether in Germany's favour. Thus Britain and France again did nothing when Hitler forced Austria into union with Germany (the *Anschluss*) – forbidden under the Versailles Treaty – in March 1938. He next demanded, on the grounds of national self-determination, the severing of Sudetenland, with its German population, from Czechoslovakia and its incorporation with Germany. At the Munich Conference on 29 September 1938, Britain and France acceded to this demand, although the loss of Sudetenland destroyed Czechoslovakia's defences and demoralized the Czechoslovak army. In March 1939 German troops occupied the rest of Czechoslovakia. Chamberlain reacted by guaranteeing Poland's independence – after Hitler demanded the transfer of Danzig and the Polish Corridor to Germany – and joined France in mutual support of Poland. Chamberlain also opened negotiations in Moscow for an alliance with the Soviet Union. These measures failed to prevent war: on 23 August Hitler and Stalin signed a non-aggression pact, and confident that Britain and France would not now intervene, Germany invaded Poland on 1 September. Britain and France declared war on Germany on 3 September.

None of the Western democracies emerged with much credit from these events. An earlier and more determined Allied response might have stopped Hitler but by 1939 he was buoyed up by his previous successes and convinced that he had little to fear from France and Britain. The United States remained aloof from Europe, and did nothing to resist acts of aggression which would ultimately threaten American security. Indeed, during the 1930s, Congress strengthened isolationism by passing neutrality legislation making it impossible for the Allies to raise American loans in the event of war.

Chronology 1919–1939

EUROPE	AMERICAS

EUROPE

May	• Bavarian government troops capture Munich from communists: civil war breaks out and a right-wing government is established
June	• Peace Treaty signed at Versailles, after German–Austrian protests over its terms
June	• German fleet scuttled at Scapa Flow
Aug	• Hungarian Socialist regime under Béla Kun overthrown by Admiral Horthy
Dec	• German troops evacuate Latvia and Lithuania
Apr	• Russo–Polish war (to Oct)
Nov	• First full-time session of League of Nations
Jan	• Paris Conference: Germany to pay £11,300 million in reparations over 42 years
Mar	• Treaty of Riga ends Soviet–Polish war
Dec	• Anglo–Irish Treaty creates the Irish Free State
Mar	• End of civil war in USSR
Apr	• Civil war in Ireland (to Apr 1923)
Aug	• Greco–Turkish war ends in Greek defeat (Sept)
Oct	• Italian fascists march on Rome and Benito Mussolini becomes Italian Prime Minister
Jan	• Default by Germany on reparation payments
Feb	• France and Belgium occupy Ruhr to obtain reparations from Germany
July	• Non-fascist parties dissolved in Italy
Nov	• Failure of Adolf Hitler's coup d'état in Munich
Jan	• First British Labour government formed under Ramsay Macdonald
Oct	• 'Zinoviev letter' allegedly urging revolution in Britain brings down Labour government
July	• France and Belgium evacuate Ruhr after Dawes Plan proposals compromise on reparations
Oct	• Adolf Hitler publishes *Mein Kampf*
Oct	• Treaty of Locarno guarantees Germany's western frontiers
May	• General strike in Britain
May	• General Pilsudski instigates coup d'état in Poland
Sept	• Germany admitted to League of Nations
July	• Socialist riots in Vienna following acquittal of Nazis for political murder
Jan	• Leon Trotsky deported to Siberia: Stalin emerges as sole ruler in USSR
Feb	• Vatican City becomes independent state within Italy
May	• General Election in Britain won by Labour: Ramsay MacDonald forms his second administration (to 1931)
Dec	• Unemployment in Germany exceeds three million

AMERICAS

Mar	• Bankruptcy of Canadian Grand Trunk Pacific Railway
Apr	• Rioting against conscription in Quebec
June	• Nicaragua asks USA for protection against Costa Rica
July	• Race riots in Chicago
Sept	• Steel strike in USA
Dec	• US House of Representatives moves to curtail immigration
Jan	• Prohibition of alcohol in USA
May	• Venustiano Carranza, President of Mexico, deposed and replaced by General Aluaro Obrezon
Mar	• Warren Harding (Republican) becomes US President
Aug	• USA makes peace treaties with Germany, Austria and Hungary
Aug	• Calvin Coolidge (Republican) becomes President of USA on sudden death of Harding
Sept	• USA resumes relations with Mexico
Feb	• US troops land in Honduras
July	• Elias Calles elected President of Mexico
Dec	• Freehold of oil companies in Mexico abolished, replaced by 50-year leases
May	• Mexico nationalizes minerals and oils
July	• Anti-church legislation in Mexico
Apr	• Carlos Ibanez assumes dictatorship in Chile and is elected President (May)
July	• Carlos Ibanez, President of Chile, resigns and is succeeded by Montero (Oct)
Nov	• Herbert Hoover (Republican) elected President of USA
Sept	• Peace between Paraguay and Bolivia
Oct	• Wall Street Crash: 'Black Friday' heralds beginning of world economic crisis
Nov	• Ortez Rubio elected President of Mexico

AFRICA, ASIA, AUSTRALASIA

Mar	• Nationalist riots in Cairo against British rule following deportation of Said Zaghul Pasha
Apr	• Amritsar massacre in Punjab as British troops fire on nationalist rioters
May	• War between British India and Afghanistan (to Aug)
Aug	• Anglo–Persian agreement at Tehran to preserve integrity of Persia
Aug	• Treaty of Rawalpindi ends Afghan War
Sept	• China ends war with Germany

Mar	• Western Allies occupy Constantinople (Istanbul)
Apr	• British civil administration of Palestine under League of Nations mandate
Aug	• Treaty of Sèvres: Turkey loses its former Arab territories and is confined to Anatolia

Jan	• First Indian Parliament meets
July	• Mongolia declares its independence from China
July	• Communist party formed in China
Aug	• End of British mandate in Iraq after uprising: Hashemite kingdom established (to 1958)

Feb	• Nine-Power Treaty secures independence of China: Japan restores Shandong
Mar	• Britain recognizes independence of Egypt
Nov	• Turkish Republic proclaimed, bringing end to Ottoman Empire

May	• Britain declares independence of Transjordan
Aug	• Treaty of Lausanne with Turkey revises Sèvres treaty in Turkey's favour
Oct	• Kemal Ataturk becomes first President of Turkey, with Ankara as new capital

June	• Britain declines Egyptian demand for evacuation of Sudan
Nov	• Soviet advisers help reorganize Guomindang (Nationalist) party in south China: Jiang Jieshi (Chiang Kai-shek) becomes leader

Jan	• Ibn Saud proclaimed king of Hijaz: name of state changed to Saudi Arabia
May	• Lebanon proclaimed a republic
June	• Chinese Nationalist government established at Hankou

July	• Chinese Guomindang expels communists from its ranks

July	• Jiang Jieshi (Chiang Kai-shek) becomes president of China after defeating insurgents
Aug	• Coup d'état in Ethiopia: Ras Tafari (Haile Selassie) takes control
Aug	• Arab–Jewish disturbances in Palestine

Dec	• All-India National Congress demands independence

SCIENCE & CULTURE

- Ernest Rutherford splits the atom
- Alcock and Brown make first trans-Atlantic non-stop flight from Newfoundland to Ireland
- First successful helicopter flight
- Rupert Brooke *Collected Poems*
- Daily London–Paris air service begins
- Preventative serum produced to combat yellow fever
- Edward Elgar Cello Concerto
- André Gide *La Symphonie Pastorale*

- D H Lawrence *Women In Love*

- Invention of Thompson sub-machine gun
- Aldous Huxley's first novel *Chrome Yellow*
- Irving Berlin first of 'Music Box Revues'

- British Broadcasting Company founded
- Howard Carter discovers tomb of Tutankhamen
- Vaughan Williams *Pastoral Symphony*
- James Joyce *Ulysses*
- T S Eliot *The Wasteland*

- Le Corbusier *Towards a New Architecture*

- George Gershwin *Rhapsody in Blue*
- Thomas Mann *The Magic Mountain*

- Rudolf Valentino stars in *The Son of the Sheik*
- Alban Berg *Wozzeck*
- Sergei Eisenstein *Battleship Potemkin*
- Robert Millikand discovers cosmic rays
- F Scott Fitzgerald *The Great Gatsby*

- Television invented by John Logie Baird
- T E Lawrence *Seven Pillars of Wisdom*
- Charleston dance becomes new craze
- Fritz Lang produces the film *Metropolis*
- William Walton *Façade* suite

- Charles Lindbergh flies solo from New York to Paris
- *The Jazz Singer* the first talking picture, with Al Jolson
- Hermann Hesse *Steppenwolf*

- Maurice Ravel *Boléro*
- Alexander Fleming discovers penicillin
- Walt Disney produces *Plane Crazy*: first Mickey Mouse cartoon
- Bertolt Brecht and Kurt Weill *The Threepenny Opera*

- Airship *Graf Zeppelin* flies round world
- Invention of the iron lung by Cecil Drinker
- Ernest Hemingway *A Farewell to Arms*

EUROPE	AMERICAS

EUROPE | ## AMERICAS

1930

EUROPE

Sept • German elections: 107 Nazis win seats in Reichstag

AMERICAS

Jan • War breaks out again between Paraguay and Bolivia
Sept • Revolution in Argentina: Hipólito Irigoyen deposed: succeeded by General José Uriburu
Oct • Revolution in Brazil (to Nov): Getúlio Vargas becomes President (to 1945)

1931

Apr • Revolution in Spain: Republican constitution replaces monarchy
Aug • National Government formed in Britain following severe financial crisis

1932

May • President Doumer of France assassinated: Albert Lebrun succeeds
Oct • British Union of Fascists formed by Sir Oswald Mosley
Oct • Hunger marches by unemployed in Britain

July • Uprising in São Paulo, Brazil (to Oct)
Nov • Franklin Delano Roosevelt wins US Presidential election (to 1945)

1933

Jan • Hitler becomes German Chancellor and Reichstag burned
Jan • Beginning of systematic persecution of German Jews
July • Germany becomes one-party state under Nazis

Feb • US Bank crisis
June • Roosevelt enunciates 'Good Neighbour' policy: aid sent to Central and South America and US troops withdrawn from Nicaragua
Aug • Uprising in Cuba: Fulgencio Batista seizes power

1934

June • 'Night of the Long Knives' in Germany
July • Austrian Chancellor Dollfuss murdered by Nazis
Aug • President Hindenburg dies: Hitler becomes Chancellor of Germany
Dec • Purge of Bolsheviks in Russia begins

May • Cuba abrogates US right of intervention
Nov • Lázaro Cardenas becomes President of Mexico

1935

Mar • Germany reintroduces conscription and repudiates military clauses of Versailles Treaty
Apr • New constitution in Poland: Smigly-Ridz becomes virtual dictator

June • Armistice between Bolivia and Paraguay ends Gran Chaco War
Dec • Death of Juan Gomez, President of Venezuela since 1908: subsequent riots in Caracas: military intervene: Eleazar Contreras succeeds

1936

Feb • General Franco rebels against new Spanish Republican government, starting Spanish Civil War
Mar • German troops occupy demilitarized Rhineland
Nov • Rome–Berlin anti-communist axis proclaimed

Nov • F D Roosevelt re-elected US President
• Rearmament begins in Canada

1937

Apr • German bombers destroy Guernica
May • Neville Chamberlain succeeds Baldwin as British Prime Minister
Oct • Nationalist forces take Gijón and complete conquest of north-west Spain

Mar • Cardenas assumes control of Mexico's oil resources and nationalizes the largely foreign-owned railways
July • Military coup d'état in Bolivia
Nov • New constitution of Brazil promulgated
Dec • All parties dissolved in Brazil

1938

Mar • Austria declared part of German Reich after German occupation
Apr • Franco's forces enter Catalonia
Oct • German troops occupy Sudeten territory in Czechoslovakia after Anglo–French agreement

Mar • All British and US oil companies expelled from Mexico and oil nationalized
May • Nazi movements in Chile and Brazil suppressed
Oct • Labour Standards Act passed in USA to regulate minimum wages and maximum hours

1939

Mar • Hitler occupies Czechoslovakia
Mar • Madrid's surrender to General Franco ends Spanish Civil War
Mar • Britain and France pledge to support Poland
Apr • Hitler denounces Germany's pact with Poland
Apr • Italy invades Albania
May • Hitler and Mussolini sign the 'Pact of Steel'
Aug • Attempts by Chamberlain and French premier Edouard Daladier to negotiate with Hitler fail
Aug • USSR–German non-aggression pact signed

Mar • US ambassador recalled from Berlin
Apr • Roosevelt makes peace plea to Hitler
June • Brazil allows entry of 3,000 German Jewish refugees
July • President Cardenas of Mexico offers 50 acres to each peasant

<table>
<tr><td colspan="2">

AFRICA, ASIA, AUSTRALASIA

</td><td>

SCIENCE & CULTURE

</td></tr>
<tr><td>Mar
June

Nov</td><td>

- Gandhi begins civil disobedience movement (to 1931)
- Rebellion in Lower Burma led by Saya San (to 1932) who was later hanged: 10,000 rebels die
- Ras Tafari becomes Haile Selassie I of Ethiopia

</td><td>

- Amy Johnson flies solo from Britain to Australia in 19.5 days
- W H Auden *Poems 1930*
- First World Cup in soccer, won by Uruguay
- Discovery of planet Pluto

</td></tr>
<tr><td>Sept</td><td>

- Japan invades Manchuria

</td><td>

- ICI produce petrol from coal
- Walt Disney's first colour film, *Flowers and Trees*
- Boris Karloff stars in film *Frankenstein*
- Virginia Woolf *The Waves*
- William Walton *Belshazzar's Feast*

</td></tr>
<tr><td>Jan
Feb

Mar</td><td>

- Indian Congress declared illegal: Gandhi arrested
- Manchukuo Republic proclaimed in Manchuria by Japanese
- Ex-Chinese emperor, Pu Yi, becomes President of Manchukuo

</td><td>

- Karl Jansky pioneers radio astronomy
- Aldous Huxley *Brave New World*
- Vitamin D discovered

</td></tr>
<tr><td>Feb
Mar</td><td>

- Japanese occupy China north of Great Wall
- Japan leaves League of Nations after League condemns its actions in China

</td><td>

- Richard Strauss *Arabella*
- George Orwell *Down and Out in Paris and London*
- Garcia Lorca *Blood Wedding*
- The film *King Kong*
- Marx Brothers star in *Duck Soup*

</td></tr>
<tr><td>May

Oct</td><td>

- Six Week War between Saudi Arabia and Yemen (until June)
- Mao Zedong (Mao Tse-tung) leads Chinese Communists on the Long March (to Nov 1935)

</td><td>

- Evelyn Waugh *A Handful of Dust*
- Dmitri Shostakovich *Lady Macbeth of Mtensk*
- Paul Hindemith *Mathis der Mahler*

</td></tr>
<tr><td>Oct</td><td>

- Italy invades Ethiopia: Italy condemned by League of Nations and sanctions imposed

</td><td>

- George Gershwin *Porgy and Bess*
- Pan-American Airways begin trans-Pacific service from California
- First radar equipment built for detecting aircraft
- Fred Astaire and Ginger Rogers dance in *Top Hat*

</td></tr>
<tr><td>May</td><td>

- Italians take Addis Ababa, and Ethiopia is formally annexed by Italy

</td><td>

- Sergei Prokofiev *Peter and the Wolf*
- Margaret Mitchell *Gone with the Wind*
- Olympic Games are held in Berlin

</td></tr>
<tr><td>Apr
July

Dec</td><td>

- Burma becomes separate entity in British Empire
- Beginning of war between China and Japan after Likouchiao incident
- Japanese take Nanjing and Shanghai: Chinese government moves capital to Chongqing

</td><td>

- *Pithecanthropus* skull discovered in Java (Java Man)
- Alban Berg *Lulu*
- Frank Whittle builds first jet engine
- John Steinbeck *Of Mice and Men*
- Nazi exhibition of 'Degenerate Art' in Munich

</td></tr>
<tr><td>Apr</td><td>

- Civil disobedience campaign in Tunisia against French rule organized by Habib Bourguiba

</td><td>

- Ballpoint pen patented by Ladislao Biro
- J P Sartre *La Nausée*
- Christopher Isherwood *Goodbye to Berlin*

</td></tr>
<tr><td>Feb
May</td><td>

- Japanese troops occupy Chinese island of Hainan
- Fighting (until Sept) between Japanese and Russians on border of Manchukuo and Mongolia: Japanese repulsed

</td><td>

- Otto Hahn achieves nuclear fission by bombarding uranium with neutrons
- John Cobb at Bonneville Salt Flats, Utah, drives at 369.74 mph (595.04 kmh)
- DDT is invented by Paul Muller
- *Gone With The Wind* film released
- John Steinbeck *The Grapes of Wrath*
- Popular songs of the period include *Roll Out The Barrel*, and *We'll Hang Out the Washing on the Siegfried Line*

</td></tr>
</table>

THE GLOBAL WAR

After the Japanese attack on Pearl Harbor the war became a world-wide struggle.

The Second World War originated in Europe and remained confined to that continent until the Soviet Union, Japan and the United States became involved in 1941. What gave the war a global dimension in 1939 was the commitment to the struggle of the entire British Empire and the Dominions, together with France's overseas colonies.

Britain and France declared war on Germany on 3 September after Hitler's forces invaded Poland. They remained on the defensive in September while Germany defeated Poland and divided that country with the Soviet Union. There was no fighting on the Western Front during the so-called 'phoney war' until May 1940, but Germany invaded Denmark and Norway in April 1940 and defeated an Anglo–French force which landed in Norway. On 10 May 1940 Germany launched an all-out assault on Holland and Belgium and Anglo–French armies sent to defend Belgium were defeated by a German panzer assault across the Ardennes to the French coast, the remnants of the British and French forces being evacuated by sea to Britain from Dunkirk. When the Germans invaded France in June the demoralized French agreed to an armistice on 22 June. Italy declared war on France and Britain on 20 June.

Britain was now alone, facing a Germany dominant on the Continent. However, during the summer and early autumn of 1940 the Royal Air Force Fighter Command defeated a German aerial assault on Britain's aerodromes and aircraft factories (the Battle of Britain) and Hitler postponed a sea-borne invasion of the British Isles indefinitely. Thereafter, until June 1941, fighting was concentrated in the Balkans, in the Mediterranean and in North Africa, where Italy was saved from defeat by the despatch of German troops to Tripoli early in 1941. When Germany invaded Greece in April, a British Expeditionary Force sent to assist the Greeks was defeated and evacuated from Greece and then finally from Crete, by 1 June.

With Germany's invasion of the Soviet Union on 22 June 1941 and Japan's attack on Pearl Harbor on 7 December (which was followed by a German declaration of war on the United States), the war became a world-wide struggle. The Russians, taken entirely by surprise, were driven out of western Russia

Total War

to the gates of Leningrad and Moscow by the end of the year, with heavy losses of men and equipment. However, both cities held out. The Japanese sank part of the American fleet at Pearl Harbor. Simultaneously Japanese forces attacked British and Dutch possessions in the Far East, capturing the Dutch East Indies, Singapore, Malaya and most of Burma.

The year 1942 represented the furthest limit of the Axis advance. Once the United States had geared up its war industries, supplied substantial quantities of military aid to Russia and Britain and built up its own armed forces, the Allies reasserted themselves. At the end of 1942 and in early 1943, Axis forces in North Africa were routed by a two-pronged Allied advance – the British from Egypt and an Anglo–American amphibious force which had landed in Algeria and Morocco. After July 1943 the Allies seized Sicily and advanced into southern Italy. The Italian government signed an armistice in September 1943.

► Members of the French Resistance, or 'Maquis' watch for German forces at Montrachet. Resistance to the German occupation of Europe varied from country to country. In France, the Resistance impeded the movement of German reinforcements to Normandy and prepared the way for Allied armies.

During the Second World War civilians experienced the death and destruction of war on a scale never before seen in history. It was the result not only of the fighting which took place across Europe and South-East Asia, and the miseries of occupation, but also of the aerial bombing of towns and cities – intended to destroy civilian morale as well as eliminate industrial targets. The *Luftwaffe* bombed Warsaw in 1939 and Rotterdam in 1940 to force the inhabitants to surrender. From late 1940 and 1941 onwards, during the 'Blitz', German bombers attacked British towns and cities, including the industrial town of Coventry which suffered immense destruction in November 1940. In 1944 and 1945 German V1 flying bombs and V2 rockets were launched on England killing thousands. After 1942 Royal Air Force bombers pounded German population centres by night and the American Army Air Force attacked German industrial and communications targets by day. This campaign culminated in the destruction of Dresden on 13 February 1945. Some 600,000 German civilians died as a result of this bombing campaign. For six months before the dropping of the atomic bombs on Japan during August 1945, Japanese cities had also been the targets of an American air assault in which 260,000 civilians were killed.

▲ General Patch and the US 7th Army crossed the Rhine at Worms in 1945 after defeating the Germans in Alsace and the Saar.

In the Pacific the Japanese fleet suffered a series of defeats at the hands of American carrier-borne aircraft and Japan was gradually driven from its Pacific island outposts.

The Red Army forced a German army corps investing Stalingrad to surrender in February 1943 after five months of heavy fighting. Despite many set-backs and appalling losses on both sides the Red Army drove the Germans back to their 1939 frontiers by the end of 1944. In the West after 1943 British and American bombers pounded German cities and industries, while at sea the German U-boat threat to Allied merchant shipping, which had caused grievous Allied losses, was finally smashed in 1944.

By 1944 the Germans and Japanese were in retreat everywhere. On D-Day – 6 June 1944 – an Anglo–American amphibious assault on Normandy from Britain secured bridgeheads, and after heavy fighting the Germans were driven out of France and

Belgium during the late summer. Despite numerous disasters, such as a nearly successful German counter-offensive against Allied positions in Belgium between December 1944 and January 1945, Germany was gradually occupied by Soviet and Allied forces, and after the suicide of Hitler on 30 April the German High Command surrendered on 8 May 1945.

In the Pacific bitter fighting continued as the Japanese clung tenaciously to the outlying islands of Iwo Jima and Okinawa before being pushed back to their home islands in June. British and Indian forces drove the Japanese from Burma in the spring of 1945. Expecting suicidal Japanese resistance and massive Allied losses if the Allies invaded Japan, President Truman authorized the dropping of two atomic bombs on Hiroshima and Nagasaki on 6 and 9 August 1945, while the Soviet Union declared war on Japan and defeated its forces in Manchuria. The Japanese agreed to surrender on 14 August.

The German Advance

Axis territory, 1 Sept 1939

German gains to end 1939

Axis gains to end 1940

Axis gains to end 1941

Axis gains to Nov 1942

Allied territory Nov 1942

Vichy France and territories

Neutral

Axis advance

★ City bombed during Battle of Britain 1940

International boundary 1 Sept. 1939

0 km 400
0 mls 300

Ceded to US Mar 1940

FINLAND
Allied with Axis

NORWAY
Invaded April 1940

Oslo

SWEDEN

Stockholm

Gulf of Finland

ESTON

NORTH SEA

Hels

Riga

LAT

BALTIC SEA

Glasgow

Edinburgh

LITHUANIA

Kaunas

Belfast

UNITED

Newcastle

Danzig

EAST PRUSSIA

Dublin

Liverpool

KINGDOM

Hull

DENMARK
Invaded April 1940

Copenhagen

Vistula

Warsaw

Bug

Annex by USS Sept 19

IRELAND

Sheffield

Hamburg

Plymouth

Coventry

Bristol

London

Berlin

Bordeaux

Southampton

Dunkirk

NETHERLANDS
Amsterdam Invaded May 1940

Elbe

POLAND
Invaded Sept 1939

English Channel

Brussels

GERMANY

Oder

Lvov

ATLANTIC OCEAN

BELGIUM

Cologne

LUX.

Frankfurt

Prague

Krakow

Paris

Meuse

BOHEMIA-MORAVIA
Protectorate Mar 1939

Chernovts

Loire

FRANCE
Invaded May 1940

Maginot Line

Rhine

Nuremberg

Danube

SLOVAKIA
Satellite Mar 1939

Vichy

Munich

Vienna

Budapest

ROMAN
Allied with Axis

Bay of Biscay

Bordeaux

VICHY FRANCE
Neutral June 1940-Nov 42
Co-operation with Germany

SWITZERLAND

A l p s

AUSTRIA
Annexed Mar.1938

HUNGARY
Allied with Axis

Rhône

Milan

Po

Zagreb

Belgrade

Bucha

PORTUGAL

Madrid

Marseille

Corsica

ITALY

ADRIATIC SEA

YUGOSLAVIA
Invaded April 1941
Divided up between Axis states

Danube

Lisbon

SPAIN

Rome

Sofia

Tangier

Gibraltar (Br.)

Sardinia

Naples

BULGARIA
Allied with Axis

SPANISH MOROCCO

Algiers

Rabat

Oran

ALBANIA
Occupied by Italy 1939

Aege Se

GREECE
Invaded April 1941

Athe

Casablanca

Tunis

Sicily

MOROCCO
(Vichy France)

Sfax

Malta (Br.)

MEDITERRANEAN SEA

Crete
Invaded May 1941

Gabes

ALGERIA
(Vichy France)

TUNISIA
(Vichy France)
Invaded Nov 1942

Tripoli

Benghazi

Tobruk

LIBYA

72

In 1940 and 1941 the German army won a
remarkable series of victories which resulted in
Germany's domination of the European continent.
These victories were not achieved by greater
manpower or superior equipment, for in May 1940
France, Britain and Belgium fielded as many troops
as the German *Wehrmacht*, and although the French
air force was extremely weak, French tanks were of
better quality than their German equivalents.

When Germany invaded Belgium and Holland on
10 May 1940 Anglo–French forces advanced into
Belgium and established a continuous front with the
Maginot Line. However, the Germans had already
planned to send armoured or panzer divisions
through the lightly defended Ardennes Forest towards
the French coast, encircling the main Allied armies in
Belgium. The panzers, a unique combination of
tanks, aircraft and motorized infantry, moving at high
speed, crossed the Meuse near Sedan on 13 May and
by 25 May had reached Calais. The out-manoeuvred
Allies fell back on Dunkirk, and although about
340,000 troops were evacuated by every available
ship to England, they lost all their weapons and
equipment. Germany then overran France, which
signed an armistice on 22 June 1940. Germany had
won because of its superior operational skills and
command system. This defeat was a major example
of what has been described as Blitzkrieg or lightning
war. Germany next planned a victory by cross-
Channel invasion of Britain, but the *Luftwaffe*, while
attempting to knock out the Royal Air Force in
preparation for such an assault, was defeated by
Fighter Command in the Battle of Britain during the
summer and autumn of 1940. Germany then turned its
attention to the Balkans, North Africa and Russia in
1941. Yugoslavia and Greece were conquered in April
and a British Expeditionary Force, sent to help the
Greeks, was forced to evacuate in May. When
Germany sent Erwin Rommel and his Afrika Korps to
help the Italians in North Africa, Britain faced another
formidable enemy, who drove them back into Egypt
by the summer of 1942.

On 22 June 1941 Germany invaded Soviet Russia
– Operation Barbarossa – designed to conquer
European Russia to the Urals within a few months.
Spearheaded by the panzers, the German armies
swept into Russia in three directions, towards
Leningrad, towards Moscow, and towards the
Ukraine, the Caucasus and the Crimea. They
advanced 50 miles a day, capturing entire Soviet
armies and cities, but the onset of the harsh winter of
1941 slowed up their advance. By December they had
besieged Leningrad, occupied the Ukraine and most
of the Crimea, but were unable to take Moscow. Most
importantly, they had not defeated the Russians.

The Japanese Advance

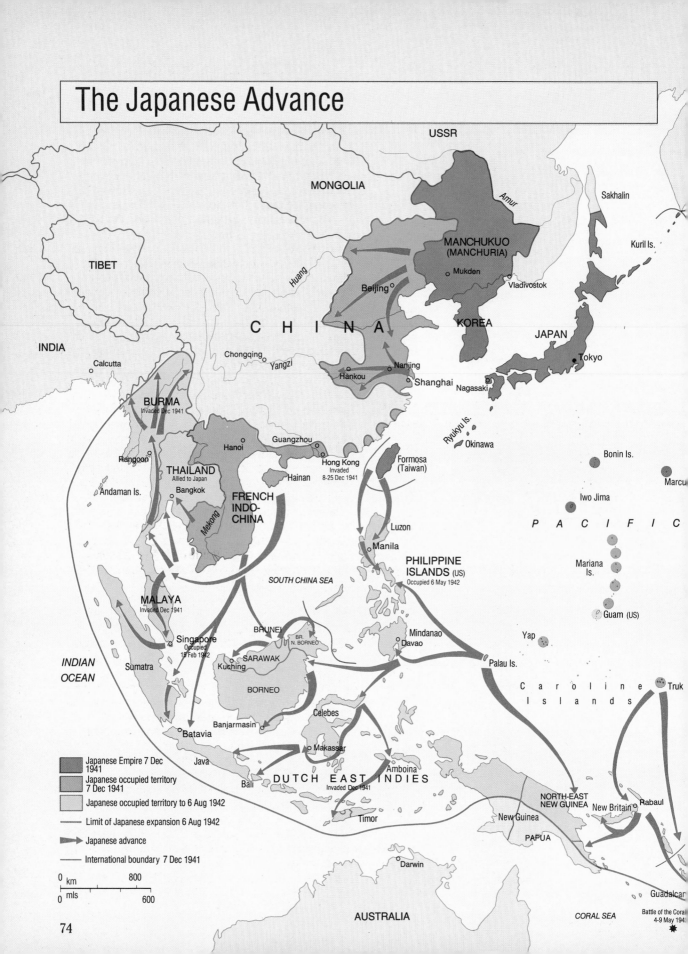

USSR

MONGOLIA

Sakhalin

Amur

MANCHUKUO
(MANCHURIA)

Mukden

Kuril Is.

TIBET

Huang

Beijing

Vladivostok

INDIA

CHINA

KOREA

JAPAN

Chongqing

Yangzi

Tokyo

Calcutta

Nanjing

Hankou

Shanghai

Nagasaki

BURMA
Invaded Dec 1941

Hanoi

Guangzhou

Rangoon

THAILAND
Allied to Japan

Hong Kong
Invaded
8-25 Dec 1941

Formosa
(Taiwan)

Ryukyu Is.

Okinawa

Bonin Is.

Marcu

Andaman Is.

Bangkok

Hainan

FRENCH
INDO-
CHINA

Iwo Jima

Mekong

PACIFIC

Luzon

Manila

MALAYA
Invaded Dec 1941

SOUTH CHINA SEA

PHILIPPINE
ISLANDS (US)
Occupied 6 May 1942

Mariana
Is.

Singapore
Occupied
15 Feb 1942

BRUNEI

BR.
N. BORNEO

Mindanao

Davao

Yap

Guam (US)

Sumatra

SARAWAK

Kuching

Palau Is.

Caroline

Islands

Truk

BORNEO

INDIAN
OCEAN

Celebes

Banjarmasin

Batavia

Makassar

Java

Amboina

Bali

DUTCH EAST INDIES
Invaded Dec 1941

NORTH-EAST
NEW GUINEA

New Britain

Rabaul

New Guinea

PAPUA

Timor

Darwin

Guadalcar

Japanese Empire 7 Dec
1941

Japanese occupied territory
7 Dec 1941

Japanese occupied territory to 6 Aug 1942

Limit of Japanese expansion 6 Aug 1942

Japanese advance

International boundary 7 Dec 1941

0 km   800
0 mls   600

AUSTRALIA

CORAL SEA

Battle of the Coral
4-9 May 194

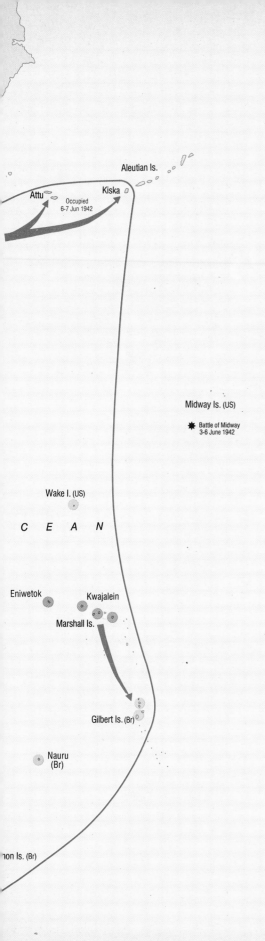

Aleutian Is.

Attu

Kiska

Occupied
6-7 Jun 1942

Midway Is. (US)

Battle of Midway
3-6 June 1942

Wake I. (US)

C E A N

Eniwetok

Kwajalein

Marshall Is.

Gilbert Is. (Br)

Nauru
(Br)

non Is. (Br)

The Japanese attack on the American naval base at Pearl Harbor on 7 December 1941 was intended to destroy the American Pacific Fleet and prevent any effective American intervention against Japan in the Far East. Inevitably this unprovoked assault caused intense anger and indignation in the United States and President Roosevelt had no difficulty in securing a declaration of war against Japan from Congress. During December the Japanese also attacked the Dutch East Indies, Hong Kong, the Philippines, Malaya, Singapore and islands in the Pacific Ocean, and sank two British battleships, the *Prince of Wales* and the *Repulse*, which had been sent to defend Singapore and Malaya. All these territories fell to the Japanese by early 1942, with an entire British Imperial army of about 80,000 men surrendering to a much smaller Japanese force besieging Singapore on 15 February. In December 1941 the Japanese invaded Burma, which they conquered by April: British casualties of 14,000 men were twice those of the Japanese. The British had now been forced back to the borders of India. Elsewhere the Japanese invaded New Guinea and occupied the northern half of the island, leading to fears in Australia of an imminent invasion. General Douglas MacArthur, former American commander in the Philippines, took command of Australian forces and repulsed a Japanese attack on Papua. In May 1942 American and Japanese carrier-borne aircraft fought in the Coral Sea, off the north-east coast of Australia, and although this was a drawn battle – both sides lost two carriers each – it prevented Japanese reinforcements reaching Papua. The Japanese tried to capture the Midway Islands, hoping to use them as a base from which to threaten America's Pacific coast. They failed, and the Americans gained the initiative. However, they still faced ferocious fighting. From August 1942 to February 1943 both sides fought for the possession of Guadalcanal, one of the Solomon Islands, which the Japanese finally abandoned after inflicting and receiving some appalling losses. Nevertheless, by January 1943 the Japanese were in occupation of a vast area in the Asian-Pacific region, from the southern Aleutian Islands in the north, through Wake Island in the east to northern New Guinea in the south and up through the Dutch East Indies, Malaya and Burma, eastern China and Manchuria to Sakhalin off the coast of Russia. They hoped to organize this area into a 'Greater South-East Asian Co-Prosperity Zone', although in practice this meant the exploitation of the human and natural resources of the conquered territories as a means of building up Japan's strength against the United States and her allies.

The World at War

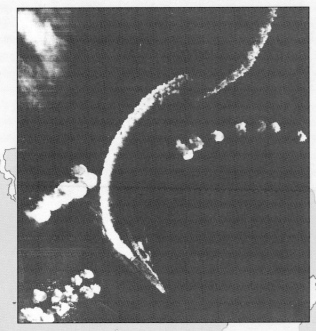

A Japanese ship under attack in the Battle of Midway, 1942.

The 1939–1945 war was truly a global one. Most countries were eventually drawn into the conflict; none could escape its effects. The most outstanding example was the worldwide assault on international commerce. The British imposed a maritime blockade on Germany in 1939 and in 1942 the United States navy began to destroy Japan's sea-going commerce. In 1941 Germany launched a submarine (U-boat or *Unterseeboot*) campaign designed to wipe out Britain's merchant shipping fleet and starve it of food and raw materials. The submarine blockade was first set up on western approaches to Britain, and later, once moved into the mid-Atlantic, it lay beyond the reach of Allied land-based craft. When the United States entered the war, the German long-range U-boats were soon to endanger shipping in US waters too. In 1942, at the height of the Battle of the Atlantic, 7.8 million gross tons of Allied merchant shipping was sunk with the loss of 26,000 merchant seamen. However, Allied counter-measures gradually defeated the submarine menace in 1943 with the breaking of Germany's radio codes by British signal intelligence, the availability of more long-range patrol aircraft and escort vessels for convoys and a massive expansion of American shipbuilding capacity. In the Far East American surface vessels and aircraft had, by 1944, destroyed Japan's merchant fleet, American signals intelligence having also broken the Japanese naval codes. Japan was accordingly cut off from vital imports.

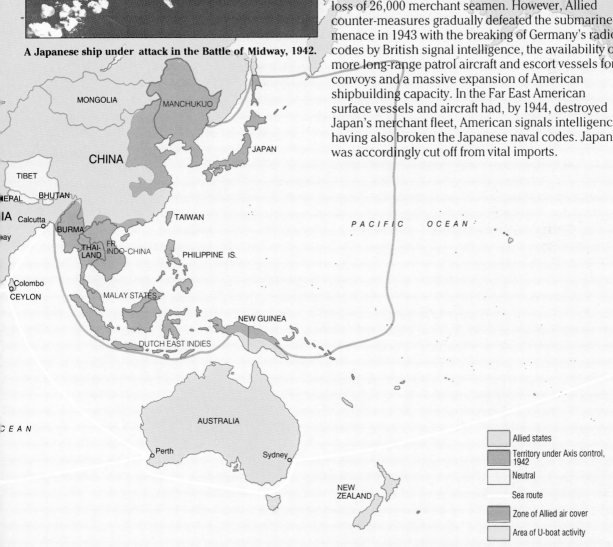

Allied states

Territory under Axis control, 1942

Neutral

Sea route

Zone of Allied air cover

Area of U-boat activity

Nazi Europe

REICHSKOMMISSARIAT
NORWAY

SWEDEN

FINLAND

Leningrad

NORTH
SEA

UNITED
KINGDOM

DENMARK

B A L T I C   S E A

Klooga
Tallinn
Vaivara

Riga

REICHSKOMMISSARIAT
OSTLAND

Kaunas

Smolen

London

Amsterdam

REICHSKOMMISSARIAT
NETHERLANDS

Vught 115

Brussels

BELGIUM

50

Cologne

Hamburg

Neuengamme

Bergen-
Belsen

Niederhagen

G E R M A N Y

565

Frankfurt

Ravensbrück

Sachsenhausen-Oranienburg

Berlin

Mittelbaudora

Buchenwald

Danzig

Stuffhof

Bialystok

Minsk

Treblinka

POLAND

Chelmno

Warsaw

Sobibor

3,500
GENERAL
GOVERNMENT
OF POLAND

Majdanek

Kiev

Paris

Drancy

FRANCE

150

Natzweiler

Rhine

Flossenburg

Theresien-
stadt

Prague

Gross Rosen

350

Auschwitz-
Birkenau

Krakow
Stryzow

Belzec

Lvov

REICHSKOMMISSAR
UKRAINE

Balanowk

Vichy

VICHY FRANCE
Occupied Nov 1942

Dachau

Munich

SWITZERLAND

300

Milan

Mauthausen

Vienna

AUSTRIA

Danube

SLOVAKIA

Plaszow

Budapest

HUNGARY

500

Dniester

Edineti

Odessa

Les
Milles

Marseille

Nice

Venice

45

ITALY

Rome

Corsica

Sardinia

Naples

Jasenovac

CROATIA

64

Belgrade

SERBIA

MONTENEGRO
(to Italy)

ROMANIA

834

Danube

Sofia

BULGARIA

46

Bucharest

M E D I T E R R A N E A N
S E A

Sicily

ALGERIA
(Vichy France)

TUNISIA
(Vichy France)

ALBANIA
(to Italy)

GREECE

110

Athens

Istanbul

78

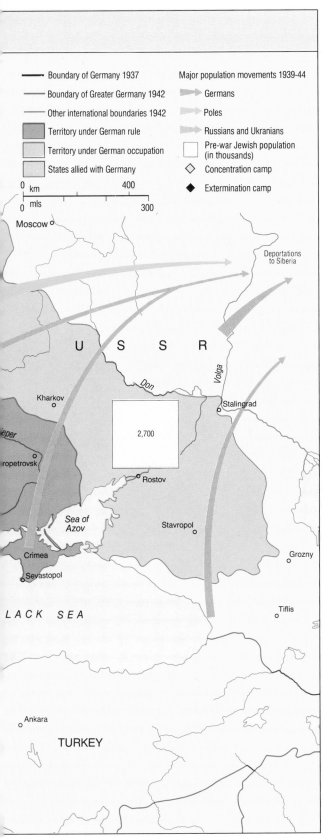

The so-called German 'New Order' in Europe was a system of economic exploitation devoted to the needs of Germany and its armed forces. Initially, the Germans plundered raw materials and machinery from conquered countries, dismantling factories and shipping them back to the Reich. Later, however, they permitted Western European industries to remain in production although the bulk of their output was sent to Germany. Agricultural produce was also requisitioned. As more Germans were drafted into the army, workers in occupied countries were forcibly recruited to work in German factories, while Soviet and Polish prisoners of war were transported to work in munitions factories and mines. Large numbers died of starvation and ill-treatment.

Hitler had preached anti-Semitism since 1920, developing the theory of an 'Aryan' master-race so that anti-Semitism and racism became the rallying cries of his regime. The Nazis' 'Final Solution' of the Jewish question began in 1939 with the occupation of Poland. Polish Jews were rounded up into ghettos, a pattern repeated in other Nazi-occupied countries. The mass murder of Jews was placed on a more systematic basis following the Wannsee Conference of leading *Schutzstaffeln* (SS) officials on 20 January 1942. An official, Adolf Eichmann, was put in charge of the transport of Europe's Jews from their homelands to the death camps in the East. In the wake of the German armies, special SS Task Forces were sent to root out and kill Jews, Gypsies, Soviet commissars and educated Slavs. The SS had already experimented with poison gas to asphyxiate their victims and mobile gas vans had been deployed in captured towns and villages for this purpose. Now specially constructed death camps were set up in Poland in which thousands of Jews were gassed daily. During the war between four to six million Jews were murdered by the Nazis.

After 1942 European resistance movements proliferated, assisted by the British Special Operations Executive and the American Office of Strategic Services. Across Europe, partisans sabotaged factories, roads and railways and ambushed German troop and supply convoys. German reprisals were savage: often, the populations of entire villages were exterminated. In 1943 heavy fighting broke out between Tito's partisans in Yugoslavia and German troops. As with similar conflicts elsewhere in Europe, the more numerous and better-equipped Germans prevailed.
In July 1944 the Polish Underground Home Army seized two thirds of Warsaw, anticipating assistance from the Red Army outside the city. Stalin refused to help them however, and in October the Germans ruthlessly crushed the revolt.

The Allied Counter-offensive

Allied territory Nov.1942
Areas liberated by Allies to July 1943
Areas liberated by Allies to June 1944
Areas liberated by Allies to Dec.1944
Areas liberated by Allies to May 1945
Areas still held by German forces at end of war
Neutral
Boundary of 'Greater Germany' 1942
Allied advances
German cities bombed
International boundary 1 Sept 1939

0 km 400
0 mls 300

NORWAY
SWEDEN
FINLAND
Allied with Germany
Oslo
Stockholm
Gulf of Finland
Hels
Tallin
ESTON
Riga
LAT
LITHUA
Kauna
BALTIC SEA
Danzig
EAST PRUSSIA
BE

NORTH SEA
Edinburgh
UNITED KINGDOM
DENMARK
Copenhagen
Dublin
IRELAND
Liverpool

ATLANTIC OCEAN

London
NETHERLANDS
Amsterdam
Bremen Hamburg
Hanover
Elbe
Antwerp
Arnhem
Brunswick
Berlin
Vistula
Warsaw
English Channel
Allied landings in Normandy, D-Day June 1944
Brussels
BELGIUM
Essen
Cologne
GERMANY
Leipzig
Dresden
Oder
POLAND
Falaise
NORMANDY
LUX.
Schweinfurt
Prague
Krakow
Lvov
Paris
Loire
Rhine
Nuremberg
Danube
Meuse
FRANCE
Munich
Vienna
SLOVAKIA
Bay of Biscay
Bordeaux
Vichy
SWITZERLAND
s
A
Rhône
Brenner Pass
AUSTRIA
Budapest
HUNGARY
ROMAN
Milan
Po
Zagreb
Belgrade
Buch
PORTUGAL
Madrid
Ravenna
Yugoslav partisans Oct 1944-May 1945
Danube
Lisbon
SPAIN
Corsica
Marseille
ADRIATIC SEA
Sofia
BULGA
Rome
ITALY
Sardinia
Anzio
Monte Cassino
Naples
Salerno
ALBANIA
Aege
Tangier
Gibraltar (Br.)
Palermo
GREECE
German forces evacuated Nov 1944
Ath
Casablanca
Rabat
SPANISH MOROCCO
Oran
Algiers
Allied advance Nov 1942
Constantine
Tunis
Sicily
Allied landing in Sicily July 1943
Malta (Br.)
Crete
MOROCCO
MEDITERRANEAN SEA
ALGERIA
TUNISIA
Tripoli
Benghazi
LIBYA

80

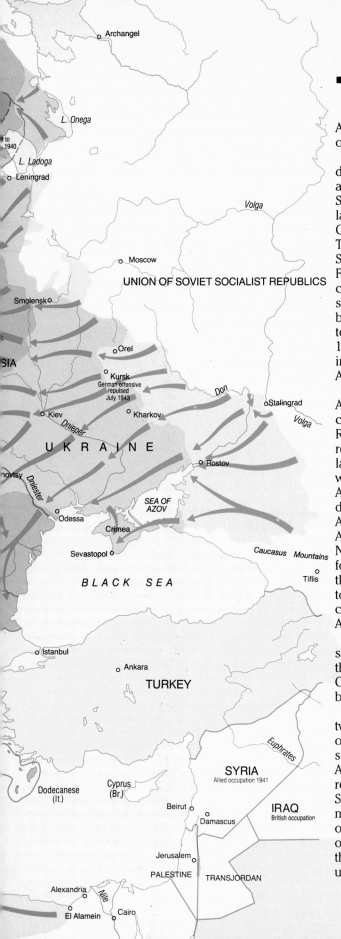

The turning point of the war for the Allies came in 1942. By the end of that year Hitler's forces had suffered severe set-backs in Russia and North Africa. In December 1941 the Russians were holding out in Leningrad, Moscow and Sevastopol.

In 1942 Hitler resumed his offensive after a break during the winter. The Germans captured Sevastopol, advanced into the Caucasus and captured most of Stalingrad. However, in November the Soviets launched a counter-offensive at Stalingrad, isolating General von Paulus and his Sixth Army inside the city. The most vicious fighting of the war took place in Stalingrad before von Paulus surrendered on 2 February 1943. The Germans next attempted a counter-offensive against the Red Army in the Kursk salient, but the Germans were defeated and they began to retreat along the entire front from the Baltic to the Black Sea. A Russian offensive in December 1943 relieved Leningrad and brought Russian troops into the Balkans and Poland. By early 1945 the Red Army had reached Berlin.

In the west the Russians pressed the British and Americans to mount a cross-Channel invasion of the continent in 1942 or 1943 to relieve pressure on the Red Army. The British refused: their army was not ready and was short of equipment. Instead an Allied landing in North Africa was agreed upon to coincide with an advance of General Montgomery's Eighth Army from Egypt. In October 1942 Montgomery destroyed Rommel's Afrika Korps at the battle of El Alamein and advanced on Tunisia, while Anglo–American forces landed in Morocco and Algeria in November. Hard fighting ensued before the Axis forces surrendered in Tunisia on 12 May. In July 1943 the Allies invaded southern Italy, causing the Italians to make peace. German occupation of northern and central Italy slowed down Allied progress and so the Allies did not reach northern Italy until April 1945.

On 6 June 1944 an Allied force landed successfully in Normandy, and after heavy fighting the Allies destroyed the German armies at the Falaise Gap. By December 1944 France and Belgium had been liberated and the Allies had reached Germany.

In the autumn of 1944 the Allied armies suffered two major setbacks: the failure of an airborne assault on Arnhem to seize a Rhine bridgehead and a surprise German counter-offensive through the Ardennes which was brought to a halt by Allied resistance in January 1945. On 12 January 1945 a Soviet offensive carried the Red Army to Berlin by mid-April. In March the Allies stormed into the heart of Germany, linking up with the Red Army on the Elbe on 25 April. Hitler committed suicide on 30 April, and the German armed services surrendered unconditionally to the Allies on 7 May.

The Defeat of Japan

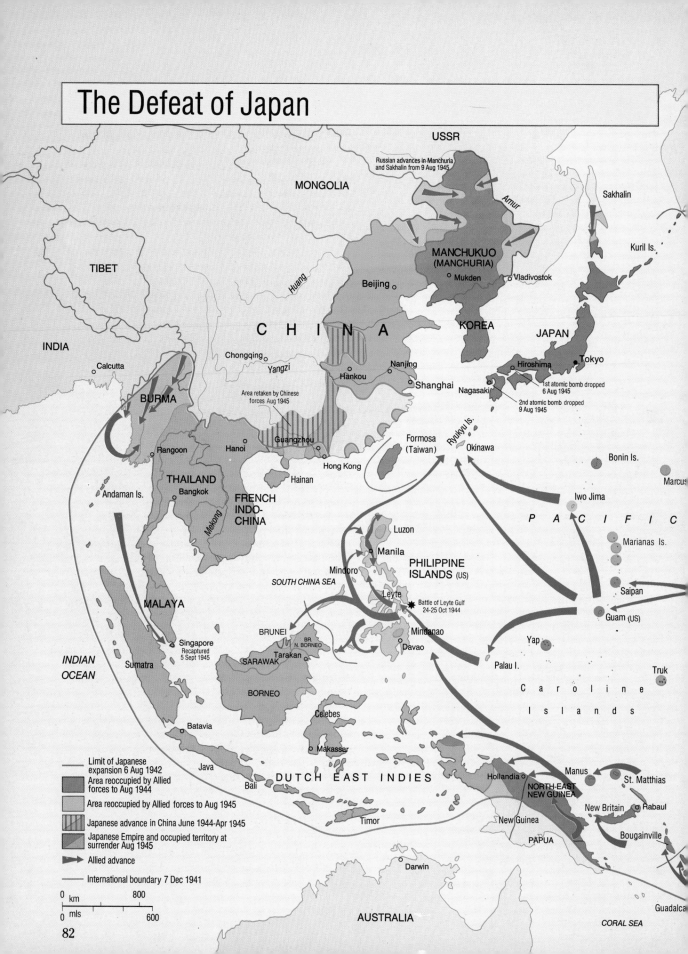

USSR

Russian advances in Manchuria
and Sakhalin from 9 Aug 1945

Sakhalin

MONGOLIA

Kuril Is.

Amur

MANCHUKUO
(MANCHURIA)

Mukden

Vladivostok

TIBET

Huang

Beijing

KOREA

JAPAN

Hiroshima

Tokyo

INDIA

C H I N A

Chongqing

Nanjing

1st atomic bomb dropped
6 Aug 1945

Calcutta

Yangzi

Hankou

Nagasaki

2nd atomic bomb dropped
9 Aug 1945

Shanghai

Area retaken by Chinese
forces Aug 1945

BURMA

Formosa
(Taiwan)

Ryukyu Is.

Okinawa

Rangoon

Hanoi

Guangzhou

Hong Kong

Bonin Is.

Marcus

THAILAND

Hainan

Bangkok

Andaman Is.

FRENCH
INDO-
CHINA

Iwo Jima

P   A   C   I   F   I   C

Mekong

Luzon

Marianas Is.

Manila

Mindoro

PHILIPPINE
ISLANDS (US)

Saipan

MALAYA

SOUTH CHINA SEA

Leyte

Battle of Leyte Gulf
24-25 Oct 1944

Guam (US)

Singapore
Recaptured
5 Sept 1945

BRUNEI

BR.
N. BORNEO

Mindanao

Yap

Truk

Sumatra

SARAWAK

Tarakan

Davao

INDIAN
OCEAN

Palau I.

C   a   r   o   l   i   n   e

BORNEO

I s l a n d s

Batavia

Celebes

Java

Bali

Makassar

DUTCH EAST INDIES

Manus

St. Matthias

Hollandia

NORTH-EAST
NEW GUINEA

Timor

New Britain

Rabaul

New Guinea

Bougainville

PAPUA

Darwin

Guadalca

AUSTRALIA

CORAL SEA

	Limit of Japanese expansion 6 Aug 1942
	Area reoccupied by Allied forces to Aug 1944
	Area reoccupied by Allied forces to Aug 1945
	Japanese advance in China June 1944-Apr 1945
	Japanese Empire and occupied territory at surrender Aug 1945
	Allied advance
	International boundary 7 Dec 1941

0   km   800

0   mls   600

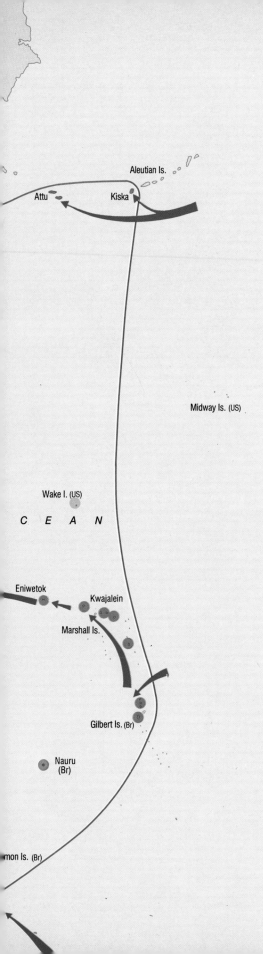

Aleutian Is.

Attu Kiska

Midway Is. (US)

Wake I. (US)

C E A N

Eniwetok

Kwajalein

Marshall Is.

Gilbert Is. (Br)

Nauru
(Br)

mon Is. (Br)

I n May 1942 the Japanese sent a carrier fleet to
capture the islands of Midway, which they hoped
to use as a base to threaten Pearl Harbor and
America's Pacific coast. American intelligence had,
however, detected their movements, and between
4–6 June, in a major action fought between aircraft
from the two carrier fleets, a United States task force
with three carriers sank four Japanese aircraft carriers
and a heavy cruiser. The United States lost one
carrier, the *Yorktown* on 7 June. This was a major
defeat for the Japanese, who could ill afford to
sustain losses on this scale. Thereafter the Japanese
were gradually pushed back to their home islands by
a combination of MacArthur's land forces and
Admiral Nimitz's Pacific Fleet, while the Japanese
merchant marine was destroyed by American
submarines, effectively ending Japan's hopes of using
the oil and raw materials of the conquered territories
to sustain its war effort.

In June 1944 the Americans occupied the island
of Saipan, 1,350 miles south of Tokyo. On 20 October
1944 MacArthur invaded the Philippines, and at the
Battle of Leyte Gulf a superior Japanese naval force
retired before a much smaller American fleet.
Gradually, during the first six months of 1945 the
Japanese hold on the Philippines was loosened.
During 1945 the Americans also captured Iwo Jima
and Okinawa, 500 miles south-west of Tokyo. The
Japanese put up suicidal resistance – 100,000 died –
and took a heavy toll in Americans killed and
wounded before Okinawa fell on 21 June. This
suggested to the Allies that a further six months or
more of bitter fighting and heavy casualties lay ahead
before the Japanese home islands would finally be
subdued. However, Japan's economic life had
already been brought to a virtual standstill by a
continuous American bombing offensive after March
1945. By the early summer Japanese politicians were
anxious to end the war, but Japan's reluctance to
endorse unconditional surrender, and fears of a coup
by Japanese military extremists, led to its approaches
for negotiations (through the Soviet Union) to be
dismissed by the United States as ambiguous and
unsatisfactory. On 6 and 9 August the United States
Air Force dropped two atomic bombs on Hiroshima
and Nagasaki, totally destroying the two cities and
killing 100,000 people. At the same time the Soviet
Union declared war on Japan and soon advanced into
Manchuria (Manchukuo). As a result of this
devastation the Japanese emperor ordered the
unconditional surrender of Japan, which took place
on 2 September 1945. Although the Americans agreed
to allow Emperor Hirohito to remain on his throne,
the real ruler of Japan was General MacArthur, the
Supreme Commander of the Allied forces.

The End of the War

NORWAY
Oslo
SWEDEN
Stockholm

FINLAND
Helsinki
L. Ladoga
Gulf of Finland
Leningrad

Tallinn
ESTONIAN
60
S.S.R.

NORTH SEA

DENMARK
Copenhagen

BALTIC SEA

125
Riga
LATVIAN S.S.R.

LITHUANIAN
80
S.S.R.
Kaunas

2400

NETHERLANDS
Amsterdam
Hamburg
Elbe

Kaliningrad
(Königsberg)
Gdansk
(Danzig)
POMERANIA
2000 (Russia)
350
1800
Vistula
Bug

oMinsk
BYELORUSSIAN
S.S.R.

WEST
Berlin
2000
650
1500
Oder
POLAND
Warsaw
U   S   S   R

EAST
Bonn
200
Frankfurt
SILESIA
2900
3800
500
3200
500

Rhine
GERMANY
Prague
Krakow
1500
Lvov
to Siberia
Kiev
Dnieper

FRANCE
400
Danube
500
1800
CZECHOSLOVAKIA
110
CARPATHO-
UKRAINE
UKRAINIAN S.S.R.
Ukrainians
Crimean Tartars
Kalmuks
Caucasians
1800

Munich
Vienna
100
100
Tisza
MOLDAVIAN
S.S.R.
Kishinev
Dniester

SWITZERLAND
AUSTRIA
200
Budapest
50
Cluj
Odessa

Milan
Trieste
220
ISTRIA
to Yugoslavia
HUNGARY
40
40
60
ROMANIA
200

300
Belgrade
Bucharest
DOBRUJA
BLACK SEA

Danube
YUGOSLAVIA

Movement of peoples, 1945-52
(figures in thousands)

130
Sofia
BULGARIA

ITALY
Tiranë
ALBANIA
90
Salonika
Istanbul

GREECE
TURKEY

from Libya
from Ethiopia and Eritrea
from Dodecanese
95
120
15
Athens

Baltic peoples
Czechs and Slovaks
Germans
Greeks
Hungarians
Italians
Poles
Romanians
Russians, White Russians and Ukrainians
Turks
Old pre-war boundary
Post-war international boundary

0   km   500
0   mls   400

With the end of the war imminent in Europe, the 'Big Three' leaders, Winston Churchill, Franklin Roosevelt and Josef Stalin met at Yalta, in the Crimea, in February 1945 to determine the future of Europe. Roosevelt had put forward no concrete American peace aims during the war, hoping that by forging personal links with Stalin their two countries would continue their war-time alliance to maintain world peace through the United Nations Organization. American ambiguity about its post-war policy resulted in vague and unsatisfactory compromises being reached at Yalta. The three powers plus France were to occupy the zones in Germany on which they had agreed in 1944 and to partition the city of Berlin between them, but the future of Germany itself was left for a later peace conference. A Soviet demand for German reparations was referred to a Reparation Commission. The Soviet Union's control of Eastern Europe was confirmed, and was promised territorial and economic compensation in the Far East when it entered the war against Japan. The results of the next 'Big Three' Conference at Potsdam in July and August were even less satisfactory, since in order to preserve the facade of Great Power unity, most substantive issues were referred to future meetings of their Foreign Ministers.

The Europe the three powers were discussing was in chaos. Most of the continent had been heavily fought over and boundaries had changed several times. Under German occupation, large population movements had taken place, while towards the end of the war, many Ukrainians and Byelorussians fled from the advancing Red Army, afraid that they would be suspected of collaborating with the Germans. In 1944–5 Germans were expelled from Czechoslovakia and Poland. Some peoples had to move several times, and many fled to the west.

The problems facing the occupying powers in Germany in 1945 were formidable. Former concentration camp prisoners had to be cared for and re-settled. Many prisoners of war were unable to return to their homes, which were under foreign rule. There were millions of displaced persons and refugees all over war-ravaged Europe, where roads, railways and water supplies had been destroyed. The food supply was also extremely limited because of the destruction of farms and transport systems.

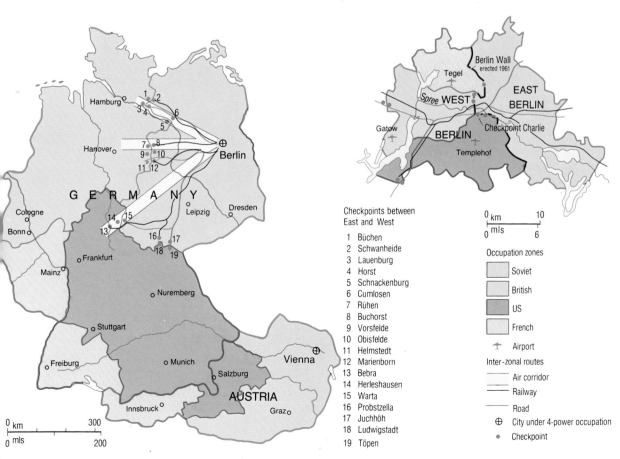

Checkpoints between
East and West

1 Büchen
2 Schwanheide
3 Lauenburg
4 Horst
5 Schnackenburg
6 Cumlosen
7 Rühen
8 Buchorst
9 Vorsfelde
10 Obisfelde
11 Helmstedt
12 Marienborn
13 Bebra
14 Herleshausen
15 Warta
16 Probstzella
17 Juchhöh
18 Ludwigstadt
19 Töpen

Occupation zones

- Soviet
- British
- US
- French
+ Airport

Inter-zonal routes

- Air corridor
- Railway
- Road
⊕ City under 4-power occupation
• Checkpoint

Soviet Expansionism

NORWAY
Oslo

FINLAND
Helsinki 1944-56
Porkkala
Soviet base
1947-56

Leningrad

SWEDEN
Stockholm
Gothenburg

Tallinn

ESTONIA
Soviet republic 1940

Riga

LATVIA
Soviet republic 1940

Moscow

NORTH
SEA

BALTIC SEA

LITHUANIA
Soviet republic 1940

Kaunas

Vilnius

Smolensk

DENMARK
Copenhagen

Kaliningrad
(Königsberg)   from Germany

Gdansk
(Danzig)

EAST
PRUSSIA

Minsk

Gomel

Hamburg

Szczecin

Poznan

Vistula

Warsaw

from Poland

NETHERLANDS

EAST
Berlin
Potsdam
GERMANY
Soviet occupation zone 1945-9,
communist 1949

Oder

Lodz

WEST
GERMANY
Cologne

Niesse

Dresden

Wroclaw

POLAND
1947

Kiev

Dnieper

Frankfurt

Prague

Krakow

Lvov

FRANCE

Nuremberg

Danube

CZECHOSLOVAKIA
1948
Brno

Rhine

Munich

Vienna
Soviet occupation zone
1945-55

Uzhgorod

from Czecho-
slovakia

Dniester

Chernovtsy

MOLDAVIA

SWITZERLAND

AUSTRIA

Budapest

HUNGARY
1947

Jassy

Odessa

from Romania

Turin

Milan

Trieste

Zagreb

Cluj

ROMANIA
1947

ITALY

ADRIATIC
SEA

Belgrade

Danube

Bucharest

Constanta

Corsica

Rome

YUGOSLAVIA
1945
left Soviet bloc 1948

Sofia

BULGARIA
1946

Varna

BLACK
SEA

Sardinia

Tirana

Skopje

Bosporus

Istanbul

ALBANIA
1946
left Soviet bloc 1961

GREECE

TURKEY

MEDITERRANEAN
SEA

Dardenelles

ICELAND

NORWAY

SWEDEN
FINL

POLAND

Kiev

Khar

Dneopret

BLACK
SEA   Yalta

TURKEY

Ardahan

Kars

Tb

SYRIA

1945

IRAQ

SAUDI ARABIA

By 1945 the Red Army had occupied Central and Eastern Europe and it was clear that the Soviet Union would insist on retaining close control over those countries after the war to prevent them ever again being used as a base for aggression against Russia. Roosevelt hoped that Stalin would allow these states at least a facade of independence. At the Yalta Conference in February 1945 Stalin signed the Declaration on Liberated Europe, a vague statement which promised democratic elections in areas freed from Axis occupation. Stalin agreed that free elections would be held in Poland. However, the setting up of an all-communist Provisional government in Poland in July 1944 had already led to Anglo–American protests and at the Potsdam Conference in 1945 a compromise was reached whereby non-communists were admitted to the Polish cabinet while Stalin repeated his promise of free elections. At Yalta, Stalin had secured Allied agreement to the Soviet annexation of Eastern Poland, and also the former German port of Königsberg (renamed Kaliningrad) in East Prussia: Poland was compensated by acquiring German territory east of the Oder and Western Neisse rivers.

After 1946 the Soviet grip on Central and Eastern Europe became total as non-communist parties were dissolved and rigid Stalinist governments installed. At Potsdam, in return for a promise that the Soviet Union would enter the war against Japan in the summer of 1945, the Allies agreed that the Soviet Union should annex the Japanese Kuril islands and southern Sakhalin, and be granted concessions in Manchuria.

The Soviets also demanded that their shipping be allowed free passage through the Dardanelles Straits, the return of Kars and Ardahan in the Caucasus, from Turkey, and a naval base on the Straits. Anglo–American suspicions of Soviet ambitions were heightened when the Soviet Union refused, until 1946, to withdraw troops from northern Iran, occupied during the war.

USSR

Volga

ARCTIC OCEAN

from Finland

ngrad

scow

UNION OF SOVIET SOCIALIST REPUBLICS

Yakutsk

Sverdlovsk

Kuybyshev

Omsk

Novosibirsk

Irkutsk

TANNU TUVA

Sakhalin

from Japan

Kuril Is.

Khabarovsk

MANCHURIA 1945-6

Vladivostok

MONGOLIA

NORTH KOREA 1948

Dairen 1945-54

Beijing

SOUTH KOREA

JAPAN

'PIAN EA

Alma Ata

Tashkent

CHINA

Shanghai

PACIFIC OCEAN

AFGHANISTAN

PAKISTAN

TIBET

INDIA

NEPAL

0 km 1200
0 mls 800

Union of Soviet Socialist Republic 1939

Territory gained 1940-1947

Soviet satellite states after Second World War

1947 Date of communist takeover

Under temporary Soviet occupation

'Iron Curtain' 1948

0 kms 400
0 mls 300

Chronology 1939–1945

EUROPE	AMERICAS

EUROPE

Sept   • Germany invades Poland and annexes Danzig: within 10 days controls western Poland
Sept   • (3rd) Britain and France declare war on Germany
Sept   • USSR invades Poland from east
Sept   • Poland partitioned between Germany and USSR
Oct   • British troops sent to France
Nov   • USSR invades Finland

Mar   • Peace treaty between USSR and Finland signed
Apr   • Germany invades Denmark and Norway
Apr   • Allies land in Norway
May   • Neville Chamberlain resigns, Winston Churchill becomes Prime Minister
May   • Germany invades Belgium and Holland: they surrender
May   • Britain occupies Iceland and the Faroe islands
May   • British army evacuated at Dunkirk (May to June)
June   • Norway surrenders
June   • Italy declares war on Britain and France
June   • German army enters Paris
June   • Henri Pétain, Prime Minister of France, requests armistice with Germany
June   • General de Gaulle founds Free French movement
June   • Armistice between France and Germany
July   • Estonia, Latvia and Lithuania vote to become Soviet republics
July   • German troops occupy Channel Islands
July   • Pro-Nazi French government of unoccupied France installed at Vichy, with Pétain as Head of State: Vichy government breaks off relations with Britain
Aug   • Churchill signs alliance with General de Gaulle
Aug   • Battle of Britain – RAF defeats German Air Force (to Oct)
Sept   • Germans bomb London: the 'Blitz' (to Oct)
Oct   • Romania allies with Germany
Nov   • Italy attacks Greece: British troops land in Greece to repel invasion

Feb   • German troops enter Bulgaria
Mar   • Yugoslavia joins tripartite pact of Germany, Italy and Japan
Mar   • Peter II overthrows pro-Axis government in Yugoslavia
Apr   • German troops enter Yugoslavia, and subsequently occupy Albania, Macedonia and Greece
Apr   • Germans crush Yugoslavia and Greece: British Expeditionary Force evacuated from Greece
May   • British forces withdraw from Crete
June   • Hitler invades USSR
June   • Battle of Bialystok–Minsk: Germans take 300,000 Russians prisoner
June   • Germans take Smolensk
July   • Anglo–Russian alliance
Sept   • Siege of Leningrad begins (lifted Jan 1944)
Sept   • (to Oct) 600,000 Russians taken prisoner after battles of Kiev and Viazma–Briansk: Orel, Kharkov and Odessa fall to Germans
Nov   • Battle for Moscow results in German stand-off (Dec)
Dec   • Russo–German front stabilized during winter months
Dec   • Germany and Italy declare war on USA
Dec   • Britain declares war on Finland, Hungary and Romania

AMERICAS

Sept   • Canadian Parliament votes to join war against Germany
Sept   • President Roosevelt declares US neutrality
Sept   • Stocks soar on Wall Street as investors predict war boom
Dec   • Battle of the River Plate: *Graf Spee* scuttled off Montevideo

June   • General Election in Canada: Mackenzie King's Liberal government confirmed in office
Sept   • USA introduces compulsory military service
Oct   • USA leases bases in Brazil and Chile
Nov   • F D Roosevelt re-elected for 3rd term

Mar   • USA introduces lease-lend system of aid to Britain and China
Mar   • USA seizes Italian, German and Danish ships in 16 ports
Apr   • US troops occupy Greenland
July   • Peru and Ecuador reach accord on border conflict
Aug   • USA extends lease-lend to USSR
Aug   • Churchill and Roosevelt meet in mid-Atlantic and issue Atlantic Charter
Dec   • Japan bombs Pearl Harbor, in effort to destroy US Pacific fleet
Dec   • USA declares war on Japan, Germany and Italy

AFRICA, ASIA, AUSTRALASIA

Sept	● Jan Smuts becomes premier of South Africa on J B Hertzog's resignation

Feb	● New five-year-old Dalai Lama enthroned in Tibet
May	● Following preaching of pacifism by Mohandas Gandhi, 40,000 Indian National Congress members imprisoned
June	● Spain occupies Tangier
July	● Italians invade Sudan
July	● British cripple French fleets at Oran and Mers el-Kebir
Aug	● Italians invade British Somaliland
Sept	● Small British force working with Ethiopian guerrillas
Sept	● Tripartite pact between Germany, Italy and Japan
Sept	● Japan invades Tonkin, northern French Indo-China
Dec	● General Wavell's British Offensive in Libya gets as far as El Agheila, expelling all Italians

Jan	● British offensive begins in East Africa: Emperor Haile Selassie re-enters Ethiopia
Feb	● Riot in Johannesburg following pro-Nazi meeting
Feb	● British take Benghazi, Libya
Feb	● German troops cross to North Africa under Field Marshal Erwin Rommel
Feb	● British take Mogadishu in Italian Somaliland
Mar	● German counter-offensive in North Africa begins
Apr	● British take Asmara, Addis Ababa and Massawa in Ethiopia
May	● Ethiopia gains independence from Italian control
June	● British and Free French invade Syria
July	● Japan occupies all French Indo-China
Aug	● Britain and USSR occupy Iran
Sept	● End of Italian operations in Libya
Nov	● British renew offensive in Libya
Dec	● Rommel begins withdrawal from Libya
Dec	● Japan attacks Pearl Harbor, Hawaii
Dec	● Japan occupies Hong Kong and Philippines

SCIENCE & CULTURE

● See page 69

● Penicillin is developed by Howard Florey as an antibiotic
● Discovery in France of Lascaux caves, famous for prehistoric wall paintings
● Glen Seaborg in California obtains plutonium by bombarding uranium with deuterons
● Sergei Prokofiev's ballet *Romeo and Juliet* played at Leningrad
● Charlie Chaplin performs in the film *The Great Dictator*
● Ernest Hemingway *For Whom the Bell Tolls*
● Graham Greene *The Power and the Glory*

● Hans Haas begins subaquatic photography
● First flight by Paul Sayer of Gloster jet fighter, Britain's first jet aircraft, based on work of Frank Whittle
● Orson Welles directs *Citizen Kane*
● Dmitri Shostakovich 7th Symphony (Leningrad)
● Michael Tippett *A Child of Our Time*
● Stanley Spencer *Shipbuilding in the Clyde*

EUROPE	AMERICAS

EUROPE

1942

Mar	• RAF 'saturation bombing' of German targets begins
May	• German offensive in Crimea
June	• In USSR, Germans smash through wide front from Kursk to Kharkhov
July	• Germans enter Sebastopol
Aug	• Allied raid on Dieppe
Aug	• Portugal and Spain form neutral 'Iberian Bloc'
Sept	• Siege of Stalingrad begins (to Jan 1943)
Nov	• Russians recover Kiev
Nov	• Vichy France occupied by Germans and Italians
Nov	• French navy scuttled in Toulon harbour

1943

Jan	• First daylight bombing of Berlin
July	• Allies land on Sicily and take Syracuse and Palermo
July	• Benito Mussolini falls: anti-fascist Marshal Badoglio forms Italian government
July	• Russians defeat German offensive at Kursk
Aug	• Russians retake Orel and Messina taken
Sept	• Donetz basin liberated
Sept	• Italy surrenders unconditionally to the Allies
Sept	• Germany occupies northern Italy and Rome: Allies invade Italian mainland at Salerno
Oct	• Free French troops liberate Corsica
Oct	• Italy declares war on Germany
Dec	• Communist government formed by Josip Broz (Tito) in Yugoslavia

1944

Jan	• Battle of Monte Cassino (to May)
May	• Crimea liberated
May	• Stalin tells Bulgaria, Romania and Hungary to declare war on Germany
June	• Allies enter Rome
June	• (6th) D-Day: Allies land in Normandy and begin invasion of German-held Western Europe
June	• Germans start to use V1 and V2 rockets to bombard Britain
June	• New Russian offensive against Finland
July	• Abortive attempt on Hitler's life
Aug	• General de Gaulle enters liberated Paris
Sept	• Battle of Arnhem: Allied progress checked
Nov	• Russian forces cross the Danube

1945

Jan	• Stalin, Roosevelt and Churchill meet at Yalta conference
Mar	• Allies reach Rhine and take Cologne
Apr	• Russians take Vienna and Berlin (23rd)
Apr	• Mussolini and mistress lynched by Italian partisans
Apr	• Hitler commits suicide
May	• Germans' unconditional surrender to Allies: end of War in Europe
June	• Germany partitioned into occupation zones between Britain, France, USA and USSR
July	• General Election in Britain: Labour Party takes office under Clement Attlee
July	• Potsdam Conference: Japan warned to make peace or suffer 'prompt and utter destruction'
Nov	• Nuremberg trials of principal Nazi leaders begin
Nov	• De Gaulle appointed head of French provisional government

AMERICAS

1942

Jan	• All American republics except Argentina sever diplomatic relations with Axis powers
May	• Negro recruits allowed in US navy for first time
May	• Japan invades Aleutian Islands
June	• Mexico declares war on Axis powers
June	• General Eisenhower appointed Commander-in-Chief of US forces in Europe
Aug	• Brazil declares war on Axis after sinking of several Brazilian ships
Nov	• USA breaks off diplomatic relations with Vichy France

1943

May	• US forces land on Attu in Aleutian Islands, held by Japanese
June	• Military coup d'état in Argentina – fascist-type government instituted

1944

Jan	• Argentina breaks with Axis powers
Feb	• More than 100 German agents captured in Chile
July	• British and US ambassadors recalled from Argentina
Nov	• F D Roosevelt re-elected US President for unprecedented 4th term

1945

Mar	• Argentina declares war on Germany
Apr	• President Roosevelt dies, succeeded by Vice President Harry Truman (to 1952)
Oct	• Military coup d'état by young officers in Venezuela: attempt at democratic government under Romulo Betancourt and Gallegos (until 1948)

AFRICA, ASIA, AUSTRALASIA

Feb	● Japanese invade Burma, Malaysia and Singapore
Mar	● Java surrenders to the Japanese
Mar	● Australia becomes Allied base in Pacific
Mar	● Sir Stafford Cripps sent by British government to India with promise of dominion status for India after war
May	● Japanese take Mandalay
June	● Battle of Midway: Japanese fleet crippled by US forces in the Pacific
June	● British lose Tobruk to Germans
Aug	● All-India Congress Committee rejects 'Cripps Offer'
Oct	● British Eighth Army defeats Germans at El Alamein
Nov	● First battle of Tunisia (to Dec)

Jan	● Eighth Army enters Tripoli, joined by Free French forces from Chad
Jan	● Casablanca Conference: Allies demand unconditional surrender from Germany, Italy and Japan
Mar	● Japanese defeated in Battle of Bismarck Sea
May	● Axis forces surrender in Tunisia
Aug	● Louis Mountbatten appointed Supreme Allied Commander, South-East Asia
Oct	● Japanese declare Burma independent
Oct	● Japanese declare Philippines independent
Nov	● Churchill, Roosevelt and Stalin meet in Tehran to plan defeat of Hitler
Dec	● Tehran Conference: second meeting of Churchill, Roosevelt and Stalin: Stalin promises to declare war on Japan after Germany's defeat
Dec	● Syria and Lebanon given independence by France

Jan	● Moroccan nationalists demand independence, riots follow
Jan	● Americans take Marshall Islands and Solomon Islands
Apr	● Allies begin to retake New Guinea
July	● US forces occupy Guam
July	● US forces seize Saipan in the Mariana Islands from Japan, 1,300 miles from Tokyo, enabling US to begin bombing Japan
Oct	● Japanese fleet heavily defeated as US forces land on Leyte in the Philippines

Feb	● Ahmed Pasha, Egyptian prime minister, assassinated after declaring war on Germany
Mar	● Arab League inaugurated in Cairo
Mar	● USA takes Iwo Jima Island, 750 miles from Tokyo
Mar	● France grants autonomy to Indo-China
Apr	● Japanese fleet destroyed in Battle of Okinawa
May	● Burma liberated by British troops
June	● British occupy Syria and Lebanon
Aug	● First atomic bomb destroys Hiroshima, second atomic bomb destroys Nagasaki
Aug	● Russia declares war on Japan: immediate advance into Manchuria
Aug	● Japan surrenders unconditionally to Allies
Sept	● Ho Chi Minh forms government in part of Indo-China (later North Vietnam)

SCIENCE & CULTURE

- ● Construction of world's first nuclear reactor at Chicago University led by Enrico Fermi
- ● Albert Camus *The Outsider* and *The Myth of Sisyphus*
- ● Richard Strauss *Capriccio*
- ● Bing Crosby sings *White Christmas*
- ● T S Eliot completes *The Four Quartets*
- ● C S Lewis *The Screwtape Letters*
- ● Magnetic recording tape is invented

- ● Chubb Crater, largest known meteorite crater, discovered at northern Ungava, Canada
- ● Rolls-Royce 'Welland' jet engine developed
- ● Humphrey Bogart and Ingrid Bergman star in *Casablanca*
- ● J P Sartre *Being and Nothingness*
- ● Rodgers and Hammerstein musical *Oklahoma!*

- ● Invention of the kidney machine
- ● Aaron Copland *Appalachian Spring*
- ● Jean Anouilh *Antigone*
- ● Tennessee Williams *The Glass Menagerie*
- ● Jackson Pollock Abstract Expressionist painting

- ● Karl Popper *The Open Society and its Enemies*
- ● George Orwell *Animal Farm*
- ● Evelyn Waugh *Brideshead Revisited*
- ● Benjamin Britten *Peter Grimes*
- ● Henry Moore *Family Group*
- ● Richard Strauss *Metamorphoses*
- ● David Lean directs *Brief Encounter*

THE END OF EMPIRE

Decolonization after the war was a haphazard, laborious and often bitter process.

Nationalist fervour in the Asian Empires of the European powers, Britain, France and the Netherlands, was running at fever pitch in 1945. Their European rulers had been humiliated by Japan, which had invaded South-East Asia in 1941–2 and had then promised the European colonies in the region their independence after the war. Furthermore, President Roosevelt was hostile to European colonialism and did not want to see the Europeans recover their empires in 1945. In 1941 he had tried to persuade Britain to sign and the other Allies to agree to the Atlantic Charter, which guaranteed world-wide democratic self-government after the war, and he believed that indigenous democratic regimes in Asia would be pro-American. Britain, France and the Netherlands, however, had as little intention in 1945 of applying the general principle of national self-

determination to their empires as they had in 1919. Although Britain granted independence to India and Pakistan in 1947 and to Burma and Ceylon in 1948 this was based as much on necessity as on conviction. Britain could no longer bear the burden of governing a huge subcontinent in which the mass of the people were in favour of independence and where the continued loyalty of the Indian Army could not be relied upon. As far as Britain was concerned, this was the end of the independence process for the foreseeable future.

▼ **On 'Black Saturday' (26 January) 1952 serious rioting against the British military presence in Egypt broke out and many British nationals were killed.**

▼ Princess Alexandra in Lagos for Nigeria's independence. Nigeria was one of the first British colonies in Africa to be granted independence.

▲ General Salan urges demonstrators in Algeria, in May 1958, to remain loyal to the French government.

With the defeat of the Japanese in 1945, British forces had re-occupied Malaya, Singapore and Hong Kong and had connived at the re-establishment of French and Dutch rule in Indo-China and the Dutch East Indies. The French and Dutch immediately found themselves faced with powerful nationalist movements. After sustained and bloody battles with Indonesian guerrillas, the Dutch abandoned Indonesia to the nationalists in 1949. The French, however, fought on in Indo-China against the Vietminh (Vietnamese nationalist) guerrillas, dominated by the communists and led by Ho Chi Minh, a veteran nationalist. In 1954, after a series of reverses in northern Vietnam, culminating in the capitulation of an entire French army corps at Dien Bien Phu to the Vietminh, France agreed to grant full independence to Laos and Cambodia, while Vietnam was split in two pending proposed all-Vietnam elections in 1956.

Britain escaped the worst manifestations of the nationalist turmoil, although its efforts to forge a zone of influence in the Middle East collapsed as a result of strenuous Egyptian resistance to continued British tutelage. At the end of 1956 Britain's position in the region was seriously undermined when an Anglo–French military expedition, which had invaded Egypt in protest against the nationalization of the Suez Canal, was forced to withdraw in humiliating circumstances after the United States imposed financial sanctions on Britain. During the 1960s Britain granted independence to most of its colonies but continued to maintain a naval presence east of Suez until 1970, and was burdened with the problem of Rhodesia (Zimbabwe) until 1980.

With the onset of the Cold War in the 1950s, the attitude of the United States towards colonialism became more ambiguous. The victory of Mao Zedong's (Mao Tse-Tung) communists in China in October 1949 convinced Washington that communism was a threat to world peace, and that nationalist movements in Indo–China, the Middle East and Africa were in danger of becoming dominated by Moscow- or Beijing-backed communists. After 1950 France began to receive substantial United States aid for its struggle in Indo–China, while Britain began to lobby for United States assistance in its conflicts with nationalists in Iran and elsewhere. However, the United States insisted that France and Britain should give their colonies real independence while also offering help to suppress communism, hoping that as a result stable, non-communist, democratic governments, would emerge. However, where the United States perceived the rise of left-wing regimes as threatening its interests, it frequently brought about their demise. Given that their successors were often military or right-wing regimes, the United States became identified with reactionary anti-democratic governments in Africa, South America and Asia. For its part the Soviet Union, after 1953, began to support nationalist anti-American leaders in the Third World who might bring their countries into the Soviet bloc.

Decolonization was a haphazard, laborious and often bitter process. France struggled for eight years to crush the nationalists in Algeria, and the outcome brought France to the brink of civil war in 1958. However, by 1955 a recognizable bloc of so-called non-aligned nations had emerged, consisting of left-wing countries like Yugoslavia and China, which had resisted Soviet domination, and newly independent countries like India, all of which wished to avoid involvement in superpower rivalries.

The British Empire after 1945

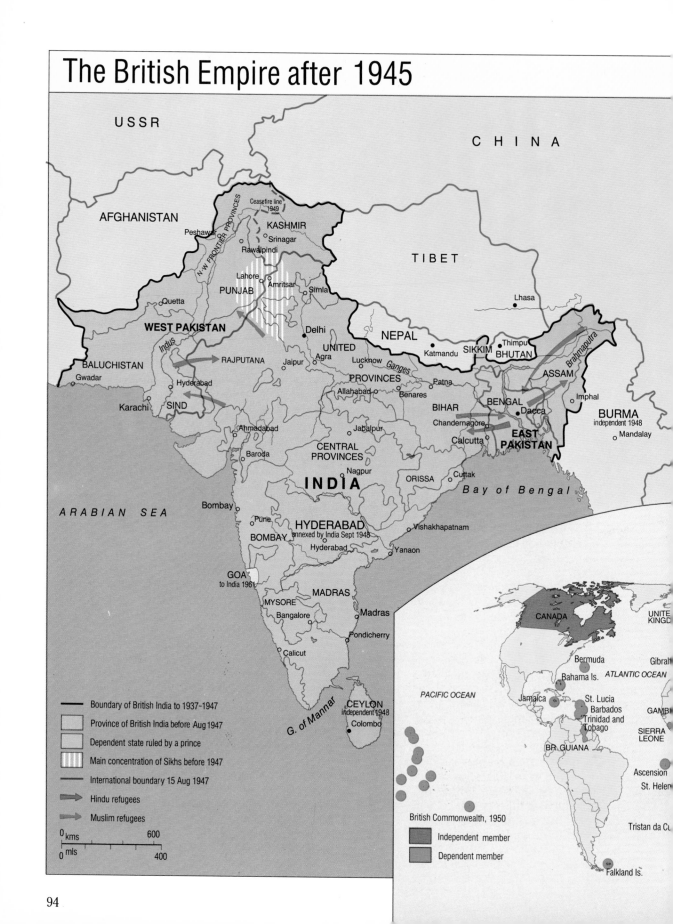

USSR

CHINA

AFGHANISTAN

Ceasefire line 1949

KASHMIR

Peshawar

Srinagar

N.W FRONTIER PROVINCES

Rawalpindi

TIBET

Lahore

PUNJAB

Amritsar

Simla

Quetta

Lhasa

WEST PAKISTAN

Delhi

NEPAL

Indus

BALUCHISTAN

RAJPUTANA

Jaipur

UNITED

Agra

Lucknow

Katmandu

SIKKIM

Thimpu

BHUTAN

Gwadar

Hyderabad

PROVINCES

Ganges

Patna

ASSAM

Brahmaputra

Karachi

SIND

Allahabad

Benares

BIHAR

BENGAL

Imphal

Chandernagore

Dacca

Ahmadabad

Jabalpur

Calcutta

EAST

BURMA
independent 1948

Baroda

CENTRAL
PROVINCES

PAKISTAN

Mandalay

ARABIAN SEA

Nagpur

INDIA

ORISSA

Cuttak

Bay of Bengal

Bombay

Pune

HYDERABAD
annexed by India Sept 1948

Vishakhapatnam

BOMBAY

Hyderabad

Yanaon

GOA
to India 1961

MADRAS

MYSORE

Bangalore

Madras

Pondicherry

Calicut

G. of Mannar

CEYLON
independent 1948

Colombo

Boundary of British India to 1937–1947

Province of British India before Aug 1947

Dependent state ruled by a prince

Main concentration of Sikhs before 1947

International boundary 15 Aug 1947

Hindu refugees

Muslim refugees

0		600
kms		
0		400
mls		

CANADA

UNITE
KINGD

Bermuda

Gibral

ATLANTIC OCEAN

PACIFIC OCEAN

Bahama Is.

Jamaica

St. Lucia

GAMB

Barbados

Trinidad and
Tobago

SIERRA
LEONE

BR. GUIANA

Ascension

St. Heler

British Commonwealth, 1950

Independent member

Dependent member

Tristan da Cu

Falkland Is.

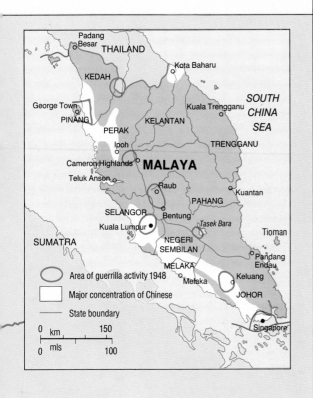

In 1939 the Viceroy of India, without consulting Indian opinion, declared war on Germany. The Indian National Congress Party campaigned against India's involvement in the war and against Britain's continued presence in India. In 1942 India was offered dominion status at the end of the war if the Congress Party would support the war effort. The Congress rejected this proposal and continued its anti-British campaign. Since Muslim opinion favoured the war, the British cultivated the Muslim League, led by Mohammed Ali Jinnah, which increased tensions between Muslims and Hindus in India.

In 1945 the British Labour government, committed to independence, sent a Cabinet delegation to India to try to resolve the differences between the Congress and the League. This effort failed and Jinnah embarked on 'Direct Action' to secure a separate Muslim state, which resulted in considerable communal violence during 1946 and 1947. In desperation the government sent Lord Louis Mountbatten to India as Viceroy, with a mandate to secure Indian independence in June 1948. Finding that the communal violence was intensifying, he advanced the independence date to 15 August 1947 and a mixed Hindu–Muslim boundary commission was set up to determine the borders between the two prospective states.

The commission's difficulties were increased by the fact that the new state of Pakistan would consist of two areas, East and West Pakistan, separated by 1,100 miles of Indian territory. Many Hindus would remain in Pakistan, while India would contain a substantial Muslim minority. Independence therefore resulted in an exodus of 13 million Sikhs and Hindus fleeing from Pakistan into India, and Muslim refugees moving in the other direction. Appalling atrocities ensued as Hindus and Muslims clashed along the borders. The rulers of the 562 princely states, were left to determine whether they wanted to join India or Pakistan. Although the majority of his people were Muslims the Hindu ruler of Kashmir opted for India and this led to clashes between India and Pakistan.

With the independence of India and Pakistan, the British Commonwealth and Empire became known more simply as the British Commonwealth and aimed to unite all of Britain's former colonies and promote economic and cultural ties.

Malayan independence followed from a long guerrilla war conducted by the Malayan Communist party, which consisted mainly of ethnic Chinese. Britain sent troops to crush the guerrillas in 1948 and its efforts were assisted by the lack of support from ethnic Malays for the uprising. In 1957 the communists were defeated and Britain granted independence to Malaya.

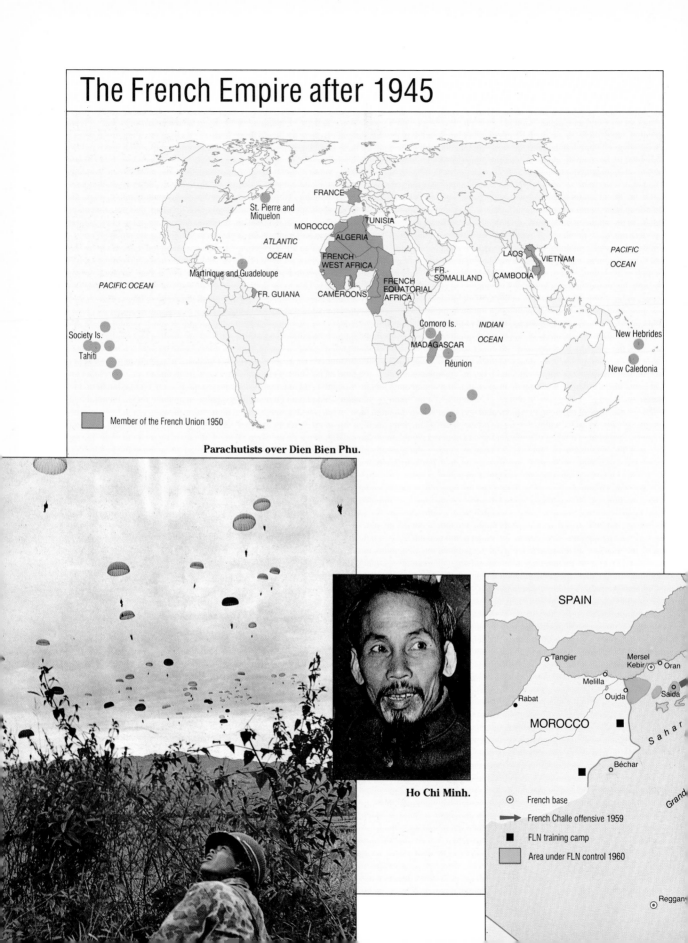

The French Empire after 1945

FRANCE

St. Pierre and Miquelon

MOROCCO   TUNISIA

ATLANTIC   ALGERIA
OCEAN

FRENCH
WEST AFRICA

Martinique and Guadeloupe

PACIFIC OCEAN

FR. GUIANA   CAMEROONS

FRENCH
EQUATORIAL
AFRICA

FR.
SOMALILAND

LAOS

CAMBODIA   VIETNAM

PACIFIC
OCEAN

Society Is.

Tahiti

Comoro Is.

MADAGASCAR

Réunion

INDIAN
OCEAN

New Hebrides

New Caledonia

Member of the French Union 1950

Parachutists over Dien Bien Phu.

Ho Chi Minh.

SPAIN

Tangier   Mersel
                 Kebir   Oran
          Melilla
Rabat   Oujda   Saida

MOROCCO   Sahar

          Béchar

                                     Grand

⊙ French base

➤ French Challe offensive 1959

■ FLN training camp

Area under FLN control 1960

⊙ Reggan

In September 1945, Ho Chi Minh, founder of the Vietnam nationalist movement, the Vietminh, set up a communist-dominated coalition government in Vietnam and declared the country independent. When French forces returned after the defeat of Japan, they discovered that Ho's government controlled most of northern Vietnam. After negotiations with the Vietminh broke down at the end of 1946, full-scale conflict broke out between the two sides, with the Vietminh initially employing guerrilla tactics, but later engaging in conventional warfare as their strength grew. The Vietminh secured military equipment and supplies from communist China after 1949 and in the following year the United States provided the French with aid.

In 1953 the French established a large garrison at Dien Bien Phu in northern Vietnam, hoping to lure the Vietminh into the open and then destroy them. The Vietminh, however, besieged the base and forced the French to surrender Dien Bien Phu in May 1954. By this time the French had wearied of the costly Indo-China imbroglio and at an international conference at Geneva in May–July 1954 agreed to grant complete independence to Laos and Cambodia, and to divide Vietnam along the 17th parallel, with the French policing the south and the Vietminh remaining in control of the north until all-Vietnamese elections could be held in 1956.

After the Second World War France was largely incapable of enforcing its rule throughout the colonies of the French Empire. Full independence was given to Morocco and Tunisia in 1956. Algeria, however, was regarded as an integral part of metropolitan France since it contained two million

French settlers. War broke out in Algeria in 1954 when Ben Bella's National Liberation Front (the FLN) began a guerrilla campaign against the French presence. This led to savage French reprisals, in which torture was used against captured communists. By May 1958 the French army in Algeria had gained the upper hand. However, on 1 June General de Gaulle was appointed Prime Minister with a mandate to prevent civil war in France. When, in 1960, he offered to negotiate with the FLN, the French army in Algeria mutinied, but this rebellion was soon crushed. While he had initially hoped that the Algerians would accept some form of autonomy, he soon realized that they would never accept this and after negotiations with the FLN at Evian in France in 1962 he agreed to Algeria's complete independence.

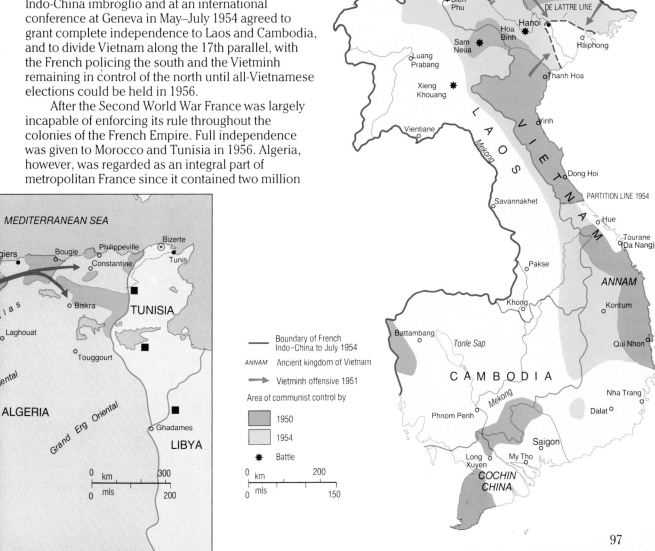

Britain and the Middle East 1945–1960

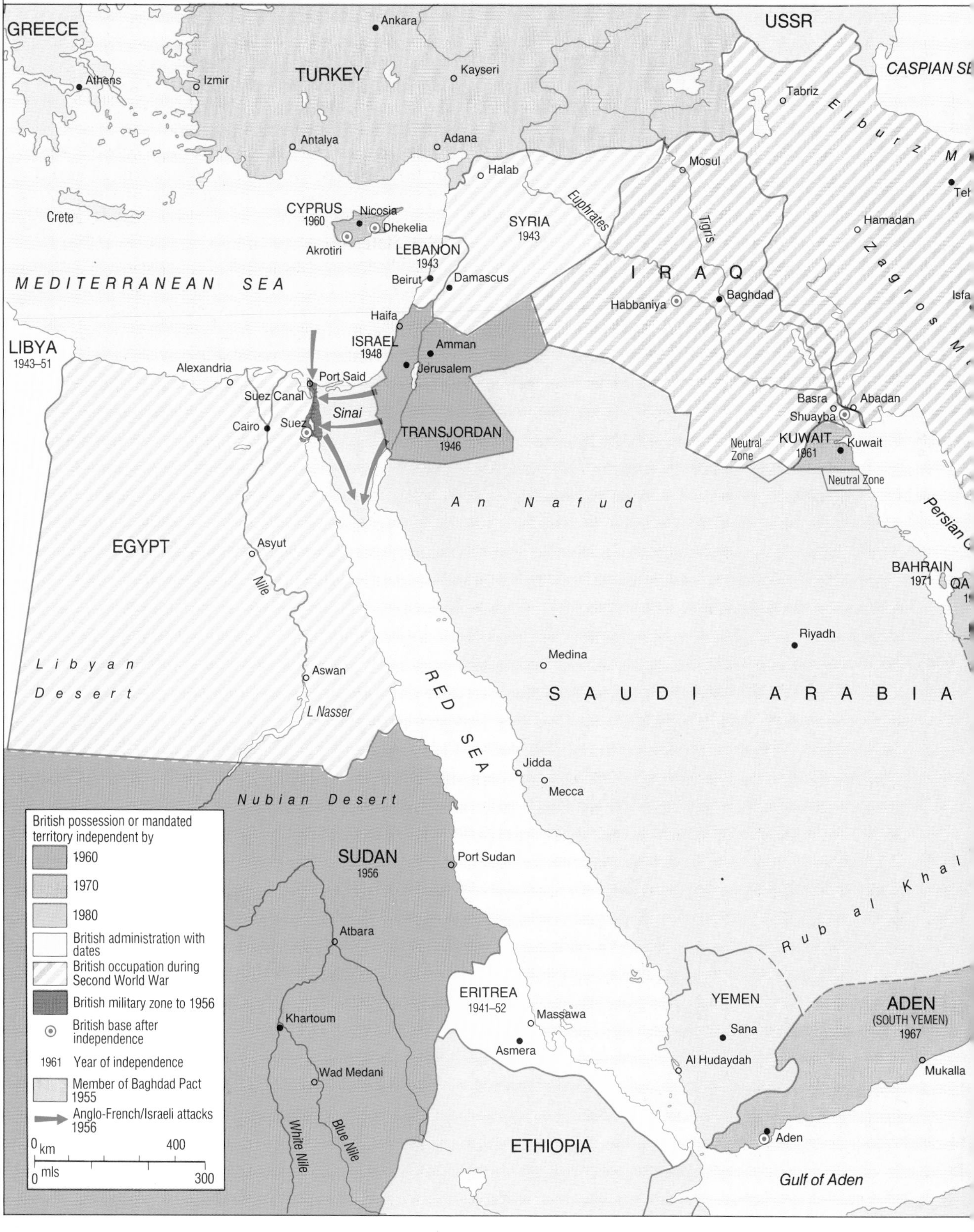

GREECE
USSR
CASPIAN SE
Ankara
TURKEY
Kayseri
Athens
Izmir
Tabriz
Elburz M
Antalya
Adana
Mosul
Hamadan
Halab
Zagros M
Crete
CYPRUS 1960
Nicosia
SYRIA 1943
Tet
Dhekelia
IRAQ
Akrotiri
LEBANON 1943
Habbaniya
Baghdad
Isfa
MEDITERRANEAN SEA
Beirut
Damascus
Haifa
Euphrates
Tigris
LIBYA 1943–51
ISRAEL 1948
Amman
Basra
Abadan
Alexandria
Port Said
Jerusalem
Shuayba
Suez Canal
Sinai
Neutral Zone
KUWAIT 1961
Kuwait
Cairo
Suez
TRANSJORDAN 1946
Neutral Zone
Persian C
An Nafud
EGYPT
Asyut
BAHRAIN 1971
QA
Nile
Riyadh
SAUDI ARABIA
Aswan
L Nasser
Libyan Desert
RED SEA
Medina
Jidda
Mecca
Nubian Desert
SUDAN 1956
Port Sudan
Rub al Khal
Atbara
ERITREA 1941–52
Massawa
YEMEN
ADEN (SOUTH YEMEN) 1967
Khartoum
Asmera
Sana
Mukalla
Wad Medani
Al Hudaydah
White Nile
Blue Nile
ETHIOPIA
Aden
Gulf of Aden

Legend

British possession or mandated territory independent by

- 1960
- 1970
- 1980

British administration with dates

British occupation during Second World War

British military zone to 1956

⊙ British base after independence

1961 Year of independence

Member of Baghdad Pact 1955

→ Anglo-French/Israeli attacks 1956

0 km 400
0 mls 300

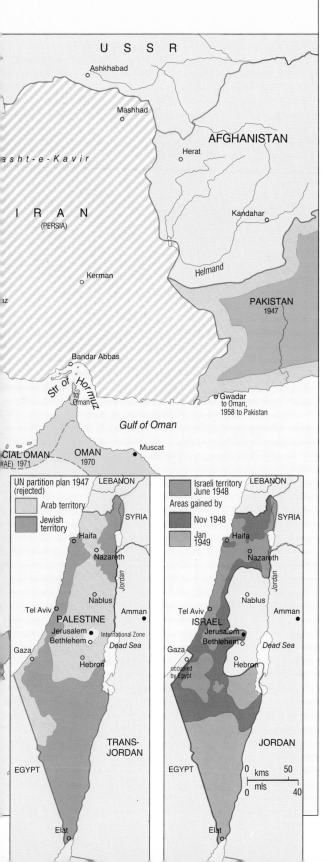

Map labels (left/main map)

U S S R

Ashkhabad

Mashhad

AFGHANISTAN

Herat

asht-e-Kavir

I R A N
(PERSIA)

Kandahar

Kerman

Helmand

PAKISTAN
1947

Bandar Abbas

Str of Hormuz
to Oman

Gwadar
to Oman,
1958 to Pakistan

Gulf of Oman

CIAL OMAN
(AE) 1971

OMAN
1970

Muscat

UN partition plan 1947 (rejected) map

UN partition plan 1947 (rejected)

Arab territory

Jewish territory

LEBANON

SYRIA

Haifa

Nazareth

Nablus

Tel Aviv

Jordan

PALESTINE

Amman

Jerusalem
Bethlehem

International Zone

Dead Sea

Gaza

Hebron

TRANS-JORDAN

EGYPT

Elat

Israel map

Israeli territory June 1948

Areas gained by

Nov 1948

Jan 1949

LEBANON

SYRIA

Haifa

Nazareth

Nablus

Tel Aviv

Jordan

ISRAEL

Amman

Jerusalem
Bethlehem

Dead Sea

Gaza
occupied
by Egypt

Hebron

JORDAN

EGYPT

0   kms   50

0   mls   40

Elat

In 1945 Britain was determined to re-establish itself as the dominant power in the Middle East. The British-garrisoned Suez Canal base was to be at the centre of this sphere of influence while Britain sought alliances with the Arab states to enable its forces to remain on their soil. The first challenge to Britain's ambitions took place in the Palestine mandate, where Zionist resentment against British restrictions on Jewish immigration led, after 1944, to increasing Jewish terrorist activities against both British forces and the Palestinian Arabs. In 1947 the United Nations proposed the partition of Palestine into an Arab and a Jewish state, but the Arabs rejected this plan. The United States supported the Jewish cause and in 1947–8 Britain, exasperated by the seemingly endless violence, withdrew its forces from the mandate. The Jews then proclaimed the new state of Israel, whereupon the neighbouring states sent troops to assist the Arabs. They were defeated by the Israelis.

Britain could not persuade Egypt to agree to the continued presence of British troops in the Suez Canal Zone, and in 1954 they agreed to evacuate the Zone, with the proviso that in the event of war they could return. Britain then moved its main base to Cyprus, but in 1955 was faced with a campaign of violence by the Greek Cypriots, who demanded *enosis* or union with Greece, rather than permanent British rule.

In Egypt a nationalist army colonel, Abdul Nasser, seized power in 1954 and began a propaganda campaign to appeal to all Arabs to unite against western imperialism and Israel. The British, alarmed by this threat to their Middle Eastern interests, joined forces with France and Israel to crush Nasser in 1956, after the Egyptian ruler nationalized the Anglo–French owned Suez Canal. An Anglo–French military expedition which landed in Egypt during the late autumn was forced to withdraw after the United States, angered by this display of Anglo–French imperialism, imposed financial sanctions on Britain. This was a major setback, but Britain did not entirely abandon the Middle East. When it gave independence to Cyprus in 1960 it retained bases on the island. Britain had also persuaded Turkey, Iraq, Iran and Pakistan to join it in the Baghdad Pact, a defensive alliance system against the Soviet Union. In 1958 Nasserite and nationalist agitation led to the downfall of the pro-British regime in Iraq, which was followed shortly by the withdrawal of that country from the Pact. In 1958 Britain and the United States sent troops to Jordan and Lebanon respectively to defend them from an alleged Nasserite coup. However, by this time, the United States was taking over Britain's role in the Middle East.

Decolonization in Africa

to Morocco 1956
Rabat
Algiers
Tunis

TUNISIA
1956
Tripoli

MOROCCO
1956

Sidi Ifni
to Morocco
1969

to Morocco 1958

Aaiun

ALGERIA
1962

LIBYA
1951
under British and French
administration 1943–51

E

**WESTERN
SAHARA**
disputed between
Morocco and
Polisario Front

CAPE VERDE IS.
1975

MAURITANIA
1960
Nouakchott

MALI
1960

NIGER
1960

CHAD
1960

SU
(ANGLO–EG

Dakar

SENEGAL
1960

Bathurst

GAMBIA
1965
Bissau

**GUINEA
BISSAU**
1974

Niger

GUINEA
1958

Conakry

**SIERRA
LEONE**
1961
Freetown

Bamako

**BURKINA
FASO**
1960
(UPPER VOLTA)
Ouagadougou

Niamey

L. Chad

to Nigeria 1961

Ndjamena
(Fort Lamy)

LIBERIA

Monrovia

**IVORY
COAST**
1960
Abidjan

Volta

GHANA
(GOLD COAST)
1957
Accra

TOGO
1960
Lomé

BENIN
(DAHOMEY)
1960

Porto
Novo
Lagos

N I G E R I A
1960

Niger

BIAFRA
independent
1967–70

to
Cameroon
1961

**CENTRAL
AFRICAN REPUBLIC**
1960

Bangui

Bioko (Fernando Póo)

**EQUATORIAL
GUINEA**
1968

CAMEROON
1960
Yaoundé

RIO MUNI

**SÃO TOME
E PRINCIPE**
1975

Annobón
(Pagalu)

Libreville

GABON
1960

CONGO
1960

Zaïre
(Congo)

Z A Ï R E
(CONGO)
1960

Brazzaville
Kinshasa
(Léopoldville)

CABINDA

Congo

Ascension I.

**SHABA
(KATANG**
independent 196

Luanda

St. Helena

A N G O L A
1975

ZAMBIA
(NORTHERN
RHODESIA)
1964

NAMIBIA
(SOUTH–WEST AFRICA)
1990
annexed by South Africa 1949

BOTSWANA
(BECHUANALAND)
1966

Walvis Bay
to South Africa

Windhoek

Gaborone

Colonial possession or protectorate prior to independence

	Belgian
	British
	French
	Italian
	Portuguese
	Spanish

1960 Year of independence

Independent state 1945

- - - Black homeland in South Africa

0 km 800

0 mls 600

**R E P U B L I C
O F
S O U T H   A F R**
British Dominion 1910–6

Orange

Cape Town

In the late 1950s and 1960s Britain, France and Belgium rapidly divested themselves of their African colonies. Britain began the process in 1957 when Ghana was given its independence, followed by Nigeria in 1960. France granted independence to Equatorial and West Africa between 1958 and 1960. The independence process in West Africa was relatively smooth because white settlers were few in number and the new ruling elites tended to be reformist and pro-Western. In East Africa, after the British crushed the Mau Mau uprising, Kenya achieved independence in December 1963 under Jomo Kenyatta, who sought to modernize Kenya and encouraged white settlers and businessmen to remain in the country. In Rhodesia, however, the situation was far more complicated. The British had established the Central African Federation in 1953, but it was unpopular with the black majority, which viewed it as a device for maintaining white supremacy. In 1963 Northern Rhodesia and Nyasaland seceded and were later granted their independence as Zambia and Malawi respectively. However, Southern Rhodesia had a substantial white settler minority which was determined not to allow black majority rule. Under Ian Smith it declared its independence of Britain in 1965 and despite economic sanctions it survived until 1979, when after prolonged guerrilla activity, the whites agreed to a constitution in which the black Africans were given overall control of the independent Zimbabwe, as Rhodesia was renamed.

Belgium suddenly abandoned the Congo in June 1960 but a few weeks after independence the Congolese army mutinied and Belgian troops returned to restore order. Thereafter, the situation became confused as Katanga, a mineral-rich province, threatened to secede and United Nations forces were sent in to replace the Belgians. Conflict between rival political leaders threatened to lead to civil war with the superpowers being drawn in on opposite sides, but the UN force managed to restore unity and was withdrawn in 1964.

Portugal retained its colonial possessions until 1974 when a change of regime in Lisbon resulted in the granting of independence to Guinea Bissau, Mozambique and Angola, although the process in Angola and Mozambique was complicated when civil war broke out. In Angola, South Africa supported the right-wing nationalists while Cuba sent troops to assist the left (see pages 116–17).

Namibia, the former German colony of South-West Africa which had been governed under mandate by South Africa since 1919, became the last colonial territory in Africa to achieve independence when its flag was finally raised in 1990.

THE POLITICS OF INDEPENDENCE

The struggle remained primarily between the United States and the Soviet Union.

During the Cold War both the United States and the Soviet Union tried to attract the newly independent and developing nations into their respective orbits. The first Third World country to be involved in conflict during the Cold War was Korea in 1950, with war breaking out between North and South Korea, communist China supporting the North and the United States backing the South. With the death of Stalin in 1953 and the eventual succession of Nikita Khrushchev to the Soviet leadership, the Soviet Union embarked on a vigorous campaign to win over the Third World, with well-publicized visits by Khrushchev to India and elsewhere, and promises of Soviet economic and military aid as an inducement to forge closer ties with the Soviet Union. In the Middle East, where Israel was known by its enemies to be a United States client, Khrushchev calculated that Nasser would respond to offers of Soviet military equipment and technical advisers by eagerly embracing the Soviet side in the Cold War. However, leaders like Nasser were nationalists as much as socialists and had no intention of becoming Soviet satellites. Thus, when Anwar Sadat succeeded Nasser as Egyptian leader, he expelled all Soviet military personnel in 1972 and turned to the United States for support. While many Middle Eastern countries accepted Soviet aid, they also persecuted communists within their borders. Egypt, India and

Yugoslavia are notable examples of the many countries which sought to avoid taking sides in the Cold War by espousing the cause of non-alignment as an alternative to close identification with either the United States or Soviet Union.

With the increasing breach between communist China and the Soviet Union in the late 1950s, Moscow found itself challenged in the Third World by a Beijing-supported brand of communism which emphasised the revolutionary potential of the peasantry against the Marxist-Leninist emphasis on the proletariat. While communist China was able to provide some assistance to Third World countries, and its emissaries had the advantage of not possessing a white skin, it could not in the last resort compete with the far greater wealth of the Soviet Union in this field. The struggle remained primarily between the United States and the Soviet Union.

The United States dwarfed both the Soviet Union and communist China in the scale of its military and economic influence world-wide after 1950. However, there was no clear victory for either side in the competition for the hearts and minds of the Third World. Most of the new states managed to preserve a precarious independence during the period, and the acceptance of aid from the East or the West did not necessarily entail complete conformity with the policies of either. While Castro was totally dependent on Soviet aid for Cuba, his country was too insignificant to be of much account in the global balance, and his cause did not prosper elsewhere in Latin America. Nor did the communist takeover of South Vietnam result in the spread of communism throughout the rest of South-East Asia, as so many Americans had feared. The influx of newly independent African countries to the United Nations after 1960 significantly altered voting patterns in the United Nations Assembly, but neither the United States nor the Soviet Union could rely on these nations supporting their respective policies. After the trauma of its defeat in Vietnam and the political turmoil of the Watergate affair the United States receded to some extent from the 'Imperial Presidency' during the 1970s as Congress showed itself disinclined to vote funds which might lead to further American involvement in Third World conflicts.

▼ **Castro and Khrushchev at the Lenin mausoleum in May 1964.**

The Growth of Terrorism

Since the 1960s terrorism has become a world-wide phenomenon. Some groups seek to publicize their cause, others to spread fear and confusion within a society so that it will collapse, allowing a new order to take its place. Assassinations, ambushes of security forces, explosions in public places, and guerrilla warfare are just a few of the tactics employed.

The most active terrorist groups in recent years have emerged from the conflict in the Middle East after 1948. Palestinian Arab extremists, deprived of their homeland by Israel's victories in wars with neighbouring Arab states, formed the Popular Front for the Liberation of Palestine (PLO) in 1964 to campaign for the establishment of an independent Arab state in Palestine. Its military wing, Al Fatah, launched commando raids into Israel and in July 1968 hijacked an El Al airliner and forced it to land at Algiers. Thereafter the seizure of airliners and the holding of their passengers as hostages became a regular terrorist activity, providing wide media coverage for various causes. International action to tighten up airport and aircraft security since 1980 has made this activity less prevalent, although in December 1988 terrorists placed a bomb on an American airliner which blew up over Scotland, killing its passengers and crew.

The revolution in Iran and the rise of Islamic fundamentalism during the 1980s gave rise to numerous terrorist groups, notably in the Lebanon, which are closely identified with the Tehran regime and are probably financed by it. The Islamic Jihad (Islamic Holy War) is one such fundamentalist organization and was responsible for the October 1983 bomb attack on the United States Marine barracks in Beirut. The Abu Nidal organization, a band of revolutionary socialist Muslims has been responsible for bomb attacks in the Lebanon, Italy and Greece, and for hijacking planes and ships. Western journalists, diplomats and businessmen in Beirut have been kidnapped and held hostage, including the special envoy of the Archbishop of Canterbury, Terry Waite, in 1987, who was in Beirut negotiating for the release of hostages.

In Europe revolutionary groups ranging from the left-wing Red Army faction or Baader-Meinhof gang in West Germany to the neo-fascist Avanguardia Nationale in Italy have been responsible for bombing and other attacks; a host of revolutionary activists and separatists across Asia and Latin America have often provoked savage reprisals by the authorities.

▶ In 1979 the Soviet Union sent troops to Afghanistan to defend a pro-Soviet, Marxist regime in Kabul. The Red Army found itself involved in a long guerrilla war with the Afghan Mujaheddin. In 1989, the Soviet Union finally announced the withdrawal of its troops.

American Influence Abroad 1945–60

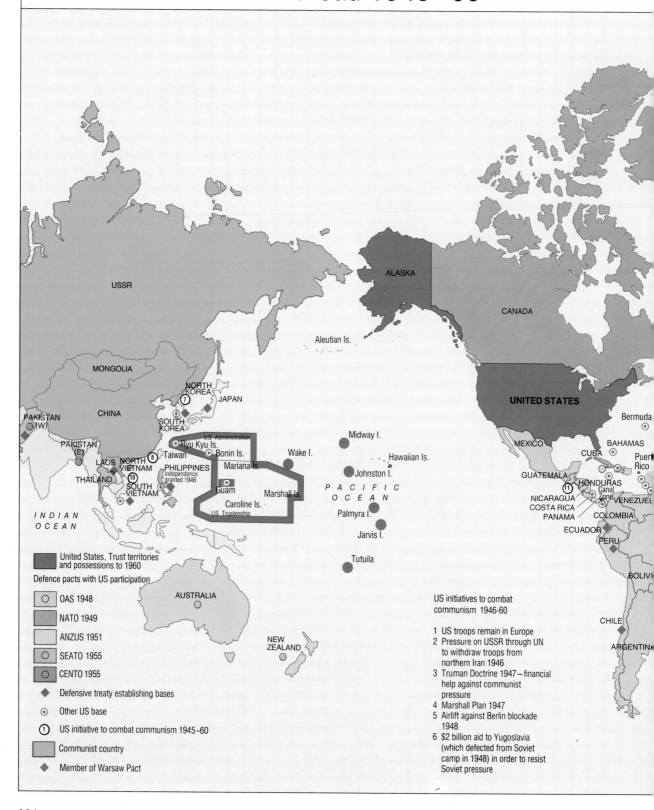

USSR

ALASKA

CANADA

Aleutian Is.

MONGOLIA

NORTH KOREA ⑦

JAPAN

CHINA

SOUTH KOREA

UNITED STATES

Bermuda

PAKISTAN (W)

PAKISTAN (E)

Ryu Kyu Is. US Administration

Taiwan ⑧ Bonin Is.

Wake I.

Midway I.

MEXICO

CUBA

BAHAMAS

Puerto Rico

LAOS NORTH VIETNAM ⑩

THAILAND

PHILIPPINES independence granted 1946

Mariana Is.

Hawaiian Is.

GUATEMALA

Canal Zone

HONDURAS ⑪

VENEZUELA

SOUTH VIETNAM

Guam

Johnston I.

PACIFIC OCEAN

NICARAGUA COSTA RICA PANAMA

COLOMBIA

Marshall Is.

INDIAN OCEAN

Caroline Is. US Trusteeship

Palmyra I.

ECUADOR

PERU

Jarvis I.

BOLIVIA

Tutuila

United States, Trust territories and possessions to 1960

Defence pacts with US participation

AUSTRALIA

CHILE

NEW ZEALAND

ARGENTINA

○	OAS 1948
	NATO 1949
	ANZUS 1951
○	SEATO 1955
○	CENTO 1955

US initiatives to combat communism 1946-60

◆ Defensive treaty establishing bases

⊙ Other US base

① US initiative to combat communism 1945–60

Communist country

◆ Member of Warsaw Pact

1 US troops remain in Europe
2 Pressure on USSR through UN to withdraw troops from northern Iran 1946
3 Truman Doctrine 1947 – financial help against communist pressure
4 Marshall Plan 1947
5 Airlift against Berlin blockade 1948
6 $2 billion aid to Yugoslavia (which defected from Soviet camp in 1948) in order to resist Soviet pressure

GREENLAND

ICELAND

oundland

LANTIC
CEAN

Azores

Madeira

dies

JYANA
NAME
R. GUIANA

LIBERIA

Fernando de
Naronha

EUROPE
① ④
NORWAY

UNITED
KINGDOM
DENMARK

NETH.
E. GER.
⑤ POLAND

BELG.
LUX.
W. GER. CZECH.
USSR

FRANCE
HUNG.
ROM.

ITALY
YUG.
⑥
BULG.
③

ALB.
TURKEY
NATO 1952

PORTUGAL SPAIN
GREECE

LEBANON ⑫
②
IRAN
⑨

LIBYA
EGYPT
Pressure on UK
France & Israel
to withdraw from
Suez 1956
SAUDI ARABIA

ETHIOPIA

GUAY

GUAY

7 US troops fight for UN in Korea
   to defend it from invasion 1950
8 Taiwan protected against
   communist Chinese threat 1950s
9 Mossadeq, left-wing Prime
   Minister of Iran deposed by CIA
   plot 1953
10 Takeover of France's
   responsibilities in Indo-China
   after 1954
11 Right-wing Guatemalans
   assisted to overthrow Marxist
   regime 1954
12 Eisenhower Doctrine
   1957 – military assistance
   against communist pressure;
   granted to Lebanon 1958

T he United States emerged from the Second World War as the richest and most powerful country in the world. Its troops were stationed across Western Europe, it dominated Japan, and it had acquired a string of bases in the Caribbean and in the Atlantic and the Pacific Oceans. Although they intended to play an active part in the United Nations, America's leaders did not plan to keep American troops in Europe for more than two years after the end of the war, which caused Britain and the other Western European powers to fear that America might return to its pre-war isolationism. Nor would it cooperate with Britain against the Soviet Union. However, when Britain planned the withdrawal of its military aid to the Greek government in March 1947, the United States, alarmed by the prospect of a communist victory in a strategically crucial country, agreed to take over Britain's financial responsibilities in both Greece and Turkey. In order to persuade a reluctant Congress to vote the money, President Truman played on its increasing fears of world communism and, on 12 March, enunciated the doctrine that the United States would "support free peoples who are resisting subjugation by armed minorities or outside pressures". This suggested that the United States had embarked on a crusade to combat communism all over the world.

In 1948, alarmed by the possibility that Europe, whose economies had not recovered from the effects of the war, might succumb to communism, the United States offered, under the Marshall Plan, financial aid to Europe, although the offer was couched in such terms as to discourage the participation of the Soviet Union and its satellites. During the Berlin blockade it showed its resistance to the Soviet Union and then, in 1949, the United States signed the North Atlantic Treaty with the Western European states, Greece, Turkey, Canada and Iceland, a radical departure from the traditional American refusal to become involved in entanglements outside its own hemisphere. The United States was now firmly committed to the containment of communism, as was demonstrated by its intervention in the Korean War in 1950.

The United States continued to support decolonization, in the expectation that this would lead to the emergence of moderate pro-American governments in the former colonies willing to encourage trade and American investment. Nevertheless anti-communism led the United States to conspire with Britain to overthrow the nationalist government of Iran in 1953 which had nationalized the British-controlled Anglo–Iranian Oil Company in 1950. Thereafter American rather than British influence prevailed in Iran.

The Korean War

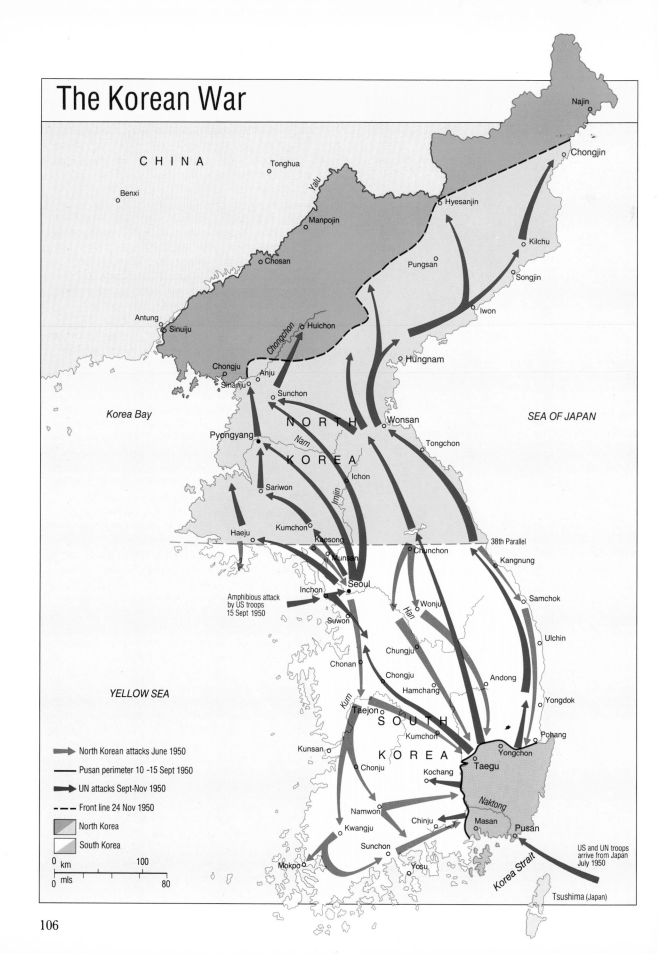

CHINA

Najin

Tonghua

Chongjin

Benxi

Manpojin

Yalu

Hyesanjin

Chosan

Pungsan

Kilchu

Songjin

Antung

Iwon

Sinuiju

Chongju

Huichon

Chongchon

Anju

Hungnam

Sinanju

Sunchon

Korea Bay

N O R T H

Wonsan

SEA OF JAPAN

Pyongyang

Nam

Tongchon

K O R E A

Sariwon

Ichon

Imjin

Kumchon

Haeju

Kaesong

Chunchon

38th Parallel

Munsan

Kangnung

Seoul

Inchon

Wonju

Samchok

Amphibious attack
by US troops
15 Sept 1950

Han

Suwon

Ulchin

Chungju

Chonan

Chongju

Andong

Hamchang

YELLOW SEA

Kum

Taejon

Yongdok

Kumchon

S O U T H

Kunsan

Pohang

Chonju

K O R E A

Yongchon

Kochang

Taegu

Naktong

Namwon

Chinju

Masan

Pusan

Kwangju

➤ North Korean attacks June 1950

Sunchon

── Pusan perimeter 10 –15 Sept 1950

Mokpo

Yosu

➤ UN attacks Sept-Nov 1950

Korea Strait

US and UN troops
arrive from Japan
July 1950

- - - Front line 24 Nov 1950

North Korea

South Korea

0   km   100

0   mls   80

Tsushima (Japan)

An M-41 tank manned by US army personnel in Korea.

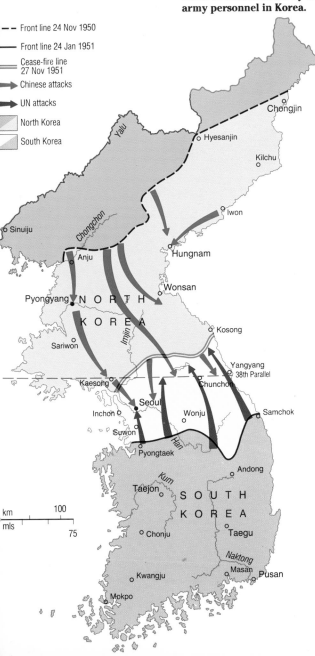

Front line 24 Nov 1950
Front line 24 Jan 1951
Cease-fire line
27 Nov 1951
Chinese attacks
UN attacks
North Korea
South Korea

When Japanese forces in Korea surrendered in 1945, the Russian Red Army occupied North Korea down to the 38th Parallel and the United States Army moved into South Korea. However, subsequent attempts to unify the country foundered on increasing Cold War suspicions, and in 1948 a United Nations Commission supervised elections in the South but was not allowed into the North. After the elections Syngman Rhee, a conservative nationalist, became head of the South Korean government, while in the North the Soviets set up a People's Republic under the Korean communist leader, Kim Il-Sung. Both the Soviet Union and the United States thereupon withdrew their troops. On 25 June 1950 North Korea, having obtained Stalin's agreement, and convinced that the United States would not intervene, invaded South Korea and drove the South Korean army back to Pusan in the far south. President Truman committed American naval and air support and later troops to South Korea, and the United Nations called on its members to send troops to South Korea. Truman believed that with the recent loss of China to communism, he could not allow South Korea to fall, especially given its close proximity to Japan. General Douglas MacArthur – Commander of the US occupation forces in Japan – was appointed Supreme Commander of the United Nations forces and, after a daring amphibious landing at Inchon, near South Korea's capital, Seoul, in September, the UN completely overwhelmed the North Koreans, forcing them to retreat across the 38th Parallel. Truman thereupon ordered MacArthur to unify Korea and United Nations forces advanced into the North and towards the Chinese border on the Yalu river. MacArthur ignored Chinese warnings that they would intervene to prevent the establishment of American positions on the Yalu. In October, under the guise of 'volunteers', the (Chinese) Peoples' Liberation Army crossed the Yalu in force and by December had driven the United Nations forces back to the South. In 1951, after heavy fighting, the United Nations forces fought their way back to the 38th Parallel, where the front stabilized for the rest of the war. MacArthur was relieved of all his commands in April after calling on Truman to extend the war into Manchuria. Truman feared that this would lead to Soviet intervention. Armistice talks began in 1951 and dragged on until 1953, when a truce was arranged.

The death toll was considerable. The UN lost 94,000 troops, while about a million civilians were killed by ground forces and by American air attacks on North Korean cities. The Chinese communists and North Koreans lost 1.5 million, a result of the Chinese employment of 'human wave' tactics to make up for their inferiority in arms and equipment.

The Arab-Israeli Conflict

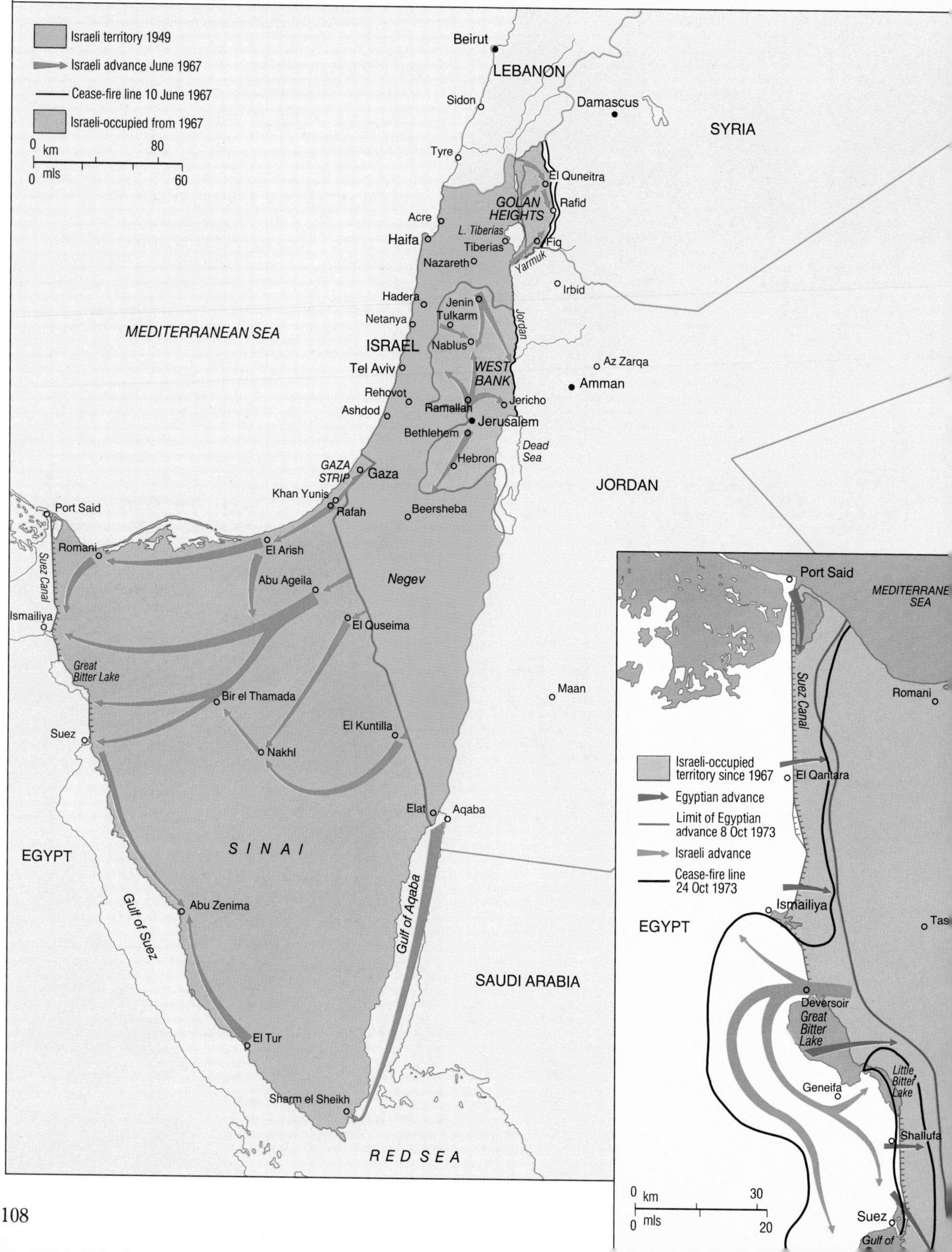

Israeli territory 1949

Israeli advance June 1967

Cease-fire line 10 June 1967

Israeli-occupied from 1967

0 km 80

0 mls 60

Beirut

LEBANON

Sidon

Damascus

SYRIA

Tyre

El Quneitra

Rafid

GOLAN HEIGHTS

Acre

L. Tiberias

Fiq

Haifa

Tiberias

Nazareth

Yarmuk

Hadera

Jenin

Irbid

Netanya

Tulkarm

Jordan

MEDITERRANEAN SEA

ISRAEL

Nablus

Tel Aviv

WEST BANK

Az Zarqa

Amman

Rehovot

Jericho

Ashdod

Ramallah

Jerusalem

Bethlehem

Dead Sea

Hebron

GAZA STRIP

Gaza

JORDAN

Khan Yunis

Port Said

Rafah

Beersheba

Romani

El Arish

Suez Canal

Abu Ageila

Negev

Ismailiya

El Quseima

Maan

Great Bitter Lake

Bir el Thamada

El Kuntilla

Suez

Nakhl

Elat

Aqaba

EGYPT

S I N A I

Gulf of Aqaba

Abu Zenima

Gulf of Suez

SAUDI ARABIA

El Tur

Sharm el Sheikh

R E D S E A

Israeli-occupied territory since 1967

Egyptian advance

Limit of Egyptian advance 8 Oct 1973

Israeli advance

Cease-fire line 24 Oct 1973

Port Said

MEDITERRANEAN SEA

Suez Canal

Romani

El Qantara

Ismailiya

EGYPT

Tas

Deversoir

Great Bitter Lake

Geneifa

Little Bitter Lake

Shallufa

0 km 30

0 mls 20

Suez

Gulf of

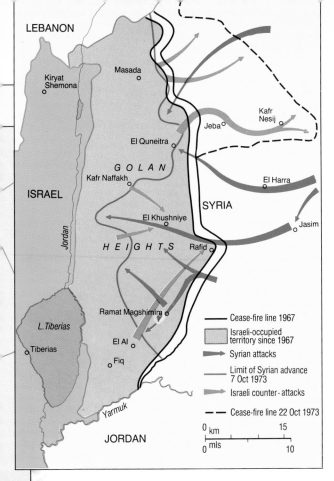

Map legend:
- Cease-fire line 1967
- Israeli-occupied territory since 1967
- Syrian attacks
- Limit of Syrian advance 7 Oct 1973
- Israeli counter-attacks
- Cease-fire line 22 Oct 1973

0 km 15
0 mls 10

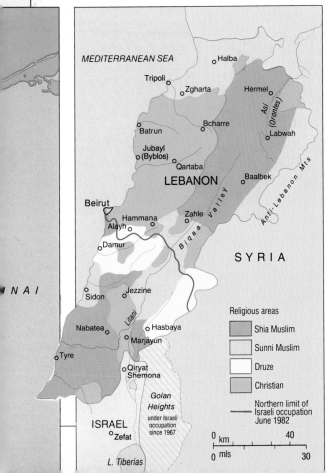

Religious areas
- Shia Muslim
- Sunni Muslim
- Druze
- Christian
- Northern limit of Israeli occupation June 1982

0 km 40
0 mls 30

In1956 Israel, colluding with Britain and France, invaded Egypt with the object of destroying Egyptian-backed Arab guerrilla bands in the Sinai Desert. Although Israel achieved its objectives, the humiliating evacuation of the Anglo–French expedition from Egypt enhanced Nasser's prestige in the Arab world and he set about trying to organize a new anti-Israeli coalition of Arab states.

The immediate occasion for renewed conflict was an Israeli attack on Jordan in early 1967 in retaliation for Jordanian-based Palestinian Arab terrorist raids into Israel. Egypt, Jordan, Syria and Iraq prepared a major offensive against Israel, which was heralded in May 1967 by Nasser's expulsion from Egyptian territory of the United Nations Emergency Force, which had been stationed in the Sinai since the Suez war. However, Israel struck first, in what became known as the 'Six Day War'. Israeli forces destroyed the Egyptian Air Force on the ground, defeated the advancing Egyptian and Jordanian forces and occupied Jerusalem, the West Bank of the River Jordan and the Sinai. They also defeated Syria and seized the Golan Heights. A Security Council resolution in November 1967 called on both sides to end the fighting. A cease-fire was arranged in 1970, but Anwar Sadat, the new Egyptian leader, organized another coalition of the front line Arab states in October 1973, launched a surprise attack on the Israeli army in the Sinai and achieved initial successes in what became known as the Yom Kippur War. The Israelis rallied, pushed back the Egyptian forces and surrounded a complete Egyptian army corps near the Canal. They also defeated a Syrian attack on the Golan Heights. The United States Secretary of State, Henry Kissinger, fearing a Soviet–American confrontation in support of their respective Middle East clients, persuaded the Soviet Union to join the United States in imposing a cease-fire and in freeing the Egyptian army corps. In September 1978 President Carter persuaded Sadat and Prime Minister Menachem Begin of Israel to sign a peace treaty whereby the Sinai was to be returned to Egypt in two stages between 1980 and 1982 and Egypt was to recognize Israel. As a result Egypt was alienated from other Arab states, which accused it of betrayal.

Lebanon became involved in the Arab–Israeli conflict in 1970 as Arab extremists launched repeated terrorist attacks into Israel from south Lebanon. In 1982, determined to destroy the Palestinian bases, Israeli troops invaded south Lebanon and reached the outskirts of Beirut. The Israelis were persuaded to withdraw in 1983, but thereafter Lebanon relapsed into anarchy as militia from factions within the various communities fought each other on the streets of Beirut.

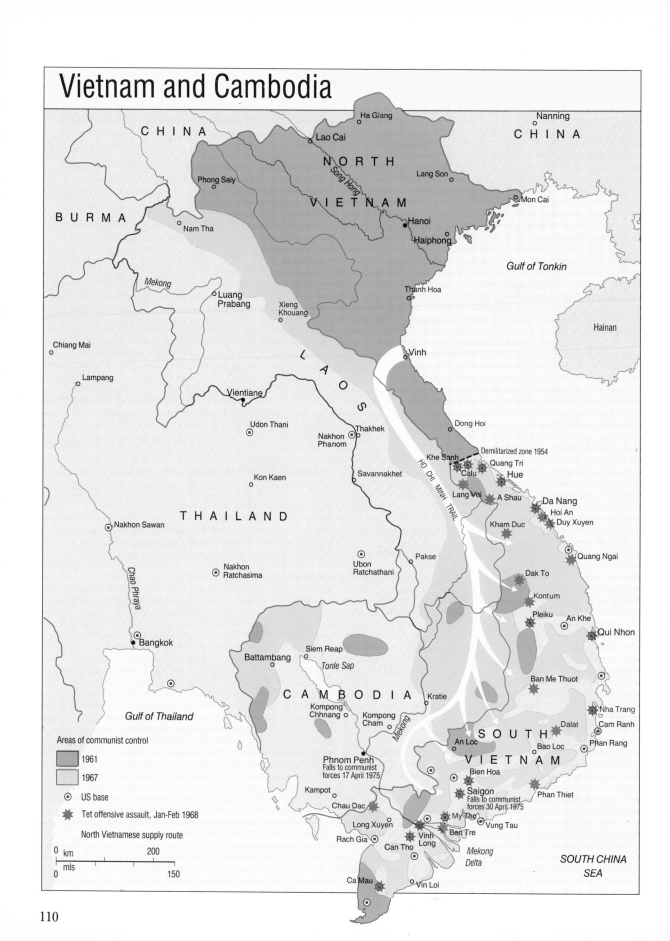

Vietnam and Cambodia

CHINA

Ha Giang

Nanning

CHINA

Lao Cai

NORTH

Lang Son

Phong Saiy

VIETNAM

Mon Cai

BURMA

Nam Tha

Hanoi

Haiphong

Song Hong

Mekong

Gulf of Tonkin

Luang
Prabang

Xieng
Khouang

Thanh Hoa

Chiang Mai

Hainan

Lampang

Vinh

L A O S

Vientiane

Udon Thani

Thakhek

Dong Hoi

Nakhon
Phanom

Demilitarized zone 1954

Savannakhet

Khe Sanh

Quang Tri

Calu

Hue

Kon Kaen

Lang Vei

A Shau

Da Nang

HO CHI MINH TRAIL

Hoi An

THAILAND

Kham Duc

Duy Xuyen

Nakhon Sawan

Quang Ngai

Nakhon
Ratchasima

Ubon
Ratchathani

Pakse

Dak To

Kontum

Chao Phraya

Pleiku

An Khe

Bangkok

Qui Nhon

Siem Reap

Battambang

Ban Me Thuot

Tonle Sap

C A M B O D I A

Kratie

Nha Trang

Cam Ranh

Gulf of Thailand

Kompong
Chhnang

Kompong
Cham

Dalat

Mekong

An Loc

S O U T H

Bao Loc

Phan Rang

Areas of communist control

Phnom Penh
Falls to communist
forces 17 April 1975

VIETNAM

Bien Hoa

1961

1967

Kampot

Saigon
Falls to communist
forces 30 April 1975

Phan Thiet

US base

Chau Dac

My Tho

Vung Tau

Tet offensive assault, Jan-Feb 1968

Long Xuyen

Ben Tre

North Vietnamese supply route

Rach Gia

Vinh
Long

Can Tho

*Mekong
Delta*

0   km   200

SOUTH CHINA
SEA

0   mls   150

Ca Mau

Vin Loi

After the 1954 Geneva Conference the United States backed Ngo Dinh Diem as prime minister of South Vietnam and the French withdrew their forces. Diem's regime, however, became increasingly repressive and corrupt. In November 1963 the United States supported a military coup, which resulted in the murder of Diem, but led to increasing political instability in Saigon. By this time the Vietcong (communist guerrillas) had begun a sustained terrorist campaign in the South, and inflicted several defeats on the demoralized South Vietnamese army. The Americans believed that if South Vietnam fell to communism the rest of South-East Asia would soon follow. President Kennedy refused to send combat troops to South Vietnam but increased the number of military advisers from 600 in 1961 to 15,000 by 1963. His successor, Lyndon Johnson, gained almost unlimited powers from Congress in 1964 to deal with the situation, and following a Vietcong attack on an American base at Pleiku on 7 February 1965, the US Air Force began a bombing campaign on the North while US combat troops were despatched to the South, increasing in number from 23,000 in 1965 to 550,000 in 1969.

The Vietnam War soon became a grinding campaign of attrition. By 1968 American public opinion was turning against the war, largely because of the rising American death toll and the initial success of the Tet Offensive, a major campaign launched from the North in early 1968 which succeeded in capturing numerous provincial towns in the South. American confidence in any prospect of victory ebbed away, opposition grew in the United States to military conscription – the Draft – and demonstrations against the war spread across American college campuses. Americans were also shaken by revelations of atrocities committed by US soldiers, such as the My Lai massacre of Vietnamese civilians which took place in 1968.

After 1969, President Richard Nixon began to wind down American involvement and forced North Vietnam to the negotiating table by stepping up the bombing campaign. In 1973 a truce was agreed: the United States was to withdraw its remaining forces while elections were to be held to unify the country. However, fighting continued until 1975 when the South was conquered by the North Vietnamese and the country was reunited.

The final agony of the Vietnam War was fought out in neighbouring Cambodia. Although supposedly neutral, Cambodia had been sucked into the war and by April 1975 was in the hands of the communist Khmer Rouge, led by Pol Pot. The Khmer Rouge evacuated the population of the cities into the countryside by force and by 1978 had killed or starved to death perhaps three million people (nearly half the population). In December 1978 frontier disputes with Kampuchea (as the country had been renamed) led Vietnam to invade Kampuchea and drive the Khmer Rouge into the jungle, replacing them with a more sympathetic government. China, which had supported the Khmer Rouge and whose relations with Vietnam had deteriorated since 1975, in turn invaded Vietnam in 1979 but its forces were driven back across the border. Faced with a failing economy at home, Vietnam withdrew its forces from Kampuchea in 1989, leaving the country precariously balanced between rival factions.

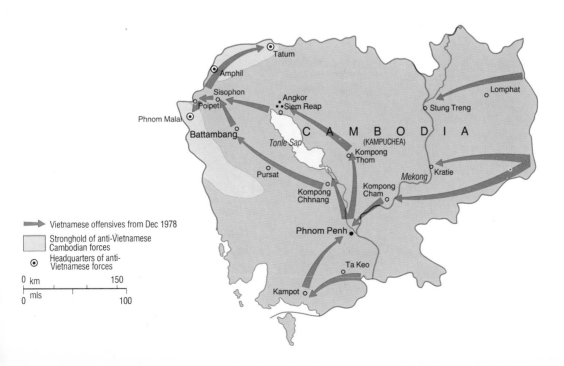

The Caribbean and South America

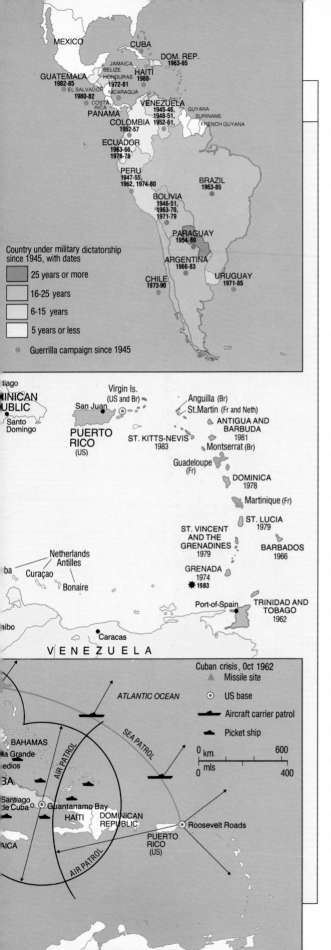

Country under military dictatorship since 1945, with dates

- 25 years or more
- 16-25 years
- 6-15 years
- 5 years or less
- ● Guerrilla campaign since 1945

MEXICO
CUBA
DOM. REP.
1963-65
JAMAICA
BELIZE
GUATEMALA
1982-85
HAITI
1988-
HONDURAS
EL SALVADOR
1972-81
1980-82
NICARAGUA
COSTA
RICA
PANAMA
VENEZUELA
1945-46,
1948-51,
1952-61,
GUYANA
SURINAME
FRENCH GUYANA
COLOMBIA
1952-57
ECUADOR
1963-66,
1976-78
PERU
1947-55,
1962, 1974-80
BRAZIL
1963-85
BOLIVIA
1946-51,
1963-70,
1971-79
PARAGUAY
1954-89
ARGENTINA
1966-83
CHILE
1973-90
URUGUAY
1971-85

tiago
INICAN
UBLIC
Santo
Domingo
San Juan
Virgin Is.
(US and Br)
Anguilla (Br)
St.Martin (Fr and Neth)
ANTIGUA AND
BARBUDA
1981
Montserrat (Br)
PUERTO
RICO
(US)
ST. KITTS-NEVIS
1983
Guadeloupe
(Fr)
DOMINICA
1978
Martinique (Fr)
ST. LUCIA
1979
ST. VINCENT
AND THE
GRENADINES
1979
BARBADOS
1966
GRENADA
1974
✶ 1983
Netherlands
Antilles
ba
Curaçao
Bonaire
Port-of-Spain
TRINIDAD AND
TOBAGO
1962
aibo
Caracas
V E N E Z U E L A

Cuban crisis, Oct 1962
- ▲ Missile site
- ⊙ US base
- ▬ Aircraft carrier patrol
- ▬ Picket ship

0 km 600
0 mls 400

ATLANTIC OCEAN
SEA PATROL
BAHAMAS
la Grande
edios
BA
AIR PATROL
Santiago
de Cuba
Guantanamo Bay
HAITI
DOMINICAN
REPUBLIC
Roosevelt Roads
PUERTO
RICO
(US)
AICA
AIR PATROL

Throughout Latin America the armed forces, traditionally conservative, have frequently intervened in politics, especially where reformers, who have sought to reduce the grip of the United States on their countries' economies and governments, threatened the status quo. In Guatemala, for example, when President Arbenz began to expropriate large holdings and moved against the United Fruit Company's monopoly, the United States in 1954 accused him of being a communist and financed an invasion by right-wing extremists, who deposed Arbenz. Thereafter, the country was ruled by military dictators.

In 1959, after a prolonged guerrilla campaign, the Cuban nationalist Fidel Castro overthrew the corrupt Batista regime. Castro's nationalization of American assets led to an American embargo on trade with Cuba, and Castro turned to the Soviet Union for aid. Soviet influence increased after the failure of an American-backed Cuban refugee invasion of Cuba at the Bay of Pigs in 1961, and in 1962 the Soviets began to build medium range inter-continental ballistic missile sites in Cuba. This escalation of the conflict led to a confrontation with the United States, but Khrushchev backed down and agreed to dismantle the missile sites.

Under President Nixon the United States had thrown its weight behind the right-wing anti-communist regimes in Latin America. After a Marxist, Salvador Allende, was elected President of Chile in 1970 and began to nationalize American companies, the United States supported a military revolt, which overthrew him in 1973 and set up a repressive military dictatorship under Augusto Pinochet. However, in the late 1970s, President Carter adopted a policy of supporting reform movements in Latin America and withdrew support from the corrupt Nicaraguan dictator, Anastasio Somoza, whose family had ruled the country for 40 years. He was overthrown by the left-wing National Liberation Front, which was dominated by the radical Sandinista guerrillas. During the 1980s President Reagan reversed Carter's Latin American policy, denounced the Sandinistas as communists, and armed anti-Sandinista guerrillas, the Contras, operating from Honduras and Costa Rica. Their efforts were not successful and Nicaragua remained under the Sandinista's control until they were defeated by a pro-American coalition in a general election held in 1990.

Elsewhere in the Caribbean, the Americans invaded Grenada and overthrew the government, suspecting it to be aligned with Cuba. Six years later, American forces invaded Panama, overthrowing a military dictator, Manuel Noriega, whom they suspected of drug trafficking.

War in the Gulf

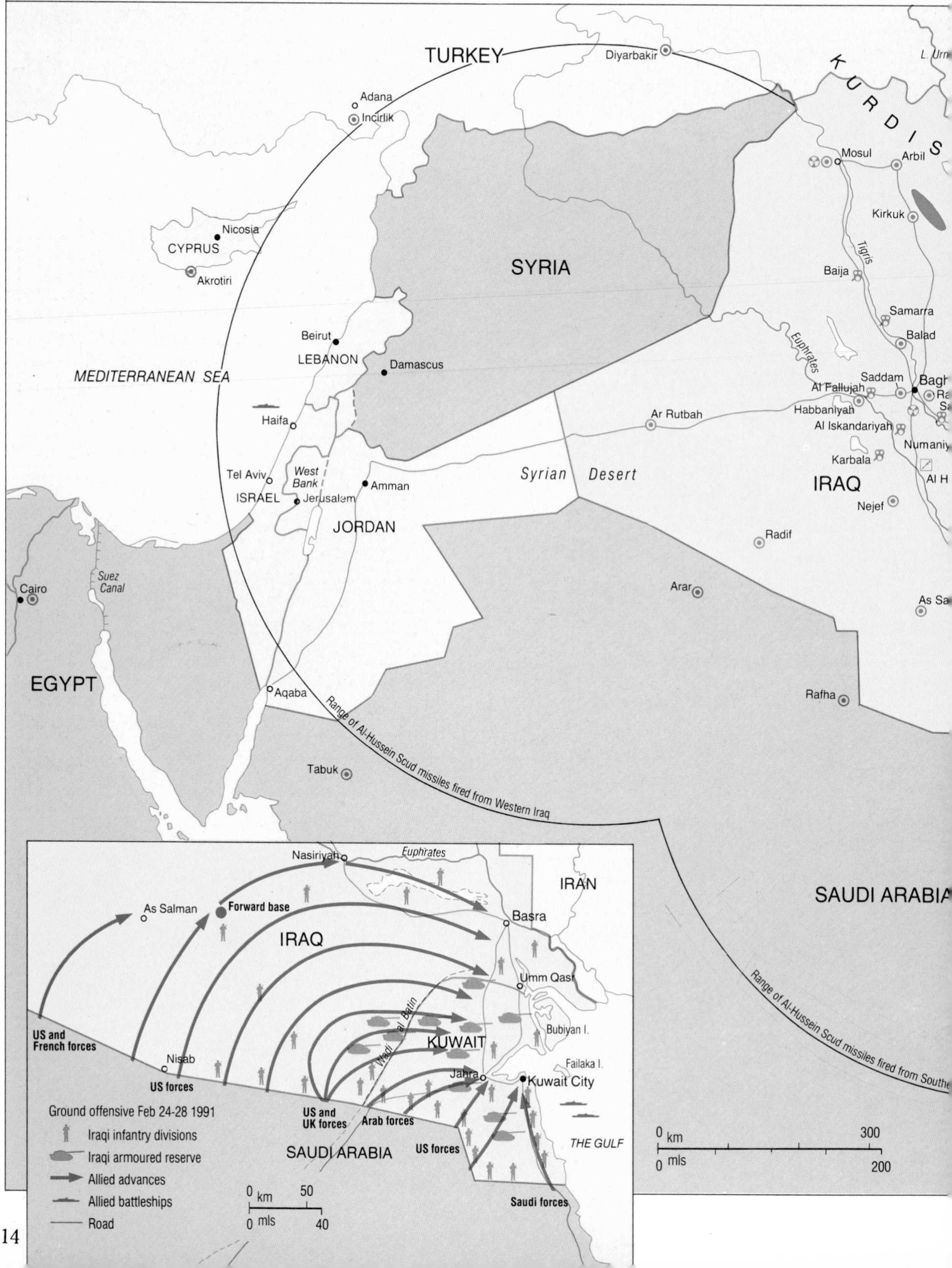

TURKEY

Diyarbakir

K U R D I S

L. Urn

Adana
Incirlik

Mosul Arbil

CYPRUS
Nicosia

Kirkuk

Akrotiri

SYRIA

Baija

MEDITERRANEAN SEA

Beirut
LEBANON Damascus

Samarra
Balad

Euphrates

Saddam

Baġh

Haifa

Al Fallujah

Ra

Si

Habbaniyah
Al Iskandariyah

Ar Rutbah

Tel Aviv
West
Bank
ISRAEL Jerusalem

Amman

Syrian Desert

Karbala

Numaniy
Al H

IRAQ

Nejef

JORDAN

Radif

Cairo

Suez
Canal

Radif

Arar

EGYPT

As Sa

Aqaba

Range of Al-Hussein Scud missiles fired from Western Iraq

Rafha

Tabuk

Nasiriyah *Euphrates*

IRAN

As Salman **Forward base**

Basra

IRAQ

Umm Qasr

Bubiyan I.

**US and
French forces**

KUWAIT

Nisab

Failaka I.

US forces

Jahra

Kuwait City

Ground offensive Feb 24-28 1991

Iraqi infantry divisions

Iraqi armoured reserve

Allied advances

Allied battleships

Road

**US and
UK forces** **Arab forces**

SAUDI ARABIA

US forces

THE GULF

Saudi forces

0 km   50
0 mls   40

SAUDI ARABIA

Range of Al-Hussein Scud missiles fired from Southe

0 km   300
0 mls   200

114

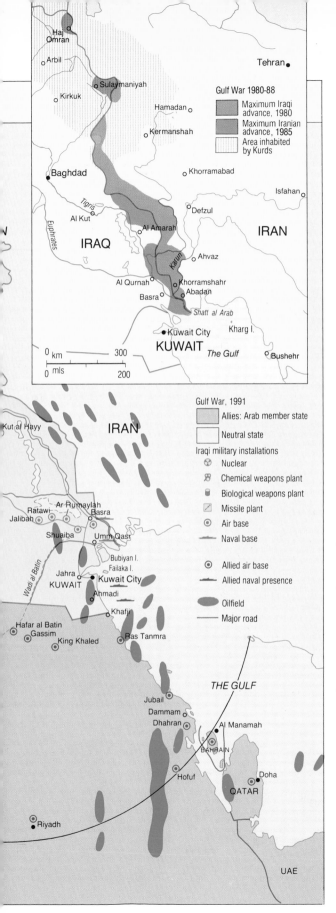

Gulf War 1980-88
- Maximum Iraqi advance, 1980
- Maximum Iranian advance, 1985
- Area inhabited by Kurds

Gulf War, 1991
- Allies: Arab member state
- Neutral state

Iraqi military installations
- ⊗ Nuclear
- 🏭 Chemical weapons plant
- 🗑 Biological weapons plant
- ▨ Missile plant
- ⊙ Air base
- ⎯ Naval base

- ⊙ Allied air base
- ⎯ Allied naval presence

- ⬮ Oilfield
- ⎯ Major road

In December 1980 the Iraqi dictator, Saddam Hussein, ordered his army to attack Iran in pursuit of long-standing Iraqi territorial claims in the Shatt al Arab region. The Iranians launched vigorous counter-offensives and war dragged on for eight years before the United Nations could arrange a cease-fire in July 1987.

On 2 August 1990 Iraq invaded Kuwait in order to secure Kuwait's valuable oilfields and thus sustain Iraq's war-torn economy. On the same day, the Security Council passed a unanimous resolution, demanding the immediate and unconditional withdrawal of Iraq's forces. On 6 August the United Nations imposed a blockade on Iraq. In Operation 'Desert Shield' the United States, Britain, France, Egypt, Syria, Morocco and twenty-two other countries sent land, sea and air forces to Saudi Arabia and the Gulf to defend Saudi Arabia against an anticipated Iraqi invasion. The blockade and frequent diplomatic efforts failed to persuade Saddam to evacuate Kuwait. On 15 January 1991, in accordance with a United Nations resolution authorizing the use of force to drive Iraq from Kuwait, the multinational coalition's air forces began a sustained air campaign against strategic targets in Iraq. Operation 'Desert Storm' succeeded in destroying Iraq's air force and severely undermined the morale of Saddam's frontline troops. In a desperate but unsuccessful effort to involve Israel in the war and to split the Arabs from the Western allies in the coalition, the Iraqis launched Scud missile attacks on Tel Aviv, and tried to link Iraq's withdrawal from Kuwait with an Israeli withdrawal from the Palestinian West Bank. Last-minute Soviet efforts to mediate an Iraqi withdrawal from Kuwait were unsuccessful and the coalition launched a land offensive against Iraqi forces on 24 February. The Iraqis were taken completely by surprise as allied deception had convinced them their attack would be from the east, but in fact their assault was launched from the west. In a lightning attack with heavy armour, the allies occupied south-east Iraq and were within 150 miles of Baghdad in a few hours, completely encircling the Iraqi armies. In a series of battles, the allies defeated the élite Iraqi Republican Guard, and on 26 February Saddam ordered his forces to withdraw from Kuwait. As they fled towards Basra, Iraqi troops suffered further losses from allied bombing. The allies liberated Kuwait City on 27 February and President Bush suspended the campaign on 28 February.

The war had serious consequences for both Iraq and Kuwait. The bulk of Kuwait's oilfields had been set on fire by the retreating Iraqi forces and Kuwait City was badly damaged. Civil war soon erupted in Iraq and hundreds of thousands of Kurdish refugees fled to the borders of Turkey and Iran.

Wars in Africa

LIBYA

○ Aozou

AOZOU STRIP
Occupied by Libya
from 1975

CHAD

○ Faya Large

Approximate division between
rebel-held north and government-
held south.

○ Abéché

● Ndjamena

Sarh ○

MOROCCO

WESTERN
SAHARA
● 1957

ALGERIA
● 1954-62

war with Polisario
front 1976-

MAURITANIA

CAPE VERDE
IS.
● 1963-74

GUINEA
BISSAU
● 1959-74

CHAD
○ 1968-

SUDAN
○ 1952-73
1983-

ETHIOPIA
○ 1962-

✳ 1963-
SOMALIA

NIGERIA
○ 1967-69
1977

LIBERIA
○ 1990

GHANA
○ 1981

CAMEROON
● 1955-60

CENTRAL
AFRICAN REPUBLIC
○ 1979

UGANDA
○ 1980
1985-86

RWANDA
○ 1962-65

○ 1978-79

○ 1962-65

BURUNDI

KENYA
● 1952-60
○ 1982

ZAÏRE
○ 1960-71
1978

TANZANIA

ANGOLA
● 1961-75
○ 1975-89

ZIMBABWE
○ 1964-80

MOZAMBIQUE
● 1964-75
○ 1981-

NAMIBIA
● 1966-89

SOUTH AFRICA
Armed struggle against
white rule, 1964-

(inset map)

ZAÏRE

○ Uige

● Luanda

○ Malanje

A N G O L A

ZAMBIA

Lobito ○
Benguela ●
○ Huambo

○ Menongue

Lubango ○
Mocamedes ●

○ Ondjiva

● Ondangua

Quedas
do
Raucana ●

Tsumeb ○
● Grootfontein

BOTSWANA

N A M I B I A

● Windhoek

● Walvis
Bay
(S.Afr.)

Keetsmanshoop

Lüderitz ○

		Area held by MPLA, Feb 1976
		Area held by UNITA, late 1980s
		Main area of European occupation
●		South African army base
→		South African incursions into Angola

0 km   500
0 mls   400

SOUTH AFRICA

● Colonial war

✳ Interstate war

○ Civil war

✳ Guerrilla activity,
late 1980s

0 km   1000
0 mls   750

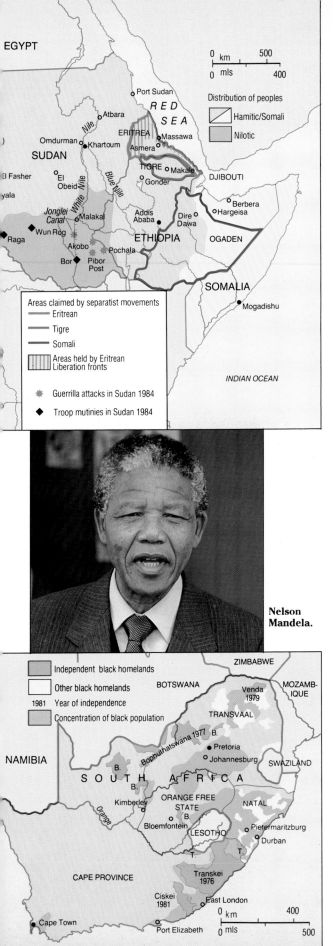

EGYPT

0 km 500
0 mls 400

Distribution of peoples

/// Hamitic/Somali

     Nilotic

Areas claimed by separatist movements
——— Eritrean
——— Tigre
——— Somali
/// Areas held by Eritrean
     Liberation fronts

✳ Guerrilla attacks in Sudan 1984
◆ Troop mutinies in Sudan 1984

RED SEA

Port Sudan
Atbara
ERITREA
Massawa
Omdurman
Khartoum
Asmera
SUDAN
TIGRE
Makale
El Fasher
El Obeid
Gonder
DJIBOUTI
yala
Jonglei Canal
Malakal
Addis Ababa
Dire Dawa
Berbera
Hargeisa
Raga
Wun Rog
Akobo
Pochala
ETHIOPIA
OGADEN
Bor
Pibor Post
SOMALIA
Mogadishu
INDIAN OCEAN
Nile
White Nile
Blue Nile

Nelson Mandela.

Independent black homelands

Other black homelands

1981 Year of independence

Concentration of black population

ZIMBABWE
BOTSWANA
MOZAMBIQUE
Venda 1979
TRANSVAAL
NAMIBIA
Bophuthatswana 1977
Pretoria
Johannesburg
SWAZILAND
SOUTH AFRICA
ORANGE FREE STATE
Kimberley
NATAL
Bloemfontein
LESOTHO
Pietermaritzburg
Durban
CAPE PROVINCE
Transkei 1976
Ciskei 1981
East London
Cape Town
Port Elizabeth
Orange
0 km 400
0 mls 500

Since the withdrawal of the European colonial powers from Africa and the granting of independence to their former colonies in the 1960s, civil wars have raged in various parts of the continent. A common feature of nearly all the wars has been the troubled inheritance of colonial boundaries that do not correspond to the loyalties of the peoples.

In 1967 the Ibos of eastern Nigeria seceded to create their own state of Biafra. Civil war ensued leading to the defeat of Biafra in 1970 by General Gowan and Muslim forces from northern Nigeria. In 1974 the Emperor of Ethiopia, Haile Selassie, was overthrown by a military coup which brought a Marxist-Leninist military regime to power. In 1977 Somalia took advantage of the confusion in Ethiopia to invade the country in order to seize the disputed Ogaden province. Ethiopia secured military aid from the Soviet Union and troops from Cuba, and defeated Somalia in 1978. Civil war also raged in Sudan and in Chad, where conflict arose between nomadic Arabs and black African Christians. After independence in 1974 both Angola and Mozambique lapsed into civil war. In Angola, the Marxist People's Movement for the Liberation of Angola (MPLA), backed by Soviet aid and 17,000 Cuban troops, fought two competing nationalist organizations, the National Union for the Total Independence of Angola (UNITA) and the National Front for the Liberation of Angola (FNLA), supported by the United States and South Africa. Although the FNLA was destroyed in 1976, the struggle between the MPLA and UNITA continued. However, under the 1989 United Nations sponsored agreement granting independence to Namibia the South Africans promised to withdraw from Namibia if Cuban troops evacuated Angola.

The situation in both Angola and Mozambique was complicated by South Africa which intervened in both countries in order to destabilize their governments and prevent them from being used as bases for black nationalist forces seeking the overthrow of apartheid in South Africa itself. For while the rest of Africa had already gained black majority rule, South Africa remained governed by its white minority population. Black 'homelands', all due to become independent, had been created within South Africa's borders, but they were still economically dependent on South Africa, and failed to receive recognition by any other country. In the late 1980s, violence broke out in the black townships against the apartheid system and it was met by repressive measures by the white government. In 1990, however, President F.W. de Klerk released the veteran African National Congress leader Nelson Mandela from prison after 26 years of captivity and began moves towards the dismantling of apartheid.

117

A NEW BALANCE OF POWER

The United States used its nuclear superiority to threaten 'massive retaliation'.

President Roosevelt's vision of 'One World' after the Second World War was shattered by the unwillingness of the Soviet Union to accept American perceptions about how the post-war order should be organized. Historians have argued endlessly about which of the two superpowers was responsible for causing the 'Cold War', but certainly Stalin's ingrained suspicions of the aims and ambitions of the United States resulted in a series of confrontations with the West which antagonized moderate opinion while convincing Western leaders that Moscow was seeking world hegemony. By 1949 the world was divided into two hostile blocs which nevertheless shrank from all-out war with its attendant risk of nuclear annihilation. The American strategy of containing the further expansion of the Soviet bloc encouraged the United States to rebuild Western Europe economically and militarily and to embark on a massive rearmament programme. The struggle between the two blocs became more intense during the 1950s. The United States adopted a rigid doctrinaire posture, which assumed that the entire communist world was centrally controlled from Moscow and even regarded nations like India, which sought to avoid taking sides, as Soviet fellow travellers. The United States used its nuclear superiority to threaten 'massive retaliation' and deter communist expansionism worldwide.

However, during the late 1950s cracks were beginning to appear on both sides. Yugoslavia had already broken away from the Soviet bloc, while the rift between the Soviet Union and communist China widened until by 1960 the two powers had become deadly rivals. France under General de Gaulle was challenging United States domination of Western Europe. New African and Asian Third World nations resisted involvement in the Cold War.

During the 1960s these divergences became more pronounced as Soviet and Chinese troops fought along their disputed borders, while in Western Europe President de Gaulle pulled French forces out of NATO's military command structure when the United States refused his demand for a greater French voice in the alliance. De Gaulle's grand design for a French-led Western Europe which could negotiate on equal terms with both superpowers did not prevail,

but it demonstrated increasing French dissatisfaction with the existing configuration of power.

The Europeans were also critical of American involvement in Vietnam, and, as the Soviet Union began to catch up with the United States during the 1960s in nuclear capability, they became concerned that the United States, fearing nuclear annihilation, might not intervene in the event of a threat to Western Europe by the Soviet Union. The bi-polar system became even more fragmented during the 1970s as the United States receded from its global role after its

Revolution in Eastern Europe

In just one year, 1989, the communist regimes which had ruled Eastern Europe since the late 1940s were swept away by a tide of revolution. Poland gained its freedom when the anti-communist Solidarity movement won control of both houses of parliament in elections held in June. In Hungary the Communist party split over political reform opening the way for free elections in April 1990 in which the conservative anti-communist parties secured a majority. In East Germany the Communist government attempted to placate mounting unrest by promising reforms but it was swept away by street demonstrations in November. The opening of the Berlin Wall and the victory of the Christian Democrats in elections held the following March resulted in overwhelming pressure for re-unification with West Germany. In Czechoslovakia Communist party rule was brought to an end by street demonstrations in November and the dissident playwright Vaclav Havel became President of a parliamentary democracy. In Bulgaria a reformist communist took power and promised free elections.

Only in Romania in the days leading up to the Christmas of 1989 was there major bloodshed when huge popular demonstrations overthrew Nicolae Ceausescu's tyrannical regime. Elections were held in May 1990 which led to a massive majority for Iliescu's National Salvation Front.

◄ **In China, April 1989, Beijing University students gathered in Tiananmen Square in support of freedom of speech and the end of corruption in the Communist Party. Martial law was declared and on 3–4 June detachments of the People's Liberation Army cleared the area by firing on unarmed crowds killing many.**

Vietnam experience, as communist China emerged as an independent nuclear power, and as France, now also a nuclear power, and the European NATO allies sought to improve their relations with the Soviet Union. West Germany recognized the 1945 territorial status quo and normalized its relations with East Germany and other Eastern European countries. The United States and communist China became reconciled while the United States also signed Strategic Arms Limitation Agreements with the Soviet Union, thus inaugurating a period of détente and friendlier East–West relations. The American Secretary of State Henry Kissinger talked of a 'pentagonal multipolar world' in which five new power centres – the United States, the Soviet Union, Western Europe, China and Japan – would form a new global balance of power.

By 1980 Soviet–American tension re-surfaced as Washington complained that the Soviet Union had used détente as a smoke-screen behind which to overtake the United States in military capability, while Moscow had taken advantage of American post-Vietnam passivity to extend its influence into Africa and the Indian Ocean. The Reagan administration revived Cold War animosities by denouncing the Soviet Union as an 'evil empire' and adopted a massive rearmament programme. By 1987, with the advent of Mikhail Gorbachev as Soviet leader, promising political and economic liberalization at home and a relaxation of tensions abroad, the dialogue between the superpowers over arms reductions was resumed and there was a revival of Western optimism about the prospects for a new détente. Gorbachev has introduced a number of reforms into the Soviet system of government, which have given the Russian people more electoral freedom than they have ever enjoyed before, but the Communist Party remains supreme. The relaxation of Party controls has, however, led to a measure of freedom of speech, but more ominously for the stability of the country it has also encouraged the re-emergence of provincial nationalism. The Red Army has been withdrawn from Afghanistan and there has also been an increasing measure of liberalization in Central and Eastern Europe.

The same has not been true of China, where the process of reform was abruptly halted in 1989. Nor, despite the increasing fragmentation of the world in the late 1980s and early in 1990, has there been any substantial change in the relative power positions of the United States and the Soviet Union. Despite the economic strains of the arms race, and the increasing economic strength of Japan and the European Community, notably West Germany, the joint military might of the two superpowers remains overwhelming and they continue to wield immense influence throughout the world.

The United Nations

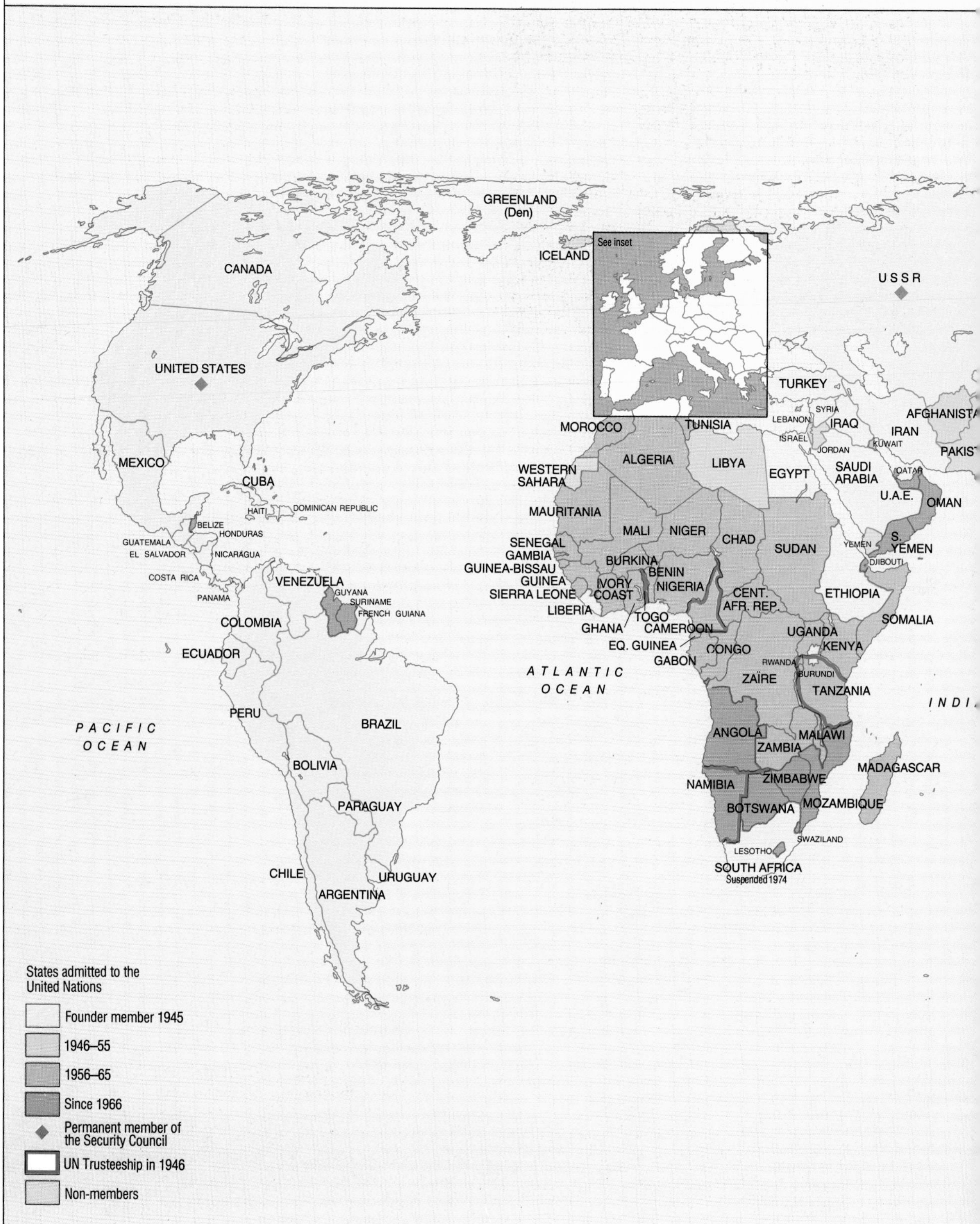

GREENLAND (Den)

ICELAND

See inset

CANADA

USSR

UNITED STATES

TURKEY

MOROCCO   TUNISIA

SYRIA
LEBANON   IRAQ
ISRAEL   JORDAN
KUWAIT

AFGHANISTA

IRAN

PAKIS

MEXICO

ALGERIA   LIBYA   EGYPT

SAUDI
ARABIA

QATAR

U.A.E.   OMAN

CUBA

WESTERN
SAHARA

HAITI   DOMINICAN REPUBLIC
BELIZE
GUATEMALA   HONDURAS
EL SALVADOR   NICARAGUA
COSTA RICA
PANAMA

MAURITANIA

MALI   NIGER   CHAD   SUDAN

YEMEN

S.
YEMEN

DJIBOUTI

SENEGAL
GAMBIA
GUINEA-BISSAU
GUINEA
SIERRA LEONE
LIBERIA

BURKINA
IVORY
COAST

BENIN
NIGERIA

CENT.
AFR. REP.

ETHIOPIA

SOMALIA

VENEZUELA

GUYANA
SURINAME
FRENCH GUIANA

COLOMBIA

GHANA
EQ. GUINEA

TOGO
CAMEROON
GABON

CONGO

UGANDA   KENYA

RWANDA
BURUNDI

ECUADOR

ZAÏRE

TANZANIA

INDI

ATLANTIC
OCEAN

PERU

BRAZIL

ANGOLA

MALAWI

ZAMBIA

MADAGASCAR

PACIFIC
OCEAN

BOLIVIA

ZIMBABWE

NAMIBIA

PARAGUAY

BOTSWANA

MOZAMBIQUE

SWAZILAND

LESOTHO

CHILE   URUGUAY
ARGENTINA

SOUTH AFRICA
Suspended 1974

States admitted to the
United Nations

Founder member 1945

1946–55

1956–65

Since 1966

◆ Permanent member of
   the Security Council

   UN Trusteeship in 1946

   Non-members

The Atlantic Charter of August 1941 made only a vague reference to the need for a permanent system of international security. Roosevelt preferred to avoid specific recommendations, fearing that to propose a new international organization to replace the League of Nations would arouse similar opposition in the United States to that which Woodrow Wilson encountered in 1919. Instead he put forward the notion of the 'Four Policemen' – the United States, the Soviet Union, Britain and China – who would act together against would-be aggressors. However, he soon discovered that this concept failed to satisfy the need for a more far-reaching and democratic body to preserve world peace. His eventual concept of a United Nations Organization retained the 'Four Policemen' in that the four powers (and later France) would have permanent seats in the Security Council, the executive organ of the United Nations. There would also be a General Assembly of all those powers who had fought against the Axis. In 1943 the Soviet Union announced its support for the proposed organization and the American Congress voted in its favour, which was crucial to its success. Detailed discussions took place at conferences at Dumbarton Oaks (near Washington DC) and San Francisco in 1944 and 1945, at which it was agreed that the five permanent members of the Security Council should each have a veto on substantive issues. The US Senate approved the United Nations Charter in July 1945 and the first meeting of the new organization took place in London in January 1946, although its permanent site was to be in New York, thus assuring continued United States membership. Other international bodies were incorporated into the United Nations, including the World Health Organization (WHO), the International Labour Organization (ILO) and the United Nations Relief and Rehabilitation Administration (UNRRA), which distributed some $4 billion worth of relief aid to Europe after the war.

Alongside the United Nations and its various affiliated bodies, a further group of organizations arose, designed to regulate the world economic order. The United States government, convinced that pre-war aggression had been caused by the collapse of world trade and financial dislocation after the depression, was the prime mover in this direction, instigating the setting up of the International Monetary Fund (IMF) and the International Bank for Reconstruction and Development (the World Bank). The task of these organizations was to provide loans and cheap credit for reconstruction purposes and help to stabilize currencies, in the expectation that this would encourage the growth of world trade.

Military and Regional Groupings

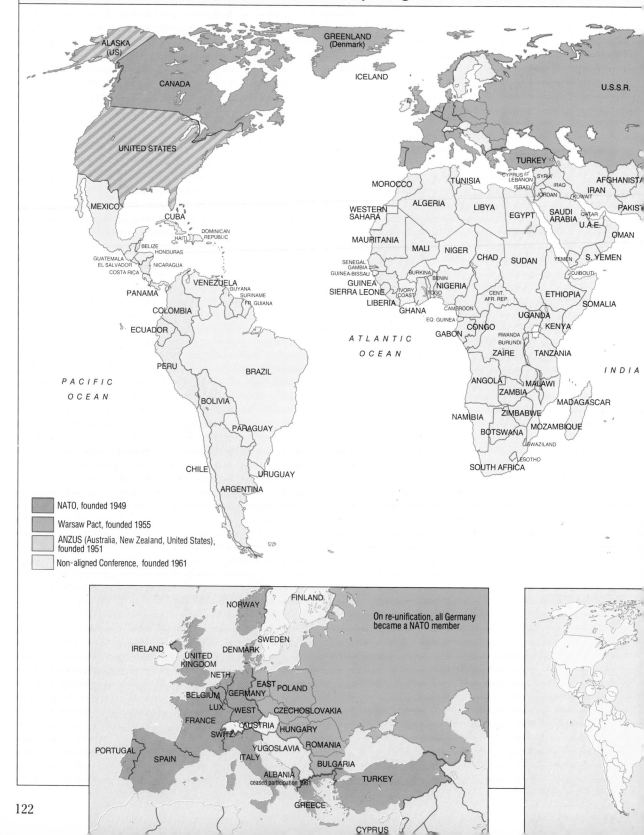

ALASKA (US)

GREENLAND (Denmark)

CANADA

ICELAND

U.S.S.R.

UNITED STATES

MEXICO

TURKEY

CYPRUS
LEBANON   SYRIA
ISRAEL   IRAQ
JORDAN   KUWAIT

AFGHANISTA

IRAN

PAKIS

CUBA

DOMINICAN REPUBLIC

HAITI

BELIZE
HONDURAS
GUATEMALA
EL SALVADOR   NICARAGUA
COSTA RICA

MOROCCO   TUNISIA

WESTERN SAHARA   ALGERIA   LIBYA   EGYPT   SAUDI ARABIA   QATAR

U.A.E.

OMAN

MAURITANIA   MALI   NIGER   CHAD   SUDAN   YEMEN   S. YEMEN

DJIBOUTI

PANAMA

VENEZUELA

GUYANA
SURINAME
FR. GUIANA

SENEGAL
GAMBIA
GUINEA-BISSAU

GUINEA
SIERRA LEONE
LIBERIA

BURKINA
IVORY COAST
GHANA

BENIN
TOGO

NIGERIA

CAMEROON

CENT. AFR. REP.

ETHIOPIA

SOMALIA

COLOMBIA

ECUADOR

EQ. GUINEA

GABON   CONGO

RWANDA
BURUNDI

ZAÏRE

UGANDA

KENYA

TANZANIA

PERU

BRAZIL

ATLANTIC OCEAN

INDIA

BOLIVIA

PACIFIC OCEAN

ANGOLA   MALAWI
ZAMBIA

MADAGASCAR

PARAGUAY

NAMIBIA   ZIMBABWE

MOZAMBIQUE

BOTSWANA

SWAZILAND

CHILE   URUGUAY

ARGENTINA

SOUTH AFRICA

LESOTHO

- ▓ NATO, founded 1949
- ▓ Warsaw Pact, founded 1955
- ▢ ANZUS (Australia, New Zealand, United States), founded 1951
- ▢ Non-aligned Conference, founded 1961

NORWAY   FINLAND

IRELAND

UNITED KINGDOM

SWEDEN

DENMARK

On re-unification, all Germany became a NATO member

NETH.

EAST GERMANY   POLAND

BELGIUM
LUX.

WEST   CZECHOSLOVAKIA

FRANCE

AUSTRIA   HUNGARY

SWITZ.

YUGOSLAVIA   ROMANIA

PORTUGAL

SPAIN   ITALY   BULGARIA

ALBANIA
ceased participation 1961

TURKEY

GREECE

CYPRUS

MONGOLIA

CHINA

N. KOREA

S. KOREA

JAPAN

PACIFIC OCEAN

BHUTAN

NEPAL

BANGLADESH

INDIA

BURMA

LAOS

TAIWAN

THAILAND

CAMBODIA

VIETNAM

PHILIPPINES

SRI LANKA

MALAYSIA

BRUNEI

SINGAPORE

INDONESIA

OCEAN

PAPUA NEW GUINEA

AUSTRALIA

NEW ZEALAND

OAS (Organization of American States), founded 1948

Arab League, founded 1945

In March 1948 Britain, France, Belgium, the Netherlands and Luxembourg signed the Treaty of Brussels, pledging that if any of them was attacked by an outside power, the others would come to its assistance. This was plainly directed against the Soviet Union, but clearly United States membership would be essential if the alliance was to possess any credibility. The United States, while increasingly suspicious of Soviet intentions after 1947, concentrated on assisting Western Europe to re-build its economic strength, and it was not until April 1949, during the Berlin blockade, that Washington agreed to the signature of the North Atlantic Treaty Organization between the United States, the Brussels Pact countries, and Canada, Iceland, Norway, Italy, and Portugal. Each signatory was obliged to assist any member which was the victim of an armed attack. United States participation in this alliance was not intended to lead to any increase in the number of US troops in Europe beyond the two divisions occupying West Germany. Its motivation was psychological: to help restore European morale and to encourage the re-building of armies and defence industries. However, the Korean War in 1950 led the United States to offer the Europeans the despatch of American reinforcements to Europe, to increase its military aid, and to appoint General Dwight D. Eisenhower as NATO Supreme Commander in return for European acceptance of West German military contribution to NATO. The French rejected the re-militarization of West Germany and it was not until 1954 that West Germany and Italy were admitted to the Brussels Pact (re-named the Western European Union) and West Germany admitted to NATO. To reassure the French, Britain promised to maintain four divisions and an air force in Europe. West Germany's admission to NATO resulted in the Soviet Union setting up the Warsaw Pact in 1955, involving Soviet and satellite armies, on the same lines as NATO and with its headquarters in Moscow.

Outside Europe, similar defence arrangements were negotiated in the 1950s between the USA and its allies in Asia and Australasia to prevent Soviet and Chinese expansion in that region. Many nations preferred, however, to remain non-aligned and joined in a grouping of nations led by Yugoslavia and India, which resisted all blandishments to support either the Soviet Union or the United States. Many of these non-aligned nations are also members of regional groupings, such as the Arab League, set up in 1945 in the Egyptian capital of Cairo to promote Arab unity, or the Organization of American States, set up in Bogotá in Colombia in 1948 to promote cooperation throughout the American continent.

Communist China

UNION OF SOVIET SOCIALIST REPUBLICS

Amur

Blagoveshchensk

Khabaro

1969

1969

Hailaer

Qiqihaer

Songhut

1969

Urumqi

Ulanhot

Ulaan Baatar

MONGOLIA

Haerbin

Vladivo

Changchun

INNER
MONGOLIA

Shenyang

Kashgar

XINJIANG-UIGHUR

Huhehot

NORTH
KOREA

SEA
JAPA

ceded to China
by Pakistan

Yumen

Baotou

Beijing

KASHMIR

Oct–Nov
1962

Ningxia

Tianjin

Lüda

Intervention in
Korean war, 1950

SOUTH
KOREA

under Chinese administration
since Nov 1962

NINGXIA-
HUI

Taiyuan

Lanzhou

Ji'nan

Qingdao

YELLOW SEA

Huang

Kaifeng

CHINESE PEOPLE'S REPUBLIC

Xi'an

Nanjing

TIBET

Invasion, 1950

Lhasa

NEPAL

Chengdu

Chongqing

Yangzi

Wuhan

Shanghai

Hangzhou

EAST CHINA SEA

BHUTAN

Oct–Nov 1962

Changsha

INDIA

ASSAM

Guiyang

Fuzhou

Matsu

Kunming

GUANGXI
ZHUANG

Xi

BURMA

Nanning

Guangzhou

Quemoy

TAIWAN
(NATIONALIST CHINA)

Mekong

Feb–Apr 1979

Hanoi

Hong Kong (Br.) to be returned to China,1997
Macau (Port.)
to be returned to China,1999

LAOS

Hainan

VIETNAM

SOUTH CHINA SEA

PHILIPPINES

THAILAND

0 km 750

0 mls 500

Boundaries of
Autonomous Regions

Territory claimed by China

Border clash

Ethno-linguistic areas

Han Chinese majority

Ethnic minorities

Hui Chinese

Turkic

Tibeto-
Burman
Thai
}Sino-
Tibetan

Mongolian
Korean
}Altaic

Others

Uninhabited

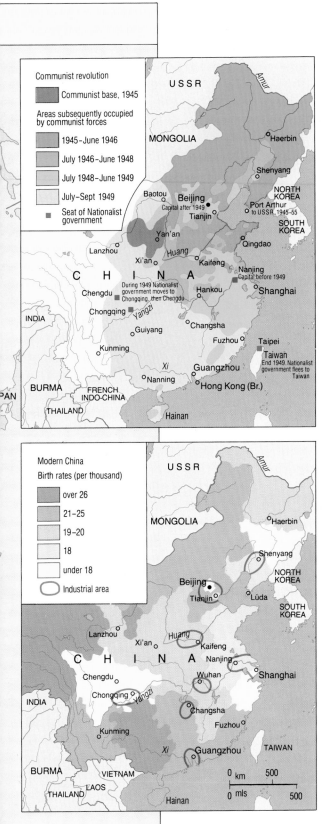

Communist revolution

Communist base, 1945

Areas subsequently occupied
by communist forces

1945–June 1946

July 1946–June 1948

July 1948–June 1949

July–Sept 1949

Seat of Nationalist
government

USSR

MONGOLIA

Haerbin

Shenyang

NORTH
KOREA

Baotou

Beijing
Capital after 1949

Tianjin

Port Arthur
to USSR 1945–55

SOUTH
KOREA

Yan'an

Qingdao

Lanzhou

Huang

Xi'an

Kaifeng

Nanjing
Capital before 1949

C H I N A

During 1949 Nationalist
government moves to
Chongqing, then Chengdu

Chengdu

Hankou

Shanghai

Chongqing

Yangzi

Changsha

Guiyang

Fuzhou

Taipei

Kunming

Taiwan
End 1949. Nationalist
government flees to
Taiwan

Xi

Guangzhou

BURMA

FRENCH
INDO-CHINA

Nanning

Hong Kong (Br.)

THAILAND

Hainan

Modern China

Birth rates (per thousand)

over 26

21–25

19–20

18

under 18

Industrial area

USSR

MONGOLIA

Haerbin

Shenyang

NORTH
KOREA

Beijing

Tianjin

Lüda

SOUTH
KOREA

Lanzhou

Huang

Xi'an

Kaifeng

C H I N A

Nanjing

Chengdu

Wuhan

Shanghai

Chongqing

Yangzi

Changsha

INDIA

Fuzhou

Kunming

TAIWAN

Xi

Guangzhou

BURMA

VIETNAM

0 km 500

LAOS

THAILAND

Hainan

0 mls 500

After the defeat of Japan at the end of the Second World War, the conflict between the Guomindang (nationalists) led by Jiang Jieshi (Chiang Kai-shek) and the communists under Mao Zedong (Mao Tse-tung) flared into open warfare. By October 1949 the communists had defeated the Guomindang and Jiang had fled to Taiwan.

The new Beijing government concentrated on the reconstruction of China's devastated economy. Agricultural production had risen, but the population increased even more rapidly; in the 1970s the government embarked on a birth control programme promoting one-child families.

In pursuit of a centralized China, the new regime tried to assimilate the various ethnic groups. The dominant Han ethnic group, concentrated in central, southern and eastern China, made up 90 per cent of China's population. The minority ethnic groups, many of whom were Muslims, lived mainly in the 'Autonomous Regions' of the far north and north-west. The persecution of these peoples and the seizure of their land led to frequent revolts in the 1950s and 1960s. In 1950 Tibetan autonomy was suppressed and a Tibetan uprising in 1959 was ruthlessly crushed. After 1978 Beijing adopted a more tolerant policy towards the cultural and religious life of the minorities.

In 1958 Mao embarked on 'The Great Leap Forward' designed to promote agricultural and industrial expansion in China, but disastrous harvests led to the failure of the programme. In 1966 Mao launched 'The Cultural Revolution', hoping to revive communist principles in Chinese society and to restore Communist party control. The ensuing violence against bourgeois and intellectual elements led by student Red Guards was only brought under control after it had done untold damage to the Chinese economy. When Mao died in 1976 political power was taken by a reformer who had been arrested during the Cultural Revolution, Deng Xiaoping. Deng purged the radical Maoists and embarked on a modernization programme, based on a limited capitalist revival and private ownership of land. However, restrictions on personal freedom were not relaxed, leading to an uprising against the regime in 1989 (see pages 118–19).

The Chinese communist regime has reacted forcibly to threats along its borders. The Chinese intervened in the Korean War (1951–3) when United Nations troops approached the Yalu frontier, defeated India during a dispute on the northern Indo-Chinese frontier in 1962, engaged in savage fighting with the Soviet Union over territory on the Usurri river boundary in 1969 and invaded North Vietnam in 1979 after the Hanoi regime occupied Kampuchea.

The Nuclear Threat

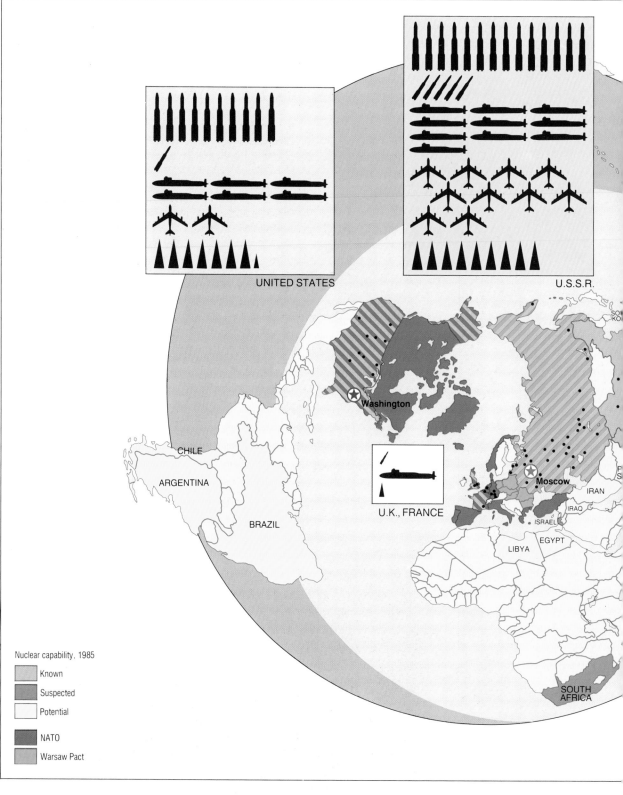

UNITED STATES

U.S.S.R.

U.K., FRANCE

Washington

Moscow

CHILE

ARGENTINA

BRAZIL

IRAN

IRAQ

ISRAEL

LIBYA

EGYPT

SOUTH
AFRICA

Nuclear capability, 1985

Known

Suspected

Potential

NATO

Warsaw Pact

126

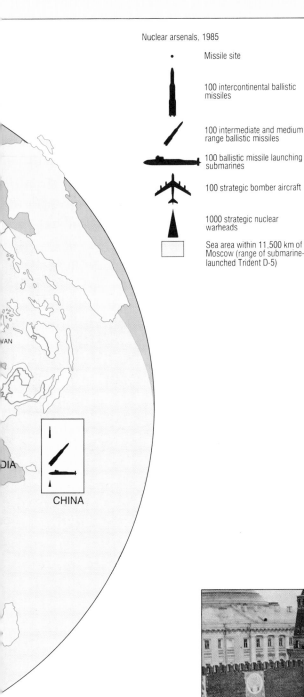

Nuclear arsenals, 1985

• Missile site

100 intercontinental ballistic missiles

100 intermediate and medium range ballistic missiles

100 ballistic missile launching submarines

100 strategic bomber aircraft

1000 strategic nuclear warheads

Sea area within 11,500 km of Moscow (range of submarine-launched Trident D-5)

VAN

DIA

CHINA

The Test Ban Treaty, signed in 1963, was the first post-war nuclear agreement. During the 1960s the Soviet Union caught up with the United States in Inter-Continental Ballistic Missiles (ICBMs). This parity between the two superpowers enabled the Soviet Union and the United States to enter into Strategic Arms Limitation Talks (SALT) in 1969. The SALT I agreement was signed in Moscow in 1972, freezing the number of ICBMs and Submarine-Launched Ballistic Missiles (SLBMs). Further Soviet–American negotiations led to the signing of SALT II in Vienna in 1979 which limited the number of Multiple Independently Targeted Re-entry Vehicles (MIRVs). The United States Senate failed to ratify this treaty, claiming that the Soviet Union had cheated on the agreement. In the 1970s the Soviet Union also replaced its short-range missiles in Eastern Europe with new medium-range ones capable of hitting any Western European target. This led the Reagan administration in 1981 to deploy Cruise and Pershing intermediate-range missiles (IRBMs) in Western Europe and to increase defence expenditure by five per cent per annum. In 1983 Reagan announced the so-called Strategic Defence Initiative (SDI) or Star Wars Programme, intended to provide space-based defences against a Soviet missile attack by the year 2000. However, with the advent of Mikhail Gorbachev as Soviet leader in 1985 and his offer of nuclear weapon reduction negotiations, there was a successful conclusion to the Intermediate Range Nuclear Force (INF) talks, which had begun at Geneva in November 1981. The INF Treaty of 1988 provided for the elimination of all land-based medium-range ballistic missiles in Europe.

In November 1990 the East and West signed a Conventional Forces Europe Agreement which halved the number of tanks on both sides in Europe and evened out the imbalance between Soviet and Western forces in Europe. By this time Russian troops had already begun to withdraw from Eastern Europe.

May Day military parade in Moscow, 1961.

Modern USSR

Franz Josef Land

BARENTS SEA

Murmansk

Novaya Zemlya

Kara Sea

Karelian A.S.S.R.

White Sea

L. Ladoga

LATVIAN S.S.R.

Tallinn

ESTONIAN S.S.R.

Kaliningrad

LITHUANIAN S.S.R.

R.S.F.S.R.

Riga

Vilnius

Leningrad

Petrozavodsk

L. Onega

Arkhangelsk

Naryan Mar

Nenets N.O.

Yamal Nenets N.O.

Vorkuta

BYELORUSSIAN

Minsk

S.S.R.

Komi A.S.S.R.

Salekhard

Gulf of Ob

Lvov

Smolensk

Kalinin

Syktyvkar

SOVIET

Ob

FEDERAL

UKRAINIAN S.S.R.

Dnjeper

Moscow

RUSSIAN

Kiev

Niżhniy Novgorod (Gorkiy)

Kirov

Komi Permyak N.O.

Khanty Mansi N.O.

MOLDAVIAN S.S.R.

Voronezh

2

3

Kazan

4

Ustinov

Perm

Khanty Mansiysk

Kishinev

Kharkov

1

Tatar A.S.S.R.

Odessa

Dnepropetrovsk

Ufa

Sverdlovsk

Tobolsk

Sevastopol

Donetsk

Don

Saratov

Kuybyshev

Bashkir A.S.S.R.

Chelyabinsk

Tyumen

Rostov

Volga

Krasnodar

Volgograd

Orenburg

Magnitogorsk

Omsk

BLACK SEA

Adygey A.O.

Kalmyk A.S.S.R.

Novosibirsk

Maykop

5

Astrakhan

Irtysh

Gorr Altay

GEORGIAN S.S.R.

6

7

8

9

10

Dagestan A.S.S.R.

Karaganda

Semipalatinsk

Ordzhonikidze

11

Makhachkala

ARMENIAN S.S.R.

Tbilisi

KAZAKH

S.S.R.

Yerevan

13

AZERBAIJAN S.S.R.

Aral Sea

Karakalpak A.S.S.R.

Kzyl Orda

L. Balkhash

12

Baku

Nukus

Syr Darya

CASPIAN SEA

Krasnovodsk

TURKMEN S.S.R.

UZBEK S.S.R.

Alma Ata

Frunze

Tashkent

KIRGIZ S.S.R.

Issyk Kul

Ashkhabad

Amu Darya

Samarkand

TAJIK S.S.R.

Dushanbe

Gorno-Badakhshan A.O.

Khorog

Ethno-linguistic areas

- Russian
- Ukrainian
- Byelorussian
- Baltic
- Romance
- Iranian
- Armenian
- Finno-Ugrian
- Turkic
- Mongolian
- Caucasian
- Sparsely populated or uninhabited areas

1. Mordovian A.S.S.R.
2. Chuvash A.S.S.R.
3. Mary A.S.S.R.
4. Udmurt A.S.S.R.
5. Karachay-Cherkess A.O.
6. Abkhaz A.S.S.R.
7. Kabardin-Balkar A.S.S.R.
8. Adzhar A.S.S.R.
9. Yugo-Ossetian A.S.S.R.
10. Severo-Ossetian A.S.S.R.
11. Chechen-Ingush A.S.S.R.
12. Nakhichevan A.S.S.R.
13. Nagorno-Karabakh A.O.

S.S.R. = Soviet Socialist Republic
A.S.S.R. = Autonomous S.S.R.
A.O. = Autonomous Oblast
N.O. = National Okrug

Autonomous regions within Soviet Republics

ARCTIC OCEAN

Severnaya Zemlya

New Siberian Is.

LAPTEV SEA

Wrangel Is.

Anadyr

Chukot N.O.

Koryak N.O.

Taimyr N.O.

Nordvik

Tiksi

Sredne Kolymsk

Kolyma

Norilsk

Verkhoyansk

Indigirka

Magadan

Kamchatka

Petropavlovsk-Kamchatskiy

SOCIALIST

REPUBLIC

Yakut A.S.S.R.

Lena

Okhotsk

SEA OF OKHOTSK

Lower Tunguska

Tura

Yakutsk

Kuril Is.

Evenk N.O.

Upper Tunguska

Aldan

Sakhalin

Lena

Amur

Komsomolsk

Sovetskaya Gavan

Krasnoyarsk

Buryat A.S.S.R.

Skovorodino

Amur

Ust Orda Buryat N.O.

L. Baykal

Aginsk Buryat N.O.

Blagoveshchensk

Birobidzhan

Jewish A.O.

Khabarovsk

vokuznetsk

akass A.O.

Abakan

Kyzyl

Tuva A.S.S.R.

Irkutsk

Ulan Ude

Chita

Aginskoye

Vladivostok

M ikhail Gorbachev became party leader on 11 March 1985 and the parlous economic state of the Soviet Union presented him with a major challenge. He introduced the twin processes of *glasnost* – the opening up of a dialogue inside the country and with the outside world – and *perestroika* – the complete restructuring of party, society and the economy. Centralized controls over the economy were relaxed and the Soviet Union sought greater access to Western capital and technology. At the same time, the Soviet people were promised greater political and press freedoms.

The relaxation of party and state controls had the

effect of encouraging the revival of nationalism in some constituent republics of the Union. Demonstrations in Georgia resulted in clashes between troops and nationalists; there was increasing unrest in the Ukraine and amongst the Romanians in Soviet Moldavia. In the Baltic republics of Latvia and Estonia the Communist party lost its monopoly of power, while early in 1990 Lithuania declared its independence from the Soviet Union. After failing to quell nationalism in the Baltic republics, Gorbachev held a referendum in March 1991. This gave qualified support for a 'renewed federation of equal sovereign republics'.

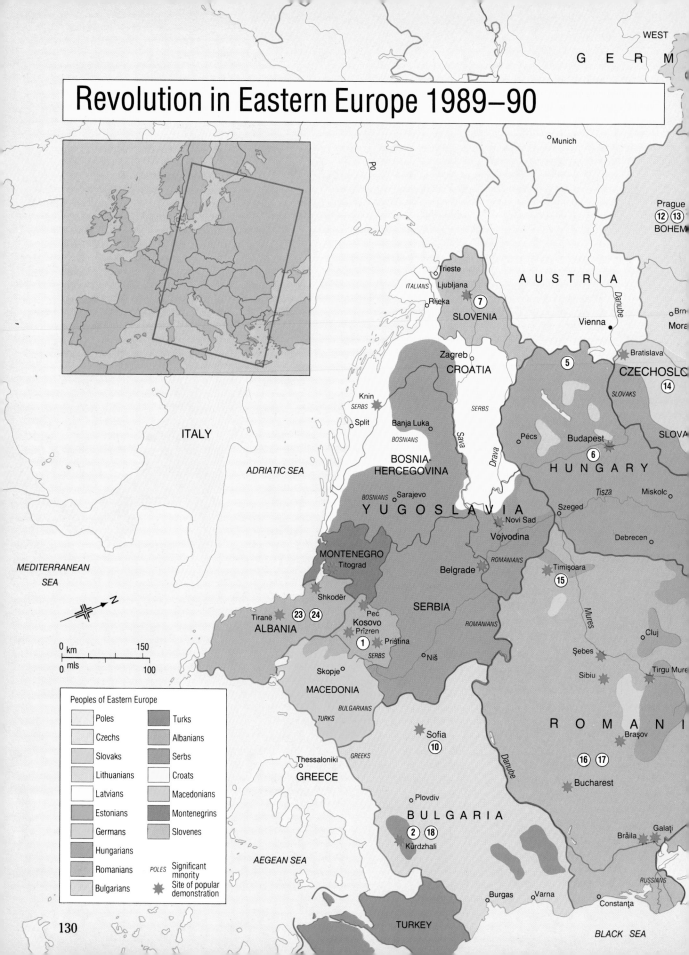

Revolution in Eastern Europe 1989–90

WEST

G E R M

Munich

Prague
⑫ ⑬
BOHEM

Po

ITALIANS
Trieste
Ljubljana
Rijeka
SLOVENIA ⑦

A U S T R I A

Danube

Vienna

Brn
Mora

⑤

Bratislava
CZECHOSL

Zagreb
CROATIA

SERBS

Knin
SERBS

Split

Banja Luka
BOSNIANS

Sava

Drava

Pécs

Budapest
⑥

H U N G A R Y

SLOVAKS

⑭

SLOVA

SLOVA

BOSNIA-
HERCEGOVINA

BOSNIANS Sarajevo

Y U G O S L A V I A

Novi Sad
Vojvodina

Tisza

Szeged

Miskolc

Debrecen

ITALY

ADRIATIC SEA

MEDITERRANEAN
SEA

MONTENEGRO
Titograd

ROMANIANS

Belgrade

Timişoara
⑮

Mureş

Cluj

Shkodër
Tiranë ㉓ ㉔
ALBANIA

Peć
Kosovo
Prîzren
① Prîstina
SERBS

SERBIA

ROMANIANS

Şebes

Sibiu

Tirgu Mure

0 km   150
0 mls   100

Niš

Skopje

R O M A N I

Braşov

MACEDONIA

BULGARIANS
TURKS

Sofia
⑩

GREEKS

⑯ ⑰

Bucharest

Peoples of Eastern Europe

Poles		Turks	
Czechs		Albanians	
Slovaks		Serbs	
Lithuanians		Croats	
Latvians		Macedonians	
Estonians		Montenegrins	
Germans		Slovenes	
Hungarians			
Romanians	*POLES*	Significant minority	
Bulgarians	★	Site of popular demonstration	

Thessaloniki

GREECE

Plovdiv

B U L G A R I A

② ⑱
Kürdzhali

AEGEAN SEA

Burgas   Varna

TURKEY

Danube

Brăila
Galaţi

RUSSIANS

Constanţa

BLACK SEA

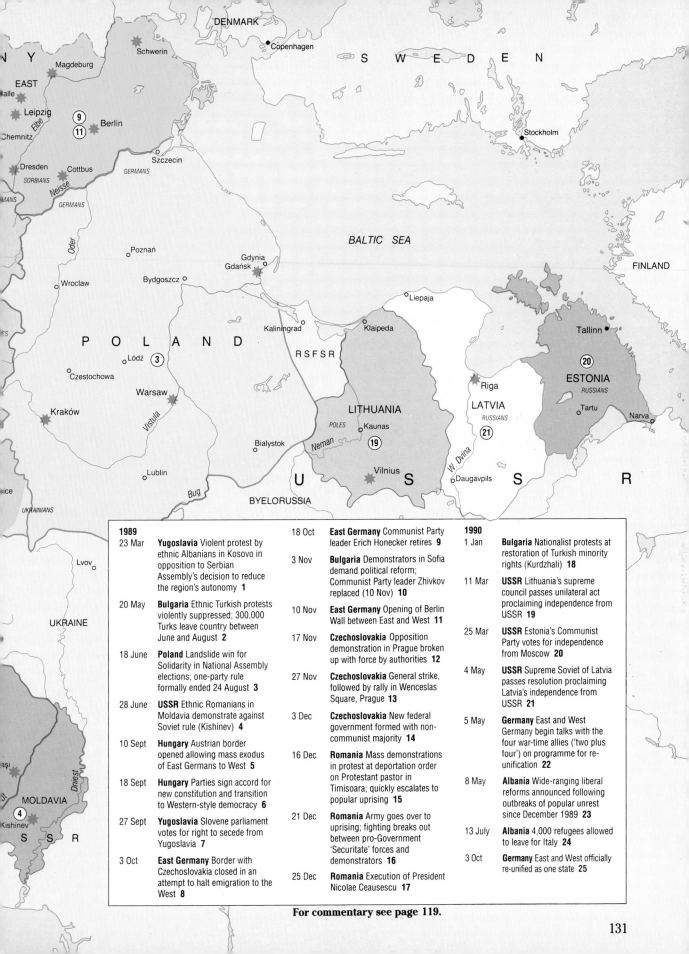

DENMARK

Copenhagen

S W E D E N

NY

EAST

Magdeburg

Schwerin

Halle

Leipzig

⑨

Berlin

Chemnitz

⑪

Elbe

Dresden

Cottbus

SORBIANS

Szczecin

Neisse

GERMANS

GERMANS

Oder

Stockholm

FINLAND

Poznań

BALTIC SEA

Wrocław

Bydgoszcz

Gdynia

Gdańsk

Liepaja

Kaliningrad

Klaipeda

Tallinn

P O L A N D

Łódź

③

R S F S R

Riga

⑳

ESTONIA

RUSSIANS

Czestochowa

Warsaw

LITHUANIA

LATVIA

Tartu

Kraków

Vistula

POLES

Kaunas

RUSSIANS

Narva

②①

Bialystok

Neman

⑲

W. Dvina

Lublin

Vilnius

Bug

Daugavpils

U

S

S

R

BYELORUSSIA

UKRAINIANS

Lvov

UKRAINE

Iaşi

Dniest

MOLDAVIA

④

Kishinev

S

S

R

1989

23 Mar **Yugoslavia** Violent protest by ethnic Albanians in Kosovo in opposition to Serbian Assembly's decision to reduce the region's autonomy **1**

20 May **Bulgaria** Ethnic Turkish protests violently suppressed; 300,000 Turks leave country between June and August **2**

18 June **Poland** Landslide win for Solidarity in National Assembly elections; one-party rule formally ended 24 August **3**

28 June **USSR** Ethnic Romanians in Moldavia demonstrate against Soviet rule (Kishinev) **4**

10 Sept **Hungary** Austrian border opened allowing mass exodus of East Germans to West **5**

18 Sept **Hungary** Parties sign accord for new constitution and transition to Western-style democracy **6**

27 Sept **Yugoslavia** Slovene parliament votes for right to secede from Yugoslavia **7**

3 Oct **East Germany** Border with Czechoslovakia closed in an attempt to halt emigration to the West **8**

18 Oct **East Germany** Communist Party leader Erich Honecker retires **9**

3 Nov **Bulgaria** Demonstrators in Sofia demand political reform; Communist Party leader Zhivkov replaced (10 Nov) **10**

10 Nov **East Germany** Opening of Berlin Wall between East and West **11**

17 Nov **Czechoslovakia** Opposition demonstration in Prague broken up with force by authorities **12**

27 Nov **Czechoslovakia** General strike, followed by rally in Wenceslas Square, Prague **13**

3 Dec **Czechoslovakia** New federal government formed with non-communist majority **14**

16 Dec **Romania** Mass demonstrations in protest at deportation order on Protestant pastor in Timisoara; quickly escalates to popular uprising **15**

21 Dec **Romania** Army goes over to uprising; fighting breaks out between pro-Government 'Securitate' forces and demonstrators **16**

25 Dec **Romania** Execution of President Nicolae Ceausescu **17**

1990

1 Jan **Bulgaria** Nationalist protests at restoration of Turkish minority rights (Kurdzhali) **18**

11 Mar **USSR** Lithuania's supreme council passes unilateral act proclaiming independence from USSR **19**

25 Mar **USSR** Estonia's Communist Party votes for independence from Moscow **20**

4 May **USSR** Supreme Soviet of Latvia passes resolution proclaiming Latvia's independence from USSR **21**

5 May **Germany** East and West Germany begin talks with the four war-time allies ('two plus four') on programme for re-unification **22**

8 May **Albania** Wide-ranging liberal reforms announced following outbreaks of popular unrest since December 1989 **23**

13 July **Albania** 4,000 refugees allowed to leave for Italy **24**

3 Oct **Germany** East and West officially re-unified as one state **25**

For commentary see page 119.

Chronology 1946–1990

EUROPE	AMERICAS
Feb '46 ● Hungary becomes a republic	Feb '46 ● Juan Perón elected President of Argentina
June '46 ● Umberto II abdicates and Italy becomes a republic	July '46 ● Atomic tests at Bikini atoll: US battleship *Arkansas* sunk by blast
May '47 ● Communist ministers excluded from French and Italian cabinets	Aug '47 ● US Secretary of State General Marshall calls for European Recovery Programme (the Marshall Plan)
Dec '47 ● King Michael of Romania abdicates: republic proclaimed	July '48 ● Communist leaders arrested in USA
Feb '48 ● Communist rule established in Czechoslovakia	Nov '48 ● Harry Truman elected President of USA
Mar '48 ● Brussels Treaty organization formed: United Kingdom, France and Benelux countries (defensive alliance)	Mar '49 ● Newfoundland becomes 10th Canadian Province
Apr '48 ● Organization for European Economic Cooperation established	Apr '49 ● NATO founded in Washington
June '48 ● Soviet blockade of West Berlin	
Jan '49 ● Council for Mutual Economic Aid (Comecon) established in Moscow	
Apr '49 ● North Atlantic Treaty signed by Brussels Treaty powers and USA, Canada, Italy, Denmark, Iceland, Norway and Portugal	
May '49 ● Council of Europe founded	
May '49 ● Federal German Republic founded: Konrad Adenauer becomes Chancellor (Sept)	
Oct '49 ● German Democratic Republic founded	
Oct '51 ● Conservative party wins British General Election: Winston Churchill re-elected Prime Minister	Feb '50 ● Senator Joseph McCarthy denounces American State Department as full of communists
Feb '52 ● George VI of Britain dies: accession of Elizabeth II	Nov '51 ● Juan Perón re-elected President of Argentina
Aug '52 ● First meeting of European Coal and Steel Community	Mar '52 ● General Batista seizes power as President of Cuba (to 1959)
Jan '53 ● Anti-Jewish campaign in Russia	Nov '52 ● General Dwight D Eisenhower (Republican) elected President of USA
Feb '53 ● Catholic Church in Poland put under state control and Cardinal Wyszynski, Primate of Poland, arrested	Jan '53 ● New constitution in Venezuela: President Jimenéz given unlimited powers
Mar '53 ● Stalin dies, succeeded by Georgy Malenkov as Chairman of Council of Ministers	July '53 ● Abortive revolt in Cuba led by Fidel Castro
June '53 ● Anti-communist riots in East Germany	June '54 ● Conservative rebellion in Guatemala: military dictatorship (to 1966)
Nov '54 ● Start of Algerian war of independence	Nov '54 ● Juan Perón's anti-clerical campaign in Argentina results in uprising
	Dec '54 ● Senator McCarthy's anti-communist witch-hunt condemned by US Senate
Feb '55 ● Malenkov resigns: collective leadership of Nikita Khrushchev and Nikolai Bulganin	Sept '55 ● Military and naval revolts in Argentina: Juan Perón resigns and flees
May '55 ● Occupation of Germany ends: Germany joins NATO and Brussels Treaty Organization	Mar '56 ● Blacks in Alabama led by Martin Luther King boycott public buses on grounds of illegality of segregation
Mar '56 ● De-Stalinization begins in Russia: Stalin's 'cult of personality' disowned by Khrushchev at Party Congress	Sept '56 ● General Somoza, President of Nicaragua, assassinated: succeeded by his son, Luis Somoza
Oct '56 ● Britain, France and Israel invade Egypt after nationalization of Suez Canal	Nov '56 ● Dwight D Eisenhower re-elected President of USA
Jan '57 ● Harold Macmillan becomes Prime Minister of Britain	Dec '56 ● Seven different governments in Haiti (to Sept '57)
Mar '57 ● Common Market comes into being: Treaty of Rome signed by 'The Six': France, West Germany, Italy, Netherlands, Belgium, Luxembourg	June '57 ● Martin Luther King emerges as leader of desegregation campaign in USA
Apr '57 ● Archbishop Makarios released by British government in return for cessation of hostilities by EOKA	June '57 ● Overwhelming Conservative victory in Canadian General Election
Feb '58 ● Benelux Economic Union formed	Aug '57 ● Federation of West Indies established by Britain
Mar '58 ● Khrushchev premier of USSR as well as First Secretary of Party	Sept '57 ● François Duvalier elected President of Haiti
June '58 ● General de Gaulle Prime Minister of France (elected President Dec)	Apr '58 ● Fidel Castro issues decree for 'total war' against President Batista
June '59 ● Eamon de Valera elected President of Ireland	Jan '59 ● Fidel Castro's guerrillas take Havana: Batista flees and Castro becomes Prime Minister
Nov '59 ● EFTA (European Free Trade Association) convention agreed: Austria, Scandinavian countries, Switzerland, UK and Portugal	Apr '59 ● St Lawrence Seaway opened in Canada
	Apr '59 ● Abortive coup attempts in Panama and Dominica with Cuban aid (to June)
	Aug '59 ● Haiti repels invasion by Cuban forces

AFRICA, ASIA, AUSTRALASIA

Mar '46 • Britain declares Transjordan independent: renamed Jordan
Dec '46 • Communist Vietminh forces open hostilities against French in Indo-China
Aug '47 • India and Pakistan become independent: Nehru becomes Prime Minister of India, Muhammed Ali Jinnah Governor General of Pakistan: thousands killed in violence between Muslims and Hindus
Sept '47 • Britain announces withdrawal from Palestine
Oct '47 • Maharaja of Kashmir accedes to India
Nov '47 • India and Pakistan at war over Kashmir
May '48 • Jan Christian Smuts defeated in South African general election: Nationalist Afrikaaner Party wins on apartheid platform
May '48 • Israel proclaimed independent state and British mandate in Palestine is terminated
July '48 • Arab League forces attack Jewish positions
Jan '49 • Jiang Jieshi resigns as President of China: Communists gain control under Mao Zedong and proclaim People's Republic (Sept): Chiang retreats to Formosa (Taiwan)
Feb '49 • Armistice between Israel and Arab states
June '49 • USA withdraws from South Korea

June '50 • Korean war begins: North Korean forces invade South Korea: US troops disembark in Korea and take Seoul (in Sept)
Oct '50 • Chinese invade Tibet
Oct '51 • Egypt denounces 1936 treaty with Britain and King Farouk is proclaimed King of Sudan
July '52 • Gamal Abdul Nasser seizes power in Egypt and King Farouk forced to abdicate
Nov '52 • Vietminh offensive begins in Laos
Feb '53 • Anglo–Egyptian agreement on Sudan
July '53 • Armistice in Korea
May '54 • French forces heavily defeated by Vietminh at Dien Bien Phu
July '54 • Anglo–Egyptian agreement: all British forces to leave Egypt by 1956
July '54 • Vietnam split at 17th parallel: north Vietnam under communist control
Nov '54 • Nationalist rising begins in Algeria: civil war follows
Dec '54 • Cambodia becomes independent from France

Apr '55 • Bandung Conference: 29 Afro-Asian non-aligned states gather to condemn colonialism
Oct '55 • South Vietnam proclaimed a republic with Ngo Dinh Diem as president
Jan '56 • Sudan proclaimed independent from Anglo–Egyptian control
Mar '56 • Morocco and Tunisia become independent from France
Apr '56 • Spanish Morocco made independent and reunited with Morocco
June '56 • Britain evacuates Canal Zone
Aug '56 • Nasser nationalizes Suez Canal
Oct '56 • Israel invades Sinai Desert: Anglo–French expedition lands at Pord Said (Nov)
Nov '56 • Anglo–French ceasefire as UN force arrives
Mar '57 • Gold Coast becomes independent from Britain: renamed Ghana
Mar '57 • Israel withdraws from Sinai and hands over Gaza strip to UN troops
July '58 • King Faisal of Iraq and other members of royal family assassinated
Aug '58 • General de Gaulle announces autonomy within 'French Community' for all French African colonies
May '59 • US reconnaisance aircraft, from base in Turkey, brought down in USSR: crisis follows

SCIENCE & CULTURE

1946 • Electronic Numerical Integrator and Calculator (ENIAC), first completely electronic computer
1947 • First supersonic flight
• Tennessee Williams *A Streetcar Named Desire*
• Discovery of the Dead Sea scrolls
1948 • Invention of long-playing record
• Invention of transistors
• Albert Camus *The Plague*
• Olivier Messiaen *Turangalîla Symphony*
• Richard Strauss *Four Last Songs*
1949 • Cortisone is discovered
• George Orwell *1984*
• Arthur Miller *Death of a Salesman*
• Simone de Beauvoir *The Second Sex*
• Rodgers and Hammerstein *South Pacific*
• T S Eliot *The Cocktail Party*

1950 • Ezra Pound *Seventy Cantos*
• Edith Piaf *La Vie en Rose*
1951 • J D Salinger *Catcher in the Rye*
• Electrical power first produced from atomic energy
• Benjamin Britten *Billy Budd*
• Salvador Dali *Crucifixion*
1952 • First atomic submarine
• USA explodes first hydrogen bomb
1953 • James Watson and Francis Crick identify structure of DNA
• Dmitri Shostakovich Tenth Symphony
• Arthur Miller *The Crucible*
1954 • Arnold Schoenberg *Moses and Aaron*
• William Golding *The Lord of the Flies*

1955 • Vaccine for polio discovered
• Vladimir Nabokov *Lolita*
• Ludwig Wittgenstein *Philosophical Investigations*
• Walter Piston Sixth Symphony
1956 • Elvis Presley *Love Me Tender*
• Transatlantic telephone service inaugurated
• John Osborne *Look Back in Anger*
1957 • Russia launches the unmanned *Sputnik I* and *II*
• Jack Kerouac *On The Road*
• Samuel Beckett *Endgame*
1958 • Hovercraft invented in UK
• USA launches *Vanguard* and *Explorer* satellites
• First US nuclear submarine passes under North Pole
• Boris Pasternak *Dr Zhivago*
• J K Galbraith *The Affluent Society*
• Harold Pinter *The Birthday Party*
1959 • USSR rocket begins orbit round Sun
• Russian satellite photographs back of the Moon
• Billy Wilder produces *Some Like It Hot* starring Marilyn Monroe

EUROPE

Jan '60 ● USSR reduces armed forces by 1.2 million to 2.4 million
Apr '60 ● Completion of collectivization in East Germany
Aug '60 ● Cyprus proclaimed independent republic
Aug '61 ● Berlin Wall erected to separate East and West Berlin
Nov '61 ● Portugal institutes a common market with its overseas territories
Mar '62 ● Evian Agreement ends Algerian War: France grants independence to Algeria
Nov '62 ● Greece joins EEC as associate member
Feb '63 ● Geneva disarmament talks
Feb '64 ● Heavy fighting between Greeks and Turks in Cyprus
Oct '64 ● Harold Wilson leads Labour Party to victory in British General Election
Oct '64 ● Khrushchev falls from power and is succeeded by Alexei Kosygin and Leonid Brezhnev

Jan '65 ● Prime Ministers of Ireland and Northern Ireland meet for first time in 40 years
Nov '65 ● Death penalty for murder abolished in Britain
Jan '66 ● Britain imposes trade sanctions on Rhodesia
Mar '67 ● First French nuclear-powered submarine launched
Apr '67 ● Military coup in Greece: King Constantine goes into exile in December
Jan '68 ● Alexander Dubček begins reforms in Czechoslovakia – the 'Prague Spring'
May '68 ● Student riots in Paris and Nanterre and serious strikes throughout France: French Assembly dissolved in Paris
Aug '68 ● Warsaw Pact troops occupy Czechoslovakia and halt 'Prague Spring'
Oct '68 ● Riots in Londonderry by civil rights demonstrators
Jan '69 ● Martial law proclaimed in Spain following riots and student unrest
Apr '69 ● Riots in Londonderry and Belfast involving Catholics and Protestants: Army ordered to guard key installations
June '69 ● Georges Pompidou elected President of France after resignation of General de Gaulle (Apr)
Oct '69 ● Willy Brandt becomes Chancellor of West Germany

June '70 ● Conservatives win British General Election and Edward Heath becomes Prime Minister (to 1974)
Oct '70 ● Major British oil find in North Sea
Dec '70 ● State of emergency in Spain following demonstrations and strikes by Basque separatists
Feb '72 ● IRA blow up British Embassy in Dublin
Mar '72 ● Parliament of Northern Ireland taken over by British government
Sept '72 ● Beginning of 'Cod War' – Iceland unilaterally extends fishing limits from 12 to 50 miles: resisted by Britain
Oct '72 ● At Munich Olympic Games, Palestinian guerrillas kill two members of Israeli team and take nine hostages
Aug '73 ● Greece proclaimed republic with George Papadopoulos as President
Apr '74 ● Left-wing coup in Portugal
July '74 ● President Makarios of Cyprus overthrown in military coup: Turks invade island
Nov '74 ● End of military dictatorship in Greece: democratic elections lead to Constantine Karamanlis becoming Prime Minister

AMERICAS

Jan '60 ● USA protests at expropriation of American property in Cuba and places embargo on shipments to Cuba (Oct)
Nov '60 ● John F Kennedy (Democrat) elected President of USA
Jan '61 ● USA breaks off diplomatic relations with Cuba
Feb '61 ● Large-scale economic and military aid agreed by USSR for Cuba
Apr '61 ● US-backed Cuban exiles, led by Jose Cardona, attempt unsuccessful invasion of Cuba at Bay of Pigs
Oct '62 ● Cuban missile crisis: US navy blockades Cuba to prevent further imports of Soviet missiles and USSR removes nuclear missiles from Cuba
Aug '63 ● Nuclear Test Ban Treaty signed by USA, USSR and Britain
Nov '63 ● President Kennedy assassinated: Vice-President Lyndon B Johnson takes over
Oct '64 ● Martin Luther King awarded Nobel Peace Prize
Nov '64 ● Lyndon Johnson elected US President in landslide victory: pledges 'Great Society' expansion of social welfare provisions

Feb '65 ● Malcolm X, Black Muslim leader, assassinated
Feb '65 ● Martin Luther King arrested in Dallas
Mar '65 ● Civil Rights march from Selma to Montgomery, Alabama: Ku Klux Klan shootings in Selma
Apr '65 ● Military junta deposes civilian government in Dominican Republic: USA sends marines to prevent establishment of communist government
Oct '65 ● Demonstrations in USA against American involvement in Vietnam War
May '66 ● British Guiana becomes independent as Guyana
June '66 ● Joaquin Balaguer elected President of Dominican Republic
July '66 ● Race riots in Chicago, Cleveland and Brooklyn, USA
Feb '67 ● General Somoza Junior, elected President of Nicaragua
Oct '67 ● 'Che' Guevara killed by Bolivian troops while waging guerrilla campaign in Andes
Apr '68 ● Pierre Trudeau (Liberal) becomes Prime Minister of Canada
Apr '68 ● Martin Luther King assassinated
June '68 ● Senator Robert Kennedy assassinated in Los Angeles
Nov '68 ● Richard Nixon (Republican) elected President of USA
Sept '69 ● President Salinas of Bolivia overthrown by General Ovando

Sept '70 ● Salvador Allende elected President of Chile heading Marxist government
Apr '71 ● President Duvalier of Haiti dies: succeeded by his son Jean-Claude Duvalier
Dec '71 ● USA devalues dollar
May '72 ● SALT I agreements signed in Moscow by Nixon and Brezhnev
June '72 ● Beginning of 'Watergate' affair with arrest of five men inside Democratic National HQ in Washington
Nov '72 ● President Nixon re-elected President of USA
Jan '73 ● USA withdraws remaining combat troops from Vietnam after cease-fire agreement
Jan '73 ● Watergate trial opens in Washington
Apr '73 ● President Nixon's chief advisers resign over Watergate bugging
Sept '73 ● Military coup in Chile: President Allende killed and General Pinochet takes over power with military government
Sept '73 ● Juan Perón re-elected President of Argentina
July '74 ● Juan Perón dies: his wife Isabel Perón succeeds
Aug '74 ● President Nixon resigns over Watergate affair to avoid impeachment: succeeded by Vice-President Ford

AFRICA, ASIA, AUSTRALASIA

Sept '60 • OPEC (Organization of Petroleum Exporting Countries) instituted in Baghdad
July '62 • Algeria becomes independent from France
Oct '62 • Uganda becomes independent from Britain
Oct '62 • China attacks India: ceasefire (in Nov)
May '63 • Organization of African Unity founded at conference in Addis Ababa
June '63 • Civil War in Iraq between Arabs and Kurds
Nov '63 • Military coup in Iraq
Apr '64 • Ian Smith becomes Prime Minister of Southern Rhodesia
Apr '64 • Tanganyika and Zanzibar united (known as Tanzania from Oct)
June '64 • Nelson Mandela and seven other black leaders sentenced to life imprisonment in South Africa
Aug '64 • North Vietnamese torpedo boats attack US warships in Gulf of Tonkin
Oct '64 • Northern Rhodesia becomes independent as Zambia with Dr Kenneth Kaunda as its first President

Mar '65 • Escalation of war in Vietnam as US ground forces sent in to aid South Vietnam
Apr '65 • Hostilities between Pakistan and India over Kashmir (to Sept)
Nov '65 • Ian Smith unilaterally declares Rhodesia independent
Jan '66 • Mrs Indira Gandhi becomes Prime Minister of India
Jan '66 • Military coup in Nigeria
Feb '66 • Milton Obote seizes power in Uganda
Aug '66 • 'Cultural Revolution' begins in China
Sept '66 • Dr Verwoerd, South African Prime Minister, assassinated: John Vorster succeeds
May '67 • Egypt closes Gulf of Aqaba to Israel
May '67 • Civil war in Nigeria with proclamation of independent republic of Biafra
June '67 • Six-day War between Israel and neighbouring Arab states
Nov '67 • People's Republic of South Yemen proclaimed in Aden
Sept '68 • Swaziland becomes an independent constitutional monarchy under King Sobhoza II
Mar '69 • Golda Meir becomes Prime Minister of Israel (to 1974)
July '69 • North Vietnam rejects US peace proposal
Sept '69 • King Idris I of Libya overthrown in military coup led by Colonel Moamer Gaddafi

Jan '70 • Biafran civil war ends in Nigeria
July '70 • Aswan High Dam begins operation
Sept '70 • General Nasser dies and is succeeded by Anwar Sadat (Oct)
Oct '70 • Kingdom of Cambodia becomes the Khmer Republic
Jan '71 • General Idi Amin leads military coup in Uganda
Mar '71 • East Pakistan declared independent as Bangladesh
Apr '72 • 50,000 killed in attempted coup in Burundi
Sept '72 • General Amin gives 8,000 Asians 48 hours to leave Uganda: European missionaries expelled from Uganda
Oct '73 • Yom Kippur 'Day of Atonement' War between Arabs and Israel begins: Sinai and Golan Heights invaded
Oct '73 • Cut in Arab oil production and increased prices cause oil crisis in USA and Europe
Apr '74 • Golda Meir resigns as Prime Minister of Israel and is succeeded by Yitzak Rabin
Sept '74 • Emperor Haile Selassie deposed in Ethiopia

SCIENCE & CULTURE

1960 • R D Laing *The Divided Self*
• Heart pacemaker developed
• Harper Lee *To Kill a Mockingbird*
1961 • Major Yuri Gagarin is the first man to travel in space round Earth
• Joseph Heller *Catch 22*
• Leonard Bernstein *West Side Story*
1962 • Second Vatican Council, attended by over 2,000 bishops, opened in Rome
• Benjamin Britten *War Requiem*
• US manned space flights
• Ken Kelsey *One Flew over the Cuckoo's Nest*
• Alexander Solzhenitsyn *One Day in the Life of Ivan Denisovich*
1963 • Vaccine for measles perfected
• Roy Lichtenstein *Whaam!*
• The Beatles *She Loves You*
1964 • China explodes an atom bomb
• Close-up photos of Moon's surface taken by *Ranger VII*
• Saul Bellow *Herzog*

1965 • US spacecraft lands on Moon: Edward White first man to walk in space
• Mao Zedong (Mao Tse-tung) *The Thoughts of Chairman Mao*
• Mary Quant introduces the miniskirt
1966 • Russian and American spacecraft made soft landings on the Moon
• Michael Tippett *The Vision of St Augustine*
• Metropolitan Opera House opens in New York
1967 • First public flight of Franco–British supersonic aircraft, *Concorde*, from Toulouse
• World's first heart-transplant carried out in South Africa by Christian Barnaard
• Desmond Morris *The Naked Ape*
• Karlheinz Stockhausen *Anthems*
1968 • Flower power in San Francisco
• Stanley Kubrick *2001, A Space Odyssey*
• Gabriel García Marquez *A Hundred Years of Solitude*
• Mies van der Rohe, National Gallery, Berlin
1969 • Neil Armstrong is first man to walk on Moon
• Fertilization in a test tube of a human ovum in Cambridge
• Woodstock pop music festival
• Vladimir Nabokov *Ada*

1970 • David Hockney *Mr & Mrs Ossie Clark and Percy*
• Germaine Greer *The Female Eunuch*
1971 • First microprocessor produced in California, USA
• Luchino Visconti directs *Death in Venice*
1972 • Liza Minnelli stars in *Cabaret*
• Steve Reich *Drumming*
1973 • Bernardo Bertolucci *Last Tango In Paris*
• Alexander Solzhenitsyn *The Gulag Archipelago*
• Ernst Schumacher *Small is Beautiful*
1974 • Philip Larkin *High Windows*
• Harrison Birtwistle *Imaginary Landscape*

EUROPE

Feb '75 • Turkish Cypriot federated state proclaimed
Nov '75 • General Franco of Spain dies: inauguration of King Juan Carlos I
Apr '76 • James Callaghan (Labour) becomes British Prime Minister
Apr '77 • Communist party legalized in Spain
June '77 • Leonid Brezhnev becomes President of USSR
Sept '77 • Catalans granted autonomy within Spanish state
Aug '78 • Pope Paul VI dies: John Paul I elected, dies (Sept): John Paul II is elected in October, the first non-Italian Pope for 450 years
May '79 • British Conservative Party wins General Election bringing Margaret Thatcher to power as first woman Prime Minister of Britain
June '79 • First direct elections to European Parliament
Aug '79 • Earl Mountbatten of Burma murdered in Ireland by IRA
Oct '79 • NATO reaffirms decision to deploy long-range nuclear weapons in Europe
Dec '79 • Soviet troops begin invasion of Afghanistan

May '80 • President Tito of Yugoslavia dies
July '80 • Olympic Games in Moscow boycotted by over 30 countries as protest against Soviet invasion of Afghanistan
Sept '80 • Solidarity union founded in Poland under Lech Walesa after two months of strikes
May '81 • François Mitterrand elected President of France
Dec '81 • Martial law declared in Poland
Oct '82 • Solidarity outlawed by Polish government
Oct '82 • Helmut Kohl elected Chancellor of West Germany
Nov '82 • President Brezhnev dies: Yuri Andropov succeeds
July '83 • Poland suspends martial law
Feb '84 • Yuri Andropov dies and is succeeded by Konstantin Chernenko

Mar '85 • Konstantin Chernenko dies and is succeeded by Mikhail Gorbachev as party general secretary
Nov '85 • Anglo-Irish agreement on Northern Ireland
Oct '87 • 'Black Monday' on London Stock Market: worst day for shares this century
Dec '88 • Bomb kills 259 on Pan-Am flight over Lockerbie in Scotland
Aug '89 • Tadeusz Mazowiecki becomes first non-communist Prime Minister of Poland since Second World War
Sept '89 • Mass exodus from East Germany as opening of Hungarian border allows entry to West Germany
Oct '89 • Erich Honecker, East German Communist Party leader forced to resign
Nov '89 • Berlin Wall comes down
Nov '89 • Czechoslovak Communist Party leaders resign
Dec '89 • Nicolae Ceausescu, Romanian dictator, executed
Mar '90 • Lithuania declares its independence from USSR
May '90 • Free elections in Romania
June '90 • Free elections in Czechoslovakia and Bulgaria
Oct '90 • Unification of East and West Germany
Nov '90 • Margaret Thatcher resigns as British prime minister: John Major succeeds
Jan '91 • Soviet troops seize nationalist defence headquarters in Lithuania, killing unarmed civilians
Mar '91 • Gorbachev seeks support for a 'renewed federation of equal sovereign republics' in Soviet referendum

AMERICAS

Nov '75 • Suriname gains independence from the Netherlands
Jan '76 • Military coup in Ecuador
Mar '76 • President Isabel Perón of Argentina overthrown: succeeded by General Videla
Nov '76 • Jimmy Carter (Democrat) elected US President
Nov '78 • Dominica gains independence from Britain
Feb '79 • USA withdraws support from President Somoza in Nicaragua
June '79 • SALT II Treaty signed by Carter and Brezhnev in Geneva
July '79 • President Somoza resigns and goes into exile: Sandinista government in Nicaragua sworn in

Oct '80 • Peace and border treaty between El Salvador and Honduras
Nov '80 • Ronald Reagan (Republican) elected President of USA
Jan '82 • Honduras ends military rule and installs President Cordova
Apr '82 • Argentina invades Falkland Islands
May '82 • British forces land on East Falklands and Argentinian forces surrender (in June)
Oct '83 • Maurice Bishop, prime minister of Grenada, overthrown and murdered: US military intervention follows
Dec '83 • Military junta dissolved in Argentina
Feb '84 • Pierre Trudeau resigns as Canadian Prime Minister
Nov '84 • Sandinistas led by Daniel Ortega win elections in Nicaragua

Jan '85 • Ronald Reagan begins second term as US President
May '85 • US trade embargo against Nicaragua
Feb '86 • Haitians overthrow President Duvalier ('Baby Doc') after years of oppressive rule
Jan '87 • Ecuadorean President and 30 others kidnapped by air force commandos demanding release of rebel leader
July '87 • Colonel Oliver North and Admiral Poindexter give testimonies over sales of arms to Iran and transfer of funds to Nicaraguan Contras
Dec '87 • USA and USSR sign historic INF (Intermediate-range Nuclear Forces) treaty to reduce nuclear arsenals
July '88 • 200,000 march on National Palace in Mexico City to protest against fraudulent elections in which Salinas de Gortari becomes President
Nov '88 • George Bush (Republican) wins US Presidency
Dec '89 • US invasion of Panama
Jan '90 • USA begins to reduce defence budget and withdraw troops from Europe and elsewhere
Feb '90 • Sandinista government in Nicaragua defeated in general elections
July '90 • Attempted coup in Trinidad and Tobago by Muslim extremists

AFRICA, ASIA, AUSTRALASIA

Apr '75 • Vietnam war ends with South falling to communists
Nov '75 • Angola gains its independence from Portugal: civil war breaks out between rival independence movements
Sept '76 • Death of Mao Zedong
Mar '77 • Indira Gandhi resigns and is replaced by Morarji Desai
July '77 • General Zia becomes President of Pakistan after military coup
Sept '77 • Steve Biko dies in South African jail
Apr '78 • President of Afghanistan overthrown: left-wing Democratic Republic established
Sept '78 • Camp David summit between Anwar Sadat of Egypt, Menachem Begin of Israel and Jimmy Carter of the USA
Dec '78 • Vietnamese invade Cambodia and capture Phnom Penh (Jan '79)
Jan '79 • Shah of Iran goes into exile
Feb '79 • Ayatollah Khomeini returns to Iran from exile in Paris and Iran adopts Islamic constitution (Dec)
Mar '79 • Egypt and Israel sign peace treaty ending state of war existing since 1948
July '79 • Former President Bhutto executed in Pakistan
Dec '79 • Soviet troops airlifted into Afghanistan

Apr '80 • Republic of Zimbabwe declared independent
Sept '80 • Conflict escalates between Iran and Iraq
Nov '80 • Trial of 'Gang of Four' in Beijing (to Dec)
Jan '81 • Iran releases American Embassy hostages after 444 days
Oct '81 • President Sadat of Egypt assassinated: Hosni Mubarak succeeds
June '82 • Israeli forces invade Lebanon
Sept '82 • Massacre of Palestinians in Beirut refugee camps
Sept '82 • President Bashir Gemayel of Lebanon assassinated in Beirut
June '83 • Yasser Arafat expelled from Syria
Oct '84 • Indian Prime Minister Indira Gandhi assassinated by Sikh bodyguards

Apr '86 • US planes bomb five sites in Libya in retaliation for Berlin disco bombing
Jan '87 • Truce declared in Afghan war
May '88 • Soviets begin withdrawal from Afghanistan
Aug '88 • Ceasefire agreed to in Iran–Iraq war
Nov '88 • Benazir Bhutto claims victory in Pakistani general elections
Dec '88 • Treaty signed agreeing to withdrawal of Cuban troops from Angola
May '89 • Mass demonstrations for democracy by Chinese students in Tiananmen Square, Beijing, ends in massacre (June)
Sept '89 • Vietnamese troops complete withdrawal from Cambodia after 10-year occupation
Feb '90 • South African President, F W de Klerk lifts ban on ANC and South African Communist party and promises reforms to dismantle apartheid
Feb '90 • Nelson Mandela, deputy leader of the ANC, released after 26 years in prison
Feb '90 • Civil war breaks out in Liberia
Aug '90 • Iraq invades Kuwait; US and allied countries respond by sending forces to the Gulf region
Jan '91 • Operation Desert Storm commences: Arab and Western allied airforces attack strategic targets in Iraq; allied land offensive liberates Kuwait (Feb) and civil war erupts in Iraq

SCIENCE & CULTURE

1975 • Anthony Powell *A Dance to the Music of Time*
       • Gabriel García Marquez *Autumn of The Patriarch*
       • Stephen Spielberg directs *Jaws*
       • US/Soviet astronauts link up in space
1976 • First commercial *Concorde* flight
1977 • Pompidou Centre opens in Paris
       • George Lucas directs *Star Wars*
       • Woody Allen directs and stars in *Annie Hall*
1978 • World's first 'test-tube baby' is born in Oldham, England
1979 • Nobel Peace Prize awarded to Mother Teresa of Calcutta
       • Two Voyager spacecrafts fly past Jupiter sending back close-up views
       • James Baldwin *Just Above My Head*
       • Francis Ford Coppola directs *Apocalypse Now*

1980 • Scientists at Harvard University synthesize interferon, a natural virus-fighting agent, by genetic engineering
       • WHO announces elimination in world of smallpox
1981 • French high-speed train makes record journey from Paris to Lyon in 2 hrs 40 mins
       • US Space Shuttle is launched: first spacecraft to be used more than once
1983 • The Compact Disc makes first appearance
       • Stephen Spielberg directs *ET*
       • Richard Nobel drives *Thrust* at 633.46 mph (1019.46 kmh)
1984 • AIDS virus is discovered
       • 15-day-old baby is given baboon's heart in California
       • Milan Kundera *The Unbearable Lightness of Being*

1985 • Pierre Boulez *Third Mallarmé Improvisation*
       • Live Aid concert at Wembley
1986 • Andrei Sakharov, physicist and Nobel Peace Prize winner, is released from exile in Gorky
       • First non-stop around the world flight completed by Dick Rutan's *Voyager*
       • Sight of Halley's Comet (last seen in 1910)
       • Nobel Prize awarded to African writer, Wole Soyinka
1988 • Russian Orthodox Church celebrates its millennium
       • USA revives space programme with successful launch of Shuttle, *Discovery*
       • Stephen Hawking *A Brief History of Time*
       • Salman Rushdie *The Satanic Verses*
       • 'Turin Shroud' pronounced of medieval origin
1989 • 12 years after launch *Voyager 2* spacecraft reaches Neptune
       • Michael Tippett *New Year*

AN UNCERTAIN FUTURE

Dramatic reversal in America's fortunes has increased global economic instability.

From 1945 until the late 1960s the United States dominated the world economy. By the early 1970s, however, its economy began to falter. The heavy expenditures on the Vietnam War and President Johnson's programme of reforms, with little corresponding increase in taxation, and the effects of the OPEC oil price rises of the early 1970s resulted in mounting budgetary deficits. Imports began to exceed exports for the first time since the 1890s. Inflation leapt from 3 per cent in 1967 to 12 per cent in 1974 while unemployment doubled to 6 per cent in 1970. Productivity also declined. The United States was experiencing the phenomenon known as 'stagflation' – high levels of inflation coupled with recession. The Nixon Administration raised interest rates in an effort to reduce the supply of money, which triggered a severe fall in stock market prices. In 1971 the US government suspended the convertibility of the dollar into gold, and the dollar fell in value on the world exchanges.

Externally American exporters faced rising competition for their products from new centres of economic strength. West Germany, Japan, Taiwan and South Korea had modernized their economies during the 1950s and 1960s and had achieved astonishing growth rates, especially in such modern industries as electronics, micro-chip and computer technology, motor car and truck manufacturing, shipbuilding and chemicals where formerly the United States had been pre-eminent. Internally many American manufacturers were driven into insolvency by the flood of imports from the newly developed Pacific Rim countries, whose high quality ensured that they found a ready market among American consumers. During the 1980s the Reagan Administration promoted tax cuts as a means of increasing incentives to greater efficiency and because it believed that the growth at the top would have a 'trickle down' effect on all sections of the economy. The deficits, which had been mounting since the 1970s, assumed astronomic proportions as the expansion of the American armed forces placed a further heavy strain on the economy. In 1982 the deficit was $110.6 billion dollars and the level of the national debt had reached $1 trillion. The United States was hit by a further recession in 1982, although

after 1984 there was a slight recovery partially attributable to a fall in oil prices. President Bush has made a start in tackling this huge deficit by imposing a one-year freeze in real growth for defence in the 1990 financial year and has cut the defence budget by a further $3,700 million.

This dramatic reversal in America's economic fortunes has resulted in increasing global economic instability. The sudden New York stock market collapse in 1987 precipitated a world-wide panic, although the markets have since managed a slow recovery. Fears have been expressed that the United States might take some dramatic step, such as imposing a wide range of import controls, in an effort to solve its economic problems, which would encourage retaliation by other countries and a dramatic shrinking of international trade in an already volatile situation.

The European Revival

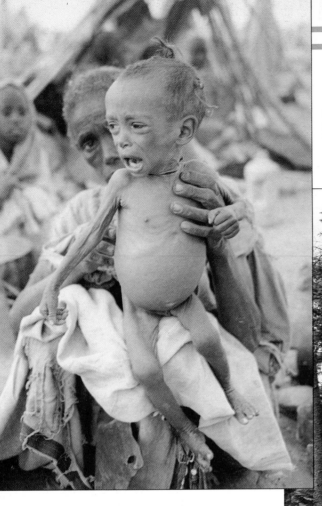

◀ In the 1980s thousands suffered and many died as a result of severe drought and famine in Ethiopia. Civil war in the northern provinces hampered relief work.

▼ Trees dying in Vosges Forest, France. It is believed that acid rain, created by the emission of nitrogen oxides and sulphur dioxide from power stations and factories, may be killing the forests of Europe.

In 1945, after the war, most of the European continent was in ruins. Roads, railways and factories had been damaged or destroyed during the fighting, and agricultural production had virtually ceased. From 1948, however, Western European recovery, which was already slowly underway, was assisted by the Marshall Plan or European Recovery Programme, whereby the United States provided dollar aid to overcome acute balance of payments difficulties in Europe. Under the Plan, the Organization of European Economic Unity (OEEC) assessed each country's needs for loans and credits. The Soviet Union and its satellites refused to participate. By 1952, when the Programme ended, European industrial production had increased by 35 per cent, and agricultural production by 10 per cent, over pre-war levels.

Economic experts recognized that West European recovery depended on the revival of the West German economy. When West Germany emerged as a separate political entity after the setting up of the Federal Republic and the election of Konrad Adenauer's pro-Western Christian Democratic Party in 1949, West Germany received Marshall Aid. Soon West Germany's trade and industry recovered from the effects of the war, and by the end of 1949 productivity had reached 1939 levels. During the 1950s West Germany became

one of the world's major industrial powers. However, the European Recovery Programme did not lead to European economic integration as many European federalists like Jean Monnet of France and Paul Henri Spaak of Belgium had anticipated. In May 1950 the French government proposed the pooling of Franco–German iron and steel production and in the following year the European Coal and Steel Community, consisting of France, West Germany, Italy, Belgium, the Netherlands and Luxembourg, came into existence. This supranational body – the precursor of the more far-reaching European Economic Community established in 1957 – supervised coal and iron production and sought the removal of internal customs barriers and quota systems. Britain, anxious not to prejudice its economic independence or its ties with the Commonwealth and the United States, refused to join, convinced that in any case the experiment would fail. During the 1950s Western Europe enjoyed an unprecedented economic boom, centred on the northern French and Ruhr industrial areas and on northern Italy. While the British economy also improved during this period, it slipped behind its European competitors, especially West Germany, and was afflicted with high inflation and frequent balance of payments crises.

American and West European banks have contributed to this problem by lending large sums of money to Third World and Eastern European countries during the 1970s. Much of this money was spent on grandiose and unprofitable projects and by the 1980s many of these debtor countries were finding it impossible to pay even the interest charges on these loans. West European banks had used the inflow of profits from the Middle East oil producers to lend money to Eastern European countries to enable them to purchase Western technology and Western industrial products in order to improve their economic prospects. With the fall in world trade these countries could not finance their growing trade imbalance with the West and had to borrow more money for this purpose: their indebtedness rose from $19 billion in 1975 to $62 billion in 1981. Fears that one of the debtor countries might default on its loans, and so begin a chain reaction, have led the banks to agree to the re-scheduling of their debts and to arrange fresh loans in order to re-pay their existing obligations which, in a decade of high interest rates, increases their predicament and merely postpones any effective solution to the problem.

▲ Hectic trading at the Tokyo stock exchange in 1987, the year of the New York stock market collapse which caused panic in markets world-wide.

The Soviet economy, which since 1945 had largely been insulated from the global economy, also faces many problems. Heavy defence expenditures, shortfalls in agricultural production necessitating large grain imports from the United States, financial aid to overseas countries, the costs of the war in Afghanistan and the bureaucracy, inefficiency and corruption which permeates the entire economic and political system led Mikhail Gorbachev to promise major structural reforms designed to reduce the increasing budget deficit and at the same time to switch resources from heavy industry and the military to consumer production. In 1988 the Soviet economy grew by only 1.5 per cent having also performed poorly in 1987, thus placing Gorbachev's reform programme in jeopardy. In 1989 Gorbachev announced defence cuts of 14.4 per cent over the next two years.

Technological change

Since 1945 the world has been transformed by great technological change. New industries – notably those based on computers – have grown quickly, while old industries, such as car manufacturing, have been revolutionized by the use of automation and robotics. Air travel has almost completely replaced ocean liners as a means of overseas travel, largely as a result of the development of jet-propelled aircraft during the 1950s, while, in the developed world at least, people's lives have been radically altered by a range of new electrical and electronic goods for both domestic and entertainment purposes. Two aspects of technological change since 1945 stand out in particular.

On 4 October 1957 the Soviet Union launched the world's first artificial satellite, *Sputnik 1*. This was the beginning of a space exploration race between the Soviet Union and the United States that resulted in America landing two men on the moon on 20 July 1969, and both countries exploring the outer planets and the rest of the solar system during the 1980s and 1990s. The United States launched its first satellite, *Explorer 1*, in 1958, France its first in 1965, Japan and China in 1970 and Britain in 1971. In total, more than 1,700 satellite and space probes have been launched over the last three decades, designed chiefly for scientific, meterological, photographic and navigational research, reconnaissance purposes, and the provision of world-wide telephone and television links.

Nuclear power has been developed from research on the atomic bomb since 1945, with nuclear energy

▲ The space shuttle *Columbia* takes off from Kennedy Space Centre.

▼ The nuclear reactor at Chernobyl after it exploded in 1986.

being harnessed to produce electricity. While a number of nuclear power plants have been constructed throughout the world, progress in the generation of cheap electricity has been slow. Disasters like the explosion of a nuclear power plant at Chernobyl in the Soviet Union in 1986, which caused widespread radioactive contamination, and the problem of nuclear waste disposal have alarmed many conservationists about the dangers to people and the environment of continuing nuclear development.

International Economic Groupings

GREENLAND
(Denmark)

NORWAY FINLAND
ICELAND SWEDEN

CANADA

U.S.S.R.

U.K
DENMARK
IRELAND
NETH EAST POLAND
GERMANY
BELGIUM WEST CZECHOSLOVAKIA
LUX AUSTRIA HUNGARY
SWITZ ROMANIA
FRANCE YUGOSLAVIA
ITALY ALBANIA BULGARIA
PORTUGAL ceased participation
SPAIN 1961
GREECE

UNITED STATES

TURKEY

CYPRUS SYRIA
LEBANON IRAQ
ISRAEL JORDAN

AFGHANISTA

IRAN

MEXICO

MOROCCO TUNISIA
KUWAIT PAKIS
WESTERN ALGERIA LIBYA SAUDI QATAR 1961
SAHARA 1969 1962 EGYPT ARABIA U.A.E.
1967 OMAN

CUBA
1972
DOMINICAN
REPUBLIC
HAITI
BELIZE
GUATEMALA
HONDURAS
EL SALVADOR NICARAGUA
COSTA RICA
PANAMA

VENEZUELA
GUYANA
SURINAME
FR. GUIANA

MAURITANIA
MALI NIGER
CHAD SUDAN
YEMEN S. YEMEN
DJIBOUTI
SENEGAL
GAMBIA BURKINA
GUINEA-BISSAU BENIN
GUINEA TOGO NIGERIA
SIERRA LEONE IVORY 1973
COAST CENT
LIBERIA AFR REP ETHIOPIA
GHANA CAMEROON SOMALIA
EQ GUINEA
GABON CONGO UGANDA
1975 RWANDA KENYA
BURUNDI
ZAIRE TANZANIA

COLOMBIA

ECUADOR
1973

PERU

BRAZIL

ATLANTIC
OCEAN

INDIA

PACIFIC
OCEAN

BOLIVIA

PARAGUAY

ANGOLA
MALAWI
ZAMBIA
MADAGASCAR
ZIMBABWE
NAMIBIA MOZAMBIQUE
BOTSWANA
SWAZILAND
LESOTHO
SOUTH AFRICA

CHILE
URUGUAY

ARGENTINA

COMECON, founded 1949

OPEC, founded 1960

OECD, founded 1961

ASEAN, founded 1967

1986   Year of joining organization

In October 1990 East and West
Germany were reunited as a
single country within the EC

NORWAY
FINLAND
associate member
1961-85

SWEDEN

IRELAND
1973
UNITED DENMARK
KINGDOM 1973
1973 NETH.
WEST
BELGIUM GERMANY
LUX
FRANCE
SWITZ AUSTRIA
applied for EC
membership 1989

EEC, founded 1958
(from 1967, EC)

EFTA, founded 1960

1970   Year of joining organization if
later than date of foundation

PORTUGAL
1986
SPAIN
1986
ITALY

TURKEY
applied for EC
membership 1987
GREECE
1981
Athens

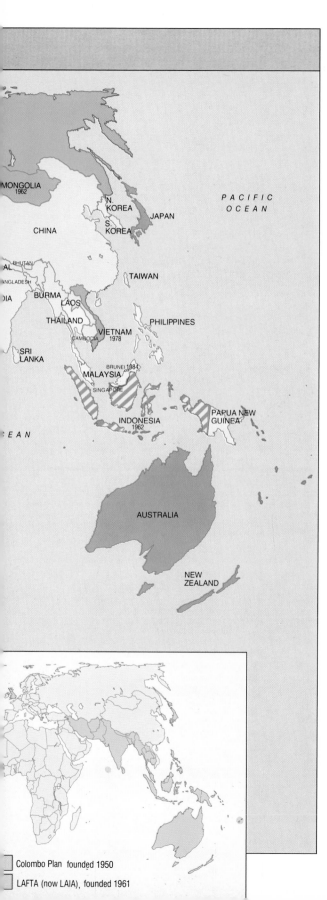

MONGOLIA
1962

N. KOREA

JAPAN

CHINA

S. KOREA

PACIFIC
OCEAN

BHUTAN

AL

ANGLADESH

TAIWAN

DIA

BURMA

LAOS

THAILAND

PHILIPPINES

VIETNAM
1978

CAMBODIA

SRI
LANKA

BRUNEI 1984

MALAYSIA

SINGAPORE

EAN

INDONESIA
1962

PAPUA NEW
GUINEA

AUSTRALIA

NEW
ZEALAND

Colombo Plan founded 1950

LAFTA (now LAIA), founded 1961

The two most influential economic groupings set up since the Second World War are the European Economic Community (EEC) and the Organization of Petroleum Exporting Countries (OPEC). The EEC (or Common Market) was established under the Treaty of Rome in 1957. The six member countries agreed to abolish their internal tariffs and institute a common external tariff within 15 years. Britain refused to join on the grounds that the common external tariff would destroy her Commonwealth trade. In 1959 Britain formed the European Free Trade Association (EFTA), initially with Norway, Sweden, Denmark, Switzerland, Austria and Portugal, to abolish internal tariffs on industrial goods, but with no common external tariff. During the 1960s, however, the EEC became increasingly successful while the British economy continued to falter. France twice refused to allow Britain to join the EEC (known as the European Community since 1967), but it eventually became a member, along with Denmark and Ireland, in January 1973; Spain, Portugal and Greece joined in the 1980s. A similar regional grouping of Eastern European countries and the Soviet Union – COMECON, later incorporating Vietnam, Mongolia and Cuba – was founded in 1949 and a Latin American Free Trade Association (renamed Latin American Integration Association, LAIA, in 1981) and a Central American Common Market were founded in 1960, all of which attempted to emulate the EEC.

The Organization of Arab Petroleum Exporting Countries, (OAPEC), part of OPEC, first met in 1971 but was strengthened by the Middle East war of 1973 when, in protest against United States and Dutch arms supplies to Israel, it cut off oil supplies to those two countries and raised oil prices generally by 70 per cent. The result was a serious recession in Western economies and a major effort was made to develop alternative sources of energy.

Groupings which exist to further development in the Third World include the Organization for Economic Cooperation and Development (OECD), founded in 1960 by the USA, Canada and 18 European states with the aim of increasing world trade and providing financial security. The Colombo Plan arose out of a desire of the old, white Commonwealth of Britain, Australia, New Zealand and Canada to help the emerging new nations of the Indian subcontinent and elsewhere. It was founded in 1950 and soon attracted American support, evolving into a Marshall Plan for Asia. In 1967, five of its main beneficiaries – Indonesia, Malaysia, Philippines, Singapore and Thailand – grouped together in the Association of South-East Asian Nations (ASEAN), designed to promote regional progress and stability.

North and South

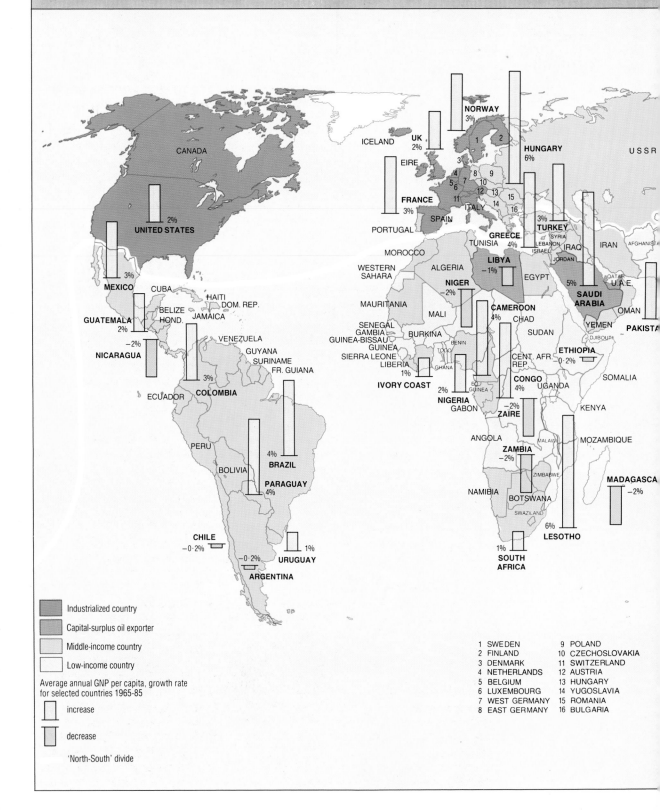

CANADA

ICELAND

UK
2%

EIRE

NORWAY
3%

1 2
3
4 8 9
7 10
5 6 12 13
11 14 16 15

HUNGARY
6%

USSR

FRANCE
3%

SPAIN

PORTUGAL

UNITED STATES

2%

MEXICO
3%

CUBA

HAITI
DOM. REP.
BELIZE
JAMAICA
HOND.

GUATEMALA
2%

NICARAGUA
−2%

VENEZUELA

GUYANA
SURINAME
FR. GUIANA

ECUADOR

COLOMBIA
3%

PERU

BRAZIL
4%

BOLIVIA

PARAGUAY
4%

CHILE
−0·2%

ARGENTINA
−0·2%

URUGUAY
1%

MOROCCO

WESTERN
SAHARA

ALGERIA

TUNISIA

GREECE
4%

SYRIA
LEBANON
ISRAEL

TURKEY
3%

IRAQ
JORDAN

IRAN

AFGHANIST

LIBYA
−1%

EGYPT

SAUDI
ARABIA
5%

QATAR
U.A.E.

OMAN

YEMEN
DJIBOUTI

PAKISTA

MAURITANIA

MALI

NIGER
−2%

CHAD

SUDAN

ETHIOPIA
−0·2%

SOMALIA

SENEGAL
GAMBIA
GUINEA-BISSAU
GUINEA
SIERRA LEONE
LIBERIA

BURKINA

BENIN
TOGO
GHANA

CAMEROON
4%

CENT. AFR.
REP.

CONGO
4%

UGANDA

KENYA

IVORY COAST

NIGERIA
2%

GABON

EQ.
GUINEA

ZAÏRE
−2%

ANGOLA

MALAWI

ZAMBIA
−2%

MOZAMBIQUE

ZIMBABWE

MADAGASCA
−2%

NAMIBIA

BOTSWANA

SWAZILAND

LESOTHO
6%

SOUTH
AFRICA
1%

Industrialized country

Capital-surplus oil exporter

Middle-income country

Low-income country

Average annual GNP per capita, growth rate
for selected countries 1965-85

increase

decrease

'North-South' divide

1	SWEDEN	9	POLAND
2	FINLAND	10	CZECHOSLOVAKIA
3	DENMARK	11	SWITZERLAND
4	NETHERLANDS	12	AUSTRIA
5	BELGIUM	13	HUNGARY
6	LUXEMBOURG	14	YUGOSLAVIA
7	WEST GERMANY	15	ROMANIA
8	EAST GERMANY	16	BULGARIA

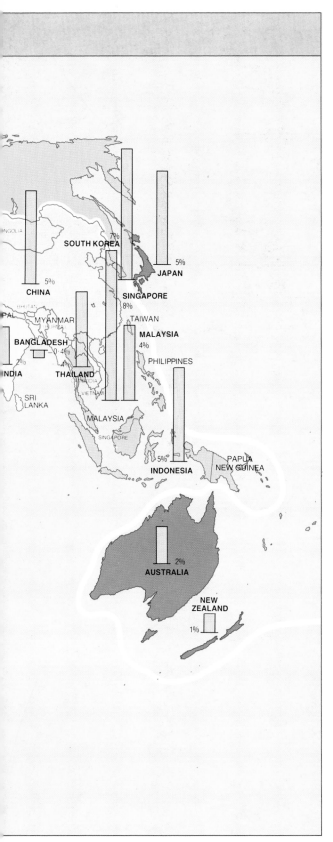

The Brandt Report (Independent Commission on International Development Issues) of 1980 divided the world economy into two. The 'North', consisting of the dominant economies of Europe, North America, the Soviet Union, Japan and Australasia, constituted 90 per cent of the world's manufacturing capacity and its multinational corporations monopolized world investment, technology and trade. The 'South', on the other hand, made up of the rest of Asia, Africa and Latin America, populated by nearly four billion people, existed on just one-fifth of the world's income. Another analysis divides the World into three: the 'First World' of the advanced capitalist economies, the 'Second World' of centrally planned economies (the Soviet bloc and China), and the 'Third World' of the developing nations. None of these definitions is entirely satisfactory since even within them there are wide variations. The Arab oil-producing countries, Taiwan, South Korea and Singapore have, for example, unlike other Third World economies, been prosperous, while American and British manufacturing output has fallen behind that of West Germany and Japan, particularly in high-technology industries.

The Third World failed to benefit from the economic boom of the 1950s and 1960s which brought the developed countries unparalleled prosperity. Furthermore, when rising prices for oil, wheat, rice and raw materials in the 1970s resulted in an economic downturn, the Third World suffered the most and the gap between the rich and poor nations widened still further. After 1960, the Third World tended to concentrate on industrialization while neglecting agriculture, so that by the 1970s many became totally dependent on food supplies from the West. Their economies were also affected by wide fluctuations in the prices of primary raw materials. In an effort to compensate for falling revenues, Third World countries borrowed heavily from Western banks during the late 1970s and rising interest rates have compounded their repayment difficulties.

In reviewing global economies, changes in gross national product are particularly significant. Middle-income countries with high growth rates are a sign of global economic development. Low-income countries with high growth rates starting from a low base, show a process of catching-up, while negative growth reflects severe problems. Growth in the industrialized countries (except Japan) is low, largely because of their high starting points.

The World Population Explosion

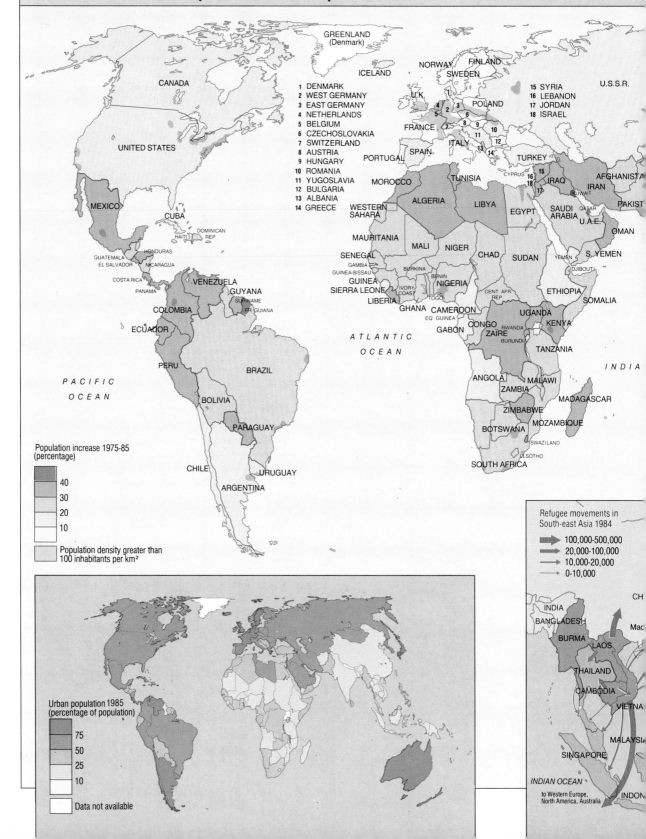

GREENLAND
(Denmark)

CANADA

NORWAY   FINLAND
SWEDEN
ICELAND

1 DENMARK
2 WEST GERMANY
3 EAST GERMANY
4 NETHERLANDS
5 BELGIUM
6 CZECHOSLOVAKIA
7 SWITZERLAND
8 AUSTRIA
9 HUNGARY
10 ROMANIA
11 YUGOSLAVIA
12 BULGARIA
13 ALBANIA
14 GREECE

15 SYRIA
16 LEBANON
17 JORDAN
18 ISRAEL

U.K.
POLAND
FRANCE
ITALY
SPAIN
PORTUGAL
TURKEY
CYPRUS
IRAQ   IRAN
KUWAIT
AFGHANISTA
PAKIST

U.S.S.R.

UNITED STATES

MEXICO
CUBA
HAITI DOMINICAN REP
GUATEMALA HONDURAS
EL SALVADOR NICARAGUA
COSTA RICA
PANAMA
VENEZUELA
GUYANA
SURINAME
FR GUIANA
COLOMBIA
ECUADOR
PERU
BRAZIL
BOLIVIA
PARAGUAY
CHILE
URUGUAY
ARGENTINA

MOROCCO
WESTERN SAHARA
MAURITANIA
SENEGAL
GAMBIA
GUINEA-BISSAU
GUINEA
SIERRA LEONE
LIBERIA
IVORY COAST
GHANA
TOGO
BENIN
NIGERIA
CAMEROON
EQ GUINEA
GABON
CONGO
ZAIRE
RWANDA
BURUNDI

TUNISIA
ALGERIA
LIBYA
EGYPT
MALI
NIGER
CHAD
SUDAN
BURKINA
CENT AFR REP
UGANDA
KENYA
TANZANIA
ANGOLA
ZAMBIA
MALAWI
ZIMBABWE
BOTSWANA
MOZAMBIQUE
SWAZILAND
LESOTHO
SOUTH AFRICA
ETHIOPIA
SOMALIA
MADAGASCAR

SAUDI ARABIA
QATAR
U.A.E.
OMAN
YEMEN
S. YEMEN
DJIBOUTI

INDIA

ATLANTIC OCEAN

PACIFIC OCEAN

INDIA

Population increase 1975-85 (percentage)

- 40
- 30
- 20
- 10

Population density greater than 100 inhabitants per km²

Urban population 1985 (percentage of population)

- 75
- 50
- 25
- 10

Data not available

Refugee movements in South-east Asia 1984

- 100,000-500,000
- 20,000-100,000
- 10,000-20,000
- 0-10,000

CH
INDIA
BANGLADESH
BURMA
LAOS
THAILAND
CAMBODIA
VIETNA
MALAYSI
SINGAPORE
Mac

INDIAN OCEAN
to Western Europe,
North America, Australia
INDON

MONGOLIA

CHINA

N. KOREA

S. KOREA

JAPAN

PACIFIC
OCEAN

TAIWAN

AL

ANGLADESH

DIA

BURMA

LAOS

THAILAND

VIETNAM

CAMBODIA

PHILIPPINES

SRI
LANKA

EAN

MALAYSIA

BRUNEI

SINGAPORE

INDONESIA

PAPUA NEW
GUINEA

AUSTRALIA

NEW
ZEALAND

m

ls

1500

1000

JAPAN

SOUTH CHINA
SEA

TAIWAN

Kong

PHILIPPINES

PACIFIC OCEAN

NEI

Country
of origin

Country
of asylum

Between 1960 and 1989 the world's population increased by more than one billion to more than five billion in 1990, largely as a result of improved health facilities and better food supplies. The United Nations has estimated that the life expectancy of individuals has increased by five years in each decade since 1945. Third World population growth has been double that of the developed West since 1950, rising from 70 per cent of the total world population in 1950 to about 75 per cent in 1985. This proportion is expected to increase in the 21st century to about 80 per cent, and world population is expected to more than double to 11.3 billion by the year 3000.

If present trends continue, by the year 2000, 48 per cent of the world's population will live in towns and cities, with the majority in Third World urban areas. Twenty-seven of the world's largest cities will be situated in the Third World against 18 in 1970. Of the world's population today 47 per cent is involved in agriculture but, of course, the proportions vary widely between the developed and developing worlds. In Africa 65 per cent of the population is engaged in agriculture, while in the United States only about 11 per cent are so employed.

There is likely to be little opportunity for emigration as an outlet for surplus populations as there had been in the 19th and early- and mid-20th centuries. During the 1950s and 1960s there was an influx of migrants to the United Kingdom from the West Indian islands and the Indian subcontinent, while Algerians went to France in search of work. During the years of economic growth in the 1960s and 1970s, countries like West Germany welcomed Greek and Turkish labour to perform tasks that the indigenous population was unwilling to perform, but during the 1970s these immigrants became increasingly unpopular in their host countries when unemployment began to rise. Britain has imposed severe restrictions on immigration and other countries have also tightened up entrance requirements. Although Australia has abandoned its 'White Australia' policy, a points system still regulates the inflow of Asian and other immigrants. The United States also operates strict immigration controls but has been unable to stem the flow of Mexican and other Latin American illegal migrants across the long United States–Mexico border. Immigration controls have been tested elsewhere by the arrival of refugees from south-east Asia. After the communist North Vietnamese victory in 1975, thousands of refugees from Vietnam took to sea in small boats making for such countries as Hong Kong and Malaysia, while other refugees fled from communist rule in Laos and Cambodia (renamed Kampuchea).

Food and Health

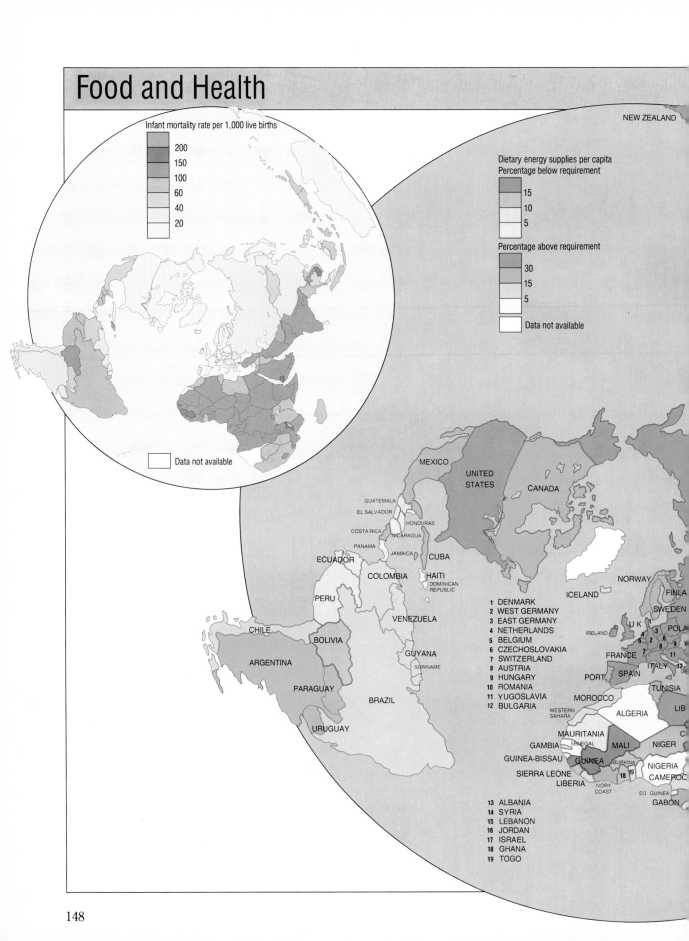

Infant mortality rate per 1,000 live births

- 200
- 150
- 100
- 60
- 40
- 20

Data not available

Dietary energy supplies per capita
Percentage below requirement

- 15
- 10
- 5

Percentage above requirement

- 30
- 15
- 5

Data not available

NEW ZEALAND

MEXICO
UNITED STATES
CANADA

GUATEMALA
EL SALVADOR
HONDURAS
COSTA RICA
NICARAGUA
PANAMA
JAMAICA
CUBA
ECUADOR
COLOMBIA
HAITI
DOMINICAN REPUBLIC

PERU
VENEZUELA

CHILE
BOLIVIA
GUYANA
SURINAME

ARGENTINA

PARAGUAY
BRAZIL

URUGUAY

NORWAY
ICELAND
FINLA
SWEDEN

1 DENMARK
2 WEST GERMANY
3 EAST GERMANY
4 NETHERLANDS
5 BELGIUM
6 CZECHOSLOVAKIA
7 SWITZERLAND
8 AUSTRIA
9 HUNGARY
10 ROMANIA
11 YUGOSLAVIA
12 BULGARIA

IRELAND
U K
FRANCE
PORT
SPAIN
ITALY
POLA

TUNISIA
MOROCCO
WESTERN SAHARA
ALGERIA
LIB

MAURITANIA
GAMBIA
SENEGAL
MALI
NIGER
C
GUINEA-BISSAU
GUINEA
BURKINA
NIGERIA
SIERRA LEONE
LIBERIA
IVORY COAST
CAMEROC
EQ GUINEA
GABON

13 ALBANIA
14 SYRIA
15 LEBANON
16 JORDAN
17 ISRAEL
18 GHANA
19 TOGO

Although the world has sufficient food for its population, many countries are still afflicted by famine, and the United Nations has estimated that 340 million of the world's population remain undernourished. Climatic changes, over-cropping and drought in North Africa have contributed to under-production, and lack of food and endemic poverty have in turn severe health implications. In a rich country such as Japan, infant mortality, at seven deaths per thousand live births, is tiny in comparison with a poor country such as Tanzania, where the rate is 90 deaths per thousand. Life expectancy is similarly different, for the average Japanese person expects to live 75 years, the average Tanzanian lives 51.4 years.

In the past 40 years, considerable advances have been made in medical technology, enabling doctors in the Third World to eliminate or control various diseases. However, the arrival of AIDS – Acquired Immune Deficiency Syndrome – during the 1980s has presented many poor nations with a major health epidemic, for there is as yet no known cure.

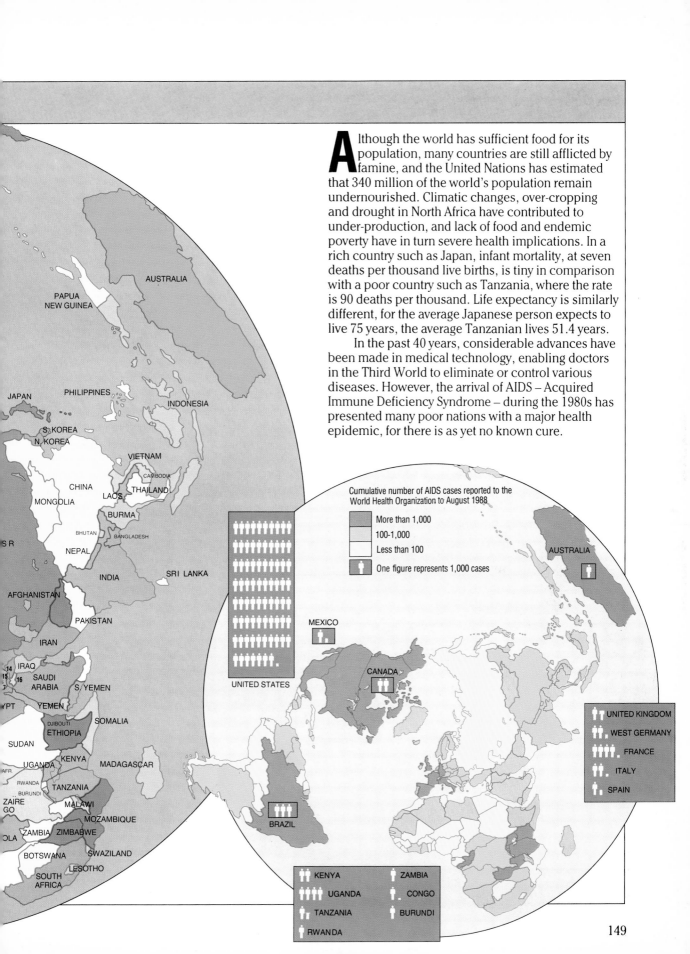

Cumulative number of AIDS cases reported to the World Health Organization to August 1988

More than 1,000
100-1,000
Less than 100
One figure represents 1,000 cases

UNITED STATES

MEXICO

CANADA

UNITED KINGDOM
WEST GERMANY
FRANCE
ITALY
SPAIN

BRAZIL

KENYA   ZAMBIA
UGANDA   CONGO
TANZANIA   BURUNDI
RWANDA

AUSTRALIA

JAPAN
PHILIPPINES
INDONESIA
S. KOREA
N. KOREA
VIETNAM
CAMBODIA
CHINA
THAILAND
MONGOLIA
LAOS
BURMA
BHUTAN
BANGLADESH
NEPAL
SR
INDIA
SRI LANKA
AFGHANISTAN
PAKISTAN
IRAN
IRAQ
SAUDI ARABIA
S. YEMEN
YEMEN
YPT
DJIBOUTI
ETHIOPIA
SOMALIA
SUDAN
UGANDA
KENYA
MADAGASCAR
AFR
RWANDA
BURUNDI
TANZANIA
ZAIRE
GO
MALAWI
MOZAMBIQUE
OLA
ZAMBIA
ZIMBABWE
BOTSWANA
SWAZILAND
LESOTHO
SOUTH AFRICA
PAPUA NEW GUINEA
AUSTRALIA

A Global Environment

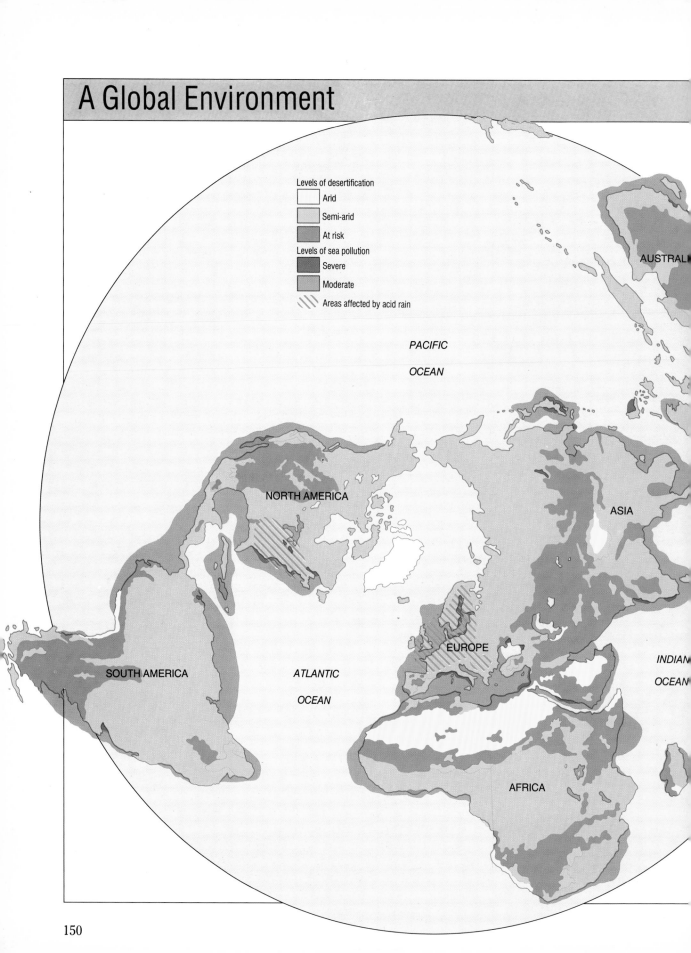

Levels of desertification
- Arid
- Semi-arid
- At risk

Levels of sea pollution
- Severe
- Moderate

Areas affected by acid rain

PACIFIC

OCEAN

AUSTRAL

NORTH AMERICA

ASIA

SOUTH AMERICA

ATLANTIC

OCEAN

EUROPE

INDIAN

OCEAN

AFRICA

In the last decade public awareness of the problem of pollution has increased dramatically as people appreciate the effects that industrial and agricultural practices have on the environment. In rural areas land clearance schemes have reduced plant and forest cover, leading to soil erosion and flooding, while the over-use of chemicals has exhausted the soil and contaminated crops. In the rain forests of Brazil and Indonesia, the desire for agricultural growth to meet the needs of an expanding population has entailed soil erosion and the extinction of wild life, but the governments of these countries are reluctant to change their policy. Industrialization and urbanization around the world have led to the release of toxic waste – gas and chemicals – into the atmosphere and these in turn threaten to destroy the ozone layer in the upper atmosphere, leading to fears of a 'greenhouse effect'. Some environmental problems have been tackled successfully. Agreements have been signed to protect endangered species and to limit the pollution of seas such as the Mediterranean. However, the Green Movement faces a long and difficult task.

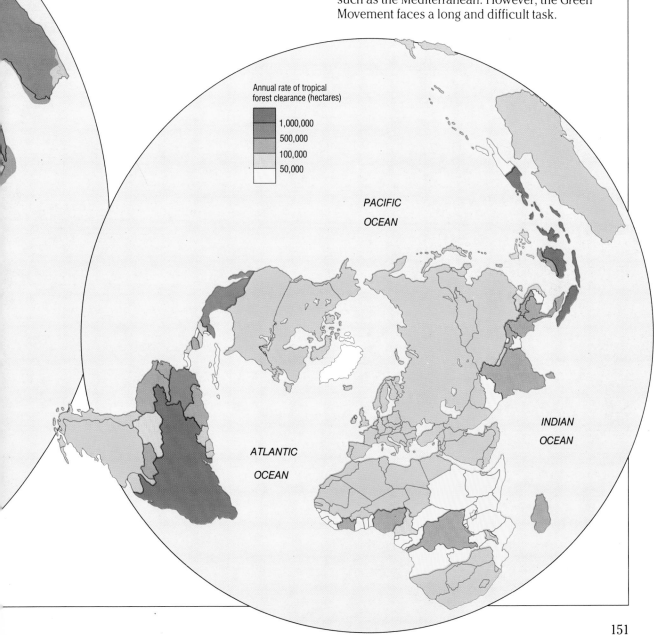

Annual rate of tropical forest clearance (hectares)

1,000,000
500,000
100,000
50,000

PACIFIC OCEAN

INDIAN OCEAN

ATLANTIC OCEAN

The World in 1990

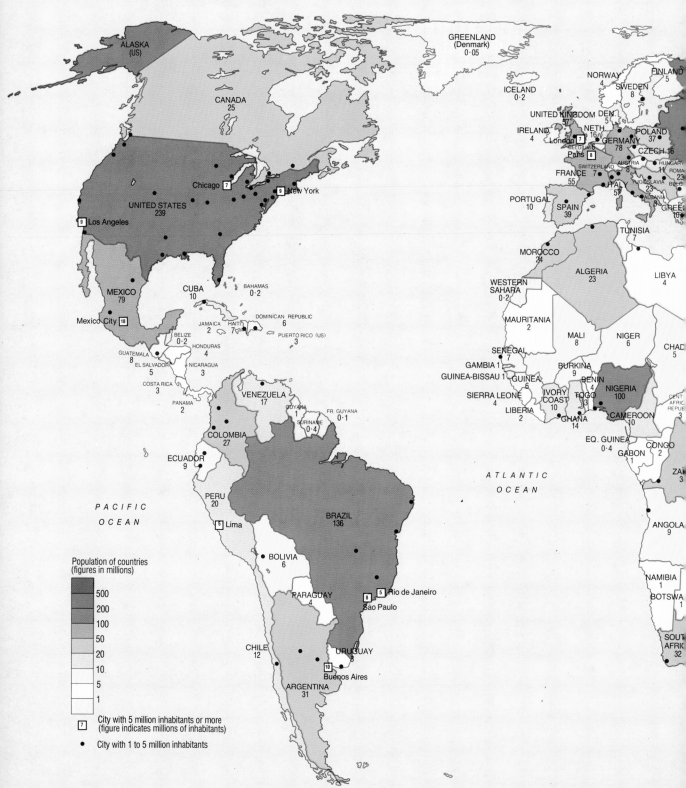

GREENLAND
(Denmark)
0·05

ICELAND
0·2

ALASKA
(US)

CANADA
25

NORWAY
4

SWEDEN
8

FINLAND
5

UNITED KINGDOM
57

DEN.
5

IRELAND
4

London 7

NETH.
16

POLAND
37

GERMANY
78

BELGIUM 6

CZECH. 16

HUNGARY
11

Paris 8

SWITZERLAND
8

AUSTRIA
8

ROMA
23

Chicago 7

New York 9

FRANCE
55

ITALY
57

YUGOSLAVIA
23

BULG

UNITED STATES
239

PORTUGAL
10

SPAIN
39

ALBANIA
GREE
10

Los Angeles 9

TUNISIA
7

MOROCCO
24

ALGERIA
23

LIBYA
4

MEXICO
79

CUBA
10

BAHAMAS
0·2

WESTERN
SAHARA
0·2

Mexico City 18

DOMINICAN REPUBLIC
6

MAURITANIA

MALI
8

NIGER
6

CHAD
5

JAMAICA HAITI
2   7

PUERTO RICO (US)
3

BELIZE
0·2

HONDURAS
4

GUATEMALA
8

EL SALVADOR
5

NICARAGUA
3

SENEGAL
7

GAMBIA 1

GUINEA-BISSAU 1

BURKINA
9

BENIN
4

NIGERIA
100

COSTA RICA
3

PANAMA
2

GUINEA
6

SIERRA LEONE
4

IVORY
COAST
10

TOGO
3

LIBERIA
2

GHANA
14

CAMEROON
10

VENEZUELA
17

GUYANA
1

FR. GUYANA
0·1

SURINAME
0·4

EQ. GUINEA
0·4

CONGO
2

CENT.
AFRIC.
REPUBI
3

COLOMBIA
27

GABON
1

ZA
3

ECUADOR
9

ATLANTIC
OCEAN

ANGOLA
9

PERU
20

PACIFIC
OCEAN

Lima 5

BRAZIL
136

Population of countries
(figures in millions)

	500
	200
	100
	50
	20
	10
	5
	1

BOLIVIA
6

PARAGUAY
4

Rio de Janeiro 5

São Paulo 8

NAMIBIA
1

BOTSWA
1

CHILE
12

URUGUAY
3

Buenos Aires 10

SOUT
AFRIC
32

ARGENTINA
31

7 City with 5 million inhabitants or more
(figure indicates millions of inhabitants)

• City with 1 to 5 million inhabitants

152

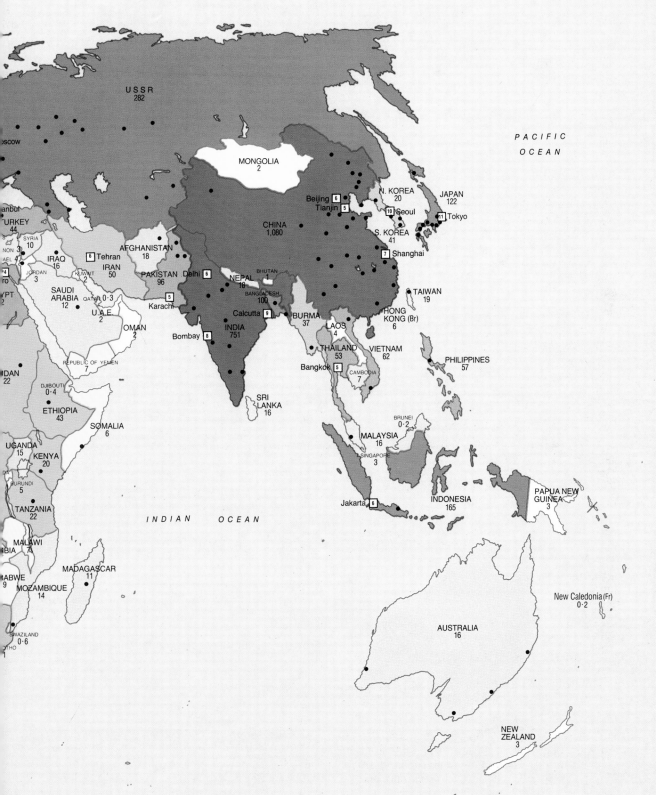

USSR
282

Moscow

MONGOLIA
2

N. KOREA
20

JAPAN
122

Beijing 6
Tianjin 5

Seoul 10

11 Tokyo

CHINA
1,080

S. KOREA
41

7 Shanghai

anbul

TURKEY
44

SYRIA
NON 3   10

AEL 4

6 Tehran

AFGHANISTAN
18

PASTAN
96

Delhi 6

NEPAL
18

BHUTAN
1

TAIWAN
19

JORDAN

IRAQ
16

KUWAIT

IRAN
50

HONG
KONG (Br)
6

PT
2

SAUDI
ARABIA
12

QATAR h 0·3

U.A.E.
2

Karachi 5

BANGLADESH
100

Calcutta 9

BURMA
37

LAOS
4

OMAN
2

Bombay 8

INDIA
751

DAN
22

REPUBLIC OF YEMEN
7

THAILAND
53

VIETNAM
62

PHILIPPINES
57

DJIBOUTI
0·4

Bangkok 5

CAMBODIA
7

SRI
LANKA
16

ETHIOPIA
43

SOMALIA
6

BRUNEI
0·2

UGANDA
15

KENYA
20

MALAYSIA
16

DA

BURUNDI
5

SINGAPORE
3

TANZANIA
22

INDIAN   OCEAN

INDONESIA
165

PAPUA NEW
GUINEA
3

Jakarta 6

MALAWI
BIA   7

ABWE
9

MADAGASCAR
11

New Caledonia (Fr)
0·2

MOZAMBIQUE
14

SWAZILAND
0·6

AUSTRALIA
16

OTHO
1

NEW
ZEALAND
3

PACIFIC

OCEAN

Glossary

AIDS Acquired Immune Deficiency Syndrome, disease of potential epidemic scale, identified 1980 and transmitted by sexual contact, shared syringes and transfusion of infected blood.

Allies The Grand Alliance of the USSR, USA and Great Britain in World War II, and later China and France. Also used to refer to the coalition of Britain, France, Russia (until 1917) and Italy against Germany in WW I.

Amnesty International Privately sponsored organization campaigning for release of political prisoners.

ANC African National Congress formed in 1912 to protect interests of black people in South Africa, made illegal by South African government between 1961–90. Nelson Mandela is its most famous leader.

Apartheid System of segregation between blacks and whites in South Africa.

Arab League Formed 1945 to increase political and economic cooperation between Arab states. Formerly, its main concern was to expel French from Arab territory, since 1967 its main activity is coordinating opposition to Israel.

Arms race Continuous competition between USSR and the West in post-war period to establish superiority in armaments.

Axis Term used by Benito Mussolini to describe relationship between Nazi Germany and fascist Italy.

Baader-Meinhof Terrorist anarchist group operating in West Germany after wave of student protests in 1968.

Balfour Declaration Issued by British Foreign Secretary in 1917, it supported Jewish homeland in Palestine, and served as a basis for the British Mandate.

Blitz Massive air attacks by night on London and other British cities between September 1940 and May 1941 by German airforce.

Blitzkrieg German term for 'lightning war' or the use of armoured vehicles supported by air power to penetrate and defeat the enemy quickly.

Boat people Refugees from Vietnam who, after communist North Vietnamese victory in 1975 in the Vietnam War, left in small boats making for Hong Kong, Malaysia and elsewhere.

Bolshevik Radical faction of Russian Social Democratic Party after it split in 1903; it seized power in October revolution of 1917.

Boxer Rebellion Uprising in Beijing in 1900 of secret society opposed to European interests in China.

Central Powers Members of Triple Alliance (Germany, Austria–Hungary and Italy) formed in 1882; on outbreak of WW I Italy remained neutral and subsequently Bulgaria and Turkey joined Germany in the war effort.

CIA US Central Intelligence Agency, established 1947 to coordinate foreign intelligence.

Cold War Political and ideological conflict between the USSR, the USA and their respective allies during the 1950s and 1960s, and saw the formation of *Warsaw Pact* and

NATO. The war occasionally went 'hot', as in Korea and Vietnam, and was gradually superseded by *détente* in the 1970s and 1980s.

Comecon Council for Mutual Economic Assistance, established in 1949 to further trade links between the USSR and *Eastern Bloc* countries.

Communism Social system in which property is communally owned by all people; many states claim such a society, including China and Cuba.

Concentration camp First used by Spanish in Cuba, and British in South Africa to detain the Boers in 1900. In Nazi Germany, camps were established in 1930s for detention of political and 'racial' enemies and many were converted into extermination camps for Jews during WW II.

Contras Nicaraguan exiles in Honduras and USA opposed to *Sandinista* government in Nicaragua during the 1980s. They received military and financial aid from USA.

D-Day landing Largest ever seaborne invasion, June 1944 when Allied troops landed on the Normandy coast.

Détente Improved relations beginning 1969 between *Warsaw Pact* countries (led by USSR) and the West (led by USA) and resulting in SALT I (Strategic Arms Limitation Treaty I).

Disarmament Reduction, limitation or abandonment of armaments (nuclear and conventional) as proposed by USSR and USA since early 1950s.

Eastern Bloc Formerly those nations in Eastern and Central Europe dominated by the USSR and forced to adopt Soviet methods of communist government. Disintegrated 1989–90.

EEC European Economic Community, also known as the Common Market, was incorporated into the European Community in 1967; formed in 1958 for the purpose of free, intra-community trade and sharing common economic and social policies.

ETA Militant Basque separatist movement responsible for violent acts against government authorities in northern Spain.

Famine Widespread food shortage and starvation caused by harvest failure, notably in Russia in 1921 and Ethiopia/Sudan during the 1980s.

Fascism Nationalist, authoritarian and anti-communist political creed founded by Benito Mussolini in Italy, 1919. Italian fascism served as a model for Spain, Germany and elsewhere.

FBI Federal Bureau of Investigation, founded 1908 as agency of US Department of Justice, responsible for general internal security. J Edgar Hoover was longest-serving director, 1924–72.

Feminism Movement for rights of women, particularly social, economic and political equality with men, which includes the British suffragettes (mainly pre-WW I), militant Women's Lib of USA in the 1960s and such theorists as Simone de Beauvoir and Germaine Greer.

Fundamentalist Christian: one who believes in literal

truth of the Bible, as in southern states of USA, popularly known as the Bible Belt; Muslim: for example Ayatollah Khomeini of Iran, one who insists on strict adherence to Islamic law rejecting non-Islamic Western or communist influences.

Gestapo Secret state police in Germany in 1930s, an instrument of terror to arrest and murder opponents of the *Nazi* regime and an arm of the SS, the Nazi storm troopers.

Global warming The rising temperature of the world's atmosphere said to be caused by an increased amount of carbon dioxide in the atmosphere.

Great Depression World economic slump of 1929–35.

Greens Environmentalists who seek a political platform to further the cause of ecological conservation world-wide; issues include greenhouse effect, nuclear power, rainforest conservation and protection of endangered species.

Guerrilla warfare Irregular forces, often acting independently behind enemy lines and avoiding direct conflict with superior armies. Actions include strikes at enemy supplies, communications and isolated army detachments.

IMF International Monetary Fund, founded 1944, makes foreign exchange resources available to members with balance of payments difficulties.

Indian National Congress Political party in India, led by Mohandas Gandhi from 1915 whose policy of non-violent civil disobedience to the Raj government characterized the party in the 1920s and 1930s.

IRA (Irish Republican Army) organized in 1919 to expel the British and establish a unified republic in Ireland. Split in late 1969, and while the Provisional wing pursued the policy of urban *guerrilla warfare*, the Official wing emphasized political rather than guerrilla activities.

Iron Curtain Armed border between Soviet-dominated eastern Europe and the West denoting strict limits placed on ideology and movement by the communist regimes of the *Eastern Bloc*.

Jihad Holy war of Muslims against infidels.

Khmer Rouge Cambodian communist movement taking its name from the Khmer people of Cambodia. It took power in 1975 and instituted a regime of genocide until removed by the Vietnamese army in 1979.

Ku Klux Klan American anti-Negro secret society. Violently active during 1920s and 1960s in mid-west and south. Attacks were broadened to include Jews, Roman Catholics and foreigners.

League of Nations International organization established in 1919 to preserve international peace through settlement of disputes by arbitration but it collapsed during WW II.

Long March 8000-mile migration in China in 1934–5 of 100,000 communists led by Mao Zedong to establish communist region in Yan'an, north-west China.

Mafia Criminal society originating in Sicily, spread to USA late 19th and early 20th century and became dominant force in organized crime during the *Prohibition* era. By 1950s it

controlled in the USA every aspect of vice, including gambling, prostitution and drugs.

Marshall Plan Arrangements for US financial help given to Europe after WW II devised by US Secretary of State General George Marshall in June 1947. The Plan offered financial aid for recovery and, in all, $17,000 million of Marshall Aid was forthcoming 1948–52.

Mau Mau Secret anti-European terrorist movement in Kenya in 1950s.

McCarthyism Name given to wave of anti-communist hysteria in USA during Cold War of 1950s, deriving from Senator Joseph McCarthy.

Mujaheddin Afghan Muslim resistance groups who fought against the Soviet military invasion of Afghanistan 1979–1989.

NATO North Atlantic Treaty Organization, established 1949 to assist any fellow signatory state suffering aggression. Arose out of western European concern over territorial ambitions of USSR.

Nazis Members of the German National Socialist Workers' Party that came to power under Hitler in 1933, espousing anti-Semitic, racialist doctrines of Aryan superiority.

Nazi–Soviet Pact Non-aggression pact agreed between Hitler and Stalin in August 1939 on eve of WW II.

Nuremberg Rallies Mass rallies staged by *Nazis* at Party Congresses in Nuremberg between 1933 and 1938.

OPEC Organization of Petroleum Exporting Countries, formed 1960 to regulate crude oil prices. By 1973 OPEC was strong enough to force four-fold increase in oil prices.

Pacific Rim Established and emerging industrial giants around edge of Pacific Ocean – notably USA, Japan, Korea, Taiwan – whose economic and trade links are now dominating the world economy.

PLO Palestine Liberation Organization, formed in Jordan 1964 to coordinate Arab efforts (including numerous guerrilla raids) to reclaim Israeli-held territory. Led by Yasser Arafat.

Privatization Policy of selling-off state-run industries to private ownership. Pioneered in Britain in 1980s and adopted by many other nations, including *Eastern Bloc* countries and, tentatively, the Soviet Union.

Prohibition The outlawing of manufacture, sale and distribution of alcoholic liquor in USA between 1920 and 1933.

Raj British rule in India, 1858–1947.

Rastafarianism Movement originating in West Indies taking name from Ras Tafari Makonnen, crowned Emperor of Ethiopia as Haile Selassie in 1930. Ethiopia is regarded as the spiritual homeland of estranged black people in the West Indies or Britain.

Red Brigades Left-wing urban terrorist organizations active in Italy since 1970s.

Resistance movements Groups of underground fighters united against a foreign occupying force. Activities include peaceful non-cooperation, sabotage of industrial and communication targets, ambush of foreign troops and outright conflict.

Sanctions Economic or diplomatic blockades used by the international community, through the *League of Nations* or United Nations *(UN)*, to force aggressor nations to reverse their policies and others to comply with United Nations resolutions. Sanctions aim to isolate a country and cripple its economy.

Sandinista National Liberation Front (FSLN) A group which opposed the Somoza dictatorship in Nicaragua. After a revolution it took over power in July 1979 but lost a majority of seats in the Assembly to anti-Sandinista parties in free elections in 1989.

Shi'ites Members of Islamic sect based in Iran who maintain Ali, son-in-law of prophet Mohammed, was true successor; Ayatollah Khomeini was its charismatic leader 1979–89.

Solidarity The non-communist, Polish trade union organization, headed by Lech Walesa, which, by a series of strikes and demonstrations, forced the resignation of the community hierarchy.

Suez Crisis (1956) Following nationalization of Suez Canal by President Nasser of Egypt, a failed attempt by the British, French and Israelis to repossess the Canal and oust Nasser.

Third World Poorer nations of the world, economically less-developed, located in Latin America, Asia and Africa.

Treaty of Versailles One of four peace settlements ending WW I. Signed June 1919 by victorious powers and reluctantly by Germany who criticized it for its harshness.

UN United Nations, international organization founded 1945 to maintain international peace and security. Member states have to provide armed forces for peace-keeping missions.

Vietminh Vietnam Independence League founded 1941, to resist Japanese occupation of Indo-China and, later, French colonial authorities.

Wall Street Site of New York stock exchange and synonym for US finance and banking.

Warsaw Pact Eastern European equivalent of *NATO*. The command structure controlled from Moscow required combined armed assistance for any member state attacked.

Watergate American political scandal of early 1970s involving bugging of Democrat's campaign HQ at Watergate complex, Washington, which led to the resignation of President Nixon in 1974.

Zionism Militant Jewish movement, launched by Theodor Herzl in 1896, to establish autonomous Jewish homeland in Palestine, named after City of Zion or Jerusalem, capital of biblical Promised Land.

Bibliography

Banks, Arthur, *A Military Atlas of the First World War* (Heinemann, 1975)

Bramwell, Anna, *Ecology in the Twentieth Century: A History* (Yale UP, 1989)

Calvocoressi, P., Wint, G. and Pritchard, J., *The Total War: The Causes and Courses of the Second World War* (Viking, 1989)

Crow, Benn, *Third World Atlas* (Open University Press, 1983)

Dockrill, Michael, *The Cold War 1945–1963* (Macmillan, 1988)

Freedman, Lawrence, *Atlas of Global Strategy: War and Peace in the Nuclear Age* (Macmillan, 1985)

Gilbert, Martin, *American History Atlas* (Weidenfeld & Nicolson, 1968)

Iriye, Akira, *The Origins of the Second World War in Asia and the Pacific* (Longman, 1987)

Keegan, John, *The Second World War: An Illustrated History* (Hutchinson, 1989)

ed., *The Times History Atlas of the Second World War* (Times Books, 1989)

Kidron, Michael, *The War Atlas: Arms Conflict, Armed Peace* (Pan, 1983)

Kidron, Michael and Segal, Ronald, *The State of the World Atlas* (Heinemann, 1981)

Kinder, Hermann and Hilgemann, Werner, *The Penguin Atlas of World History Vol. II* (Penguin, 1978)

Mercer, Derrik, ed., *Chronicle of the 20th Century* (Legrand/Longman, 1988)

Natkiel, R., Sommerville, D. and Westwood, J. N., *Atlas of 20th Century History* (Hamlyn-Bison, 1982)

Palmer, Alan, *The Penguin Dictionary of Twentieth Century History 1900–1988* (Penguin, 1990)

Pitt, B. and Pitt, F., *The Chronological Atlas of World War II* (Macmillan, 1989)

Taylor, A.J.P., *The First World War: An Illustrated History* (Penguin, 1978)

The Second World War: An Illustrated History (Penguin, 1976)

Tindall, George Brown, *America: A Narrative History (Illustrated)* (W. W. Norton, 1988)

Index

Page numbers in **bold** print refer to map entries; those in *italics* refer to captions and illustrations.

158